Civil Society and the Search for Development
Alternatives in Cameroon

Civil Society and the Search for Development Alternatives in Cameroon

Edited by
Emmanuel Yenshu Vubo

CODESRIA

Council for the Development of Social Science Research in Africa

ISBN: 978-286978-220-4

Typeset by Sériane Camara Ajavon

Cover image designed by Florent Loso Tonado

Printed by Imprimerie Graphiplus, Dakar, Senegal

CODESRIA publishes a quarterly journal, *Africa Development,* the longest standing
Africa-based social science journal; *Afrika Zamani,* a journal of history; the *African
Sociological Review; African Journal of International Affairs* (AJIA); *Africa Review of Books;*
and the *Journal of Higher Education in Africa.* It copublishes the *Africa Media Review* and
Identity, Culture and Politics: An Afro-Asian Dialogue. Research results and other activities
of the institution are disseminated through 'Working Papers', 'Monograph Series',
'CODESRIA Book Series', and the *CODESRIA Bulletin.*

CODESRIA would like to express its gratitude to the Swedish International
Development Cooperation Agency (SIDA/SAREC), the International Development
Research Centre (IDRC), Ford Foundation, MacArthur Foundation, Carnegie
Corporation, NORAD, the Danish Agency for International Development
(DANIDA), the French Ministry of Cooperation, the United Nations Development
Programme (UNDP), the Netherlands Ministry of Foreign Affairs, Rockefeller
Foundation, FINIDA, CIDA, IIEP/ADEA, OECD, OXFAM America, UNICEF
and the Government of Senegal for supporting its research, training and publication
programmes.

Contents

I: Policy Background

II: Traditional Social Movements

III: Associational Life between Traditional and Modern Society on the Path to Autonomy and Self-Reliant Development

IV: Non-Governmental Organisations

V: State-Civil Society Relations

Contributors

Robert Mbe Akoko holds an MA in Anthropology from the University of Ibadan and is currently pursuing a PhD at the African Studies Centre of the University of Leiden. He is a lecturer in Anthropology at the University of Buea and has published a wide range of articles in the domain of the anthropology of new religious movements. His research interests are in the domain of the pentecostalisation of mainline Christianity.

Wilfred Jingwa Awung holds an MA in Agricultural Economics from the Obafemi Awolowo University, Ile-Ife and is currently pursuing a PhD in Economics at the Southern Illinois University, Carbondale. He was a laureate of the 1998 cycle of Robert McNamara fellowship at the Economic Development Institute of the World Bank and a grantee of the African Economic Research Consortium.

Samah Abang-Mugwa holds a BSc in Sociology and Anthropology from the University of Buea, a post-graduate diploma in the teaching of philosophy from the Advanced Teacher Training College, Yaoundé and a Postgraduate Diploma in Political Science and Strategic Studies from the University of Yaoundé II.

Maurice Ufon Besseng holds a post-graduate diploma and an MSc in Gender Studies from the University of Buea.

John W. Forje holds a PhD in Political development from the University of Lund and another PhD in Technology and Science Policy from the University of Salford, England. He is a lecturer in the Department of Political Science of the University of Yaoundé II after having served for a long time at the Institute of Social Sciences and is the author of several books and scholarly articles. He has been Archie Mafeje Fellow at the African Institute of South Africa, Pretoria.

Charles C. Fonchingong holds an MSW (Community Development) from the University of Ibadan (1997) and has been lecturing in the Department of Women's Studies at the University of Buea. He has a wide range of scholarly publications to his credit and is currently pursuing a PhD in Social Policy Studies at the university of Canterbury.

A.V. Kini-Yen Fongot-Kinni studied a wide range of the humanities and the social sciences in Rome and at the Universities of Paris I, V and VII of the Sorbonne and obtained several qualifications among which the Doctorat d'Etat in Political Science. He worked with the United States Information Service (ISIS) of the United States Embassy in Yaoundé and the Peace Corps Service of the same country attached to Cameroon before setting up the Afhemi Museum of Anthropology and Art Gallery in Yaoundé where he serves as curator.

Emmanuel Ndenecho obtained a PhD in Geography from the University of Buea in 2003 and is a Lecturer at the Annex of the Higher Teacher Training College of the University of Yaoundé I at Bambili. Before then he was Director of the Bambili Regional School of Agriculture of the University of Dschang. Research interests: land use and problems of the ecosystem.

Max Memfi Ntangsi holds an MSc in Economics from Ahmadu Bello University. He is a Senior Lecturer in Economics and Coordinator of the Short Courses programme of the Faculty of Social and Management Sciences of the University of Buea. He is the author of several scholarly publications.

Enoh Tanjong obtained a PhD in Mass Communication from the University of Wisconsin – Madison, USA in 1986. He served in several senior capacities at the Ministry of Information and Culture which later became the Ministry of Communication, Yaoundé, Cameroon and the University of Buea. He is a consultant with several national international organisations and has published extensively in the domain of mass communication and grassroots organisations.

Joseph Nyambo Temngah obtained a Doctorate from the University of Yaoundé in 1996. He was recruited to teach in the Department of English Law of the University of Yaoundé II in 1996 and was appointed as Head of Department, Department of Common Law at the University of Douala since 1999. He has published in several scholarly journals.

Emmanuel Yenshu Vubo is a Senior Lecturer in Sociology. He obtained his Doctorate from the University of Yaoundé in 1991 and has served in several senior capacities at the University of Buea. He is a member of several scholarly societies and has published several scholarly journal articles plus book chapters in the domain of sociology and social anthropology.

Introduction

Emmanuel Yenshu Vubo

Introduction

The most crucial and endemic problem that Africa has faced since independence has been its inability to embark on a meaningful path of development and to achieve a level of well-being deemed satisfactory for a sizeable proportion of its population (Ndulu et al. 1998:4, McNamara 1991:2-4). Traditional indicators (GNP per capita) and, of recent, indicators taking into consideration general social conditions (human development index) have not been very encouraging and have at times degenerated into real misery. It has become widely accepted that some of these failures have largely been due to the insertion of the attempts at development within the confines of the state as it exists in Africa (Ake 1992:10). However, the alternatives proposed within the context of conventional liberal thinking have not only failed but have led to misery for large segments of society as structural adjustment has often resulted in de-structuring (Ben Hammouda 1998:18, Dembele 1998:10). This is happening, as there is general pressure to liberalise and to open up both political and economic space for transnational political and economic interests (Sachs 1995:2), which Dembele (op cit.:10) refers to as 'Africa's... recolonisation'. These developments are taking place in a context where people are little informed (and even misinformed) of key issues and where they can neither influence nor participate in determining what is best for them. The liberal-democratic experiment forced through during the 1990s has met with the most glaring failures and reversals to the extent that the hopes offered by the project are likely to lead to deep frustration. One needs to remark that this is occurring in a context where Africans are led to perceive this project as the only viable one, a fact which is likely to deepen the frustration when all else comes to a halt. The present context is dominated by the 'grip of ideology and doctrine, including the doctrines crafted to induce hopelessness, resignation and despair' (Chomsky 1997:243).

The euphoria that accompanied independence in Africa is thus giving way to despair as efforts at development and nation building have failed (Amin 1998:169).

Despite recent indicators of a timid progress in the economy no African country is spared the present crisis (Amin ibid., McNamara 1991:2-4). The end of the Cold War was characterised by optimism as the pressures of alignment characteristic of that era gave way to the possibility for the search for new solutions to the crisis. This was however short-lived as it was perceived by the capitalist centre as an opportunity to complete its project of creating a one-dimensional world in its own image. This explains the pressure exerted on poorer countries, which had not yet adopted market driven strategies to do so. For example, when Cameroon adopted the Structural Adjustment Programme (SAP) it did so reluctantly and has been equally reluctant in its implementation. Recourse to the Washington Consensus has meant compliance with pre-conditions, some of which are of a non-economic nature. It is in this context that political pluralism was born. In other words, the growth of political parties and the effervescence of social movements are concomitant with this process of economic adjustment. When political parties were legalised in Cameroon in the early 1990s there was optimism, as expressed in the slogans of change, as they came to be aligned with other social movements proposing a new vision for society. More than a decade after it is necessary to reflect on the balance sheet of these developments. The aim of this project is to evaluate the potential of civil society social movements in providing alternative solutions to the present development crisis that affects Cameroon as an African case study.

A multidimensional crisis rocks the very basis of the state and the nation building project in Cameroon as elsewhere in Africa. In the political domain the legitimacy of the state has been called into question with the rise of regional (cf. Nkwi and Nyamnjoh 1997) and counter-hegemonic movements (Yenshu Vubo 1998a, Burnham 1996), a crisis of democratic participation manifested in increasing voter apathy, the transformation of the single-party structure into a hegemonic party and the growth of political violence in both subtle legitimate and overt illegitimate forms. In the economic sphere the crisis manifests itself in the inability of the modern state to generate a viable strategy, project or programme for building a sustainable economy with a level of autonomy and meaningful integration into the world economy.

We can identify the following characteristics of the crisis situation. The Structural Adjustment Programme proposed by the Washington Consensus has been unable to usher in the building blocks of a viable economy without generating mass suffering. Most economic policies and programmes are dependent on external dictates and therefore are cut off from local realities or unresponsive to local needs, resulting in dependency. There is a disproportionate stress on the achievement of macro-economic indicators in total disregard of relations between these indicators and micro-level facts. The insistence on conforming to standards of performance set by the Washington Consensus, be it in the domain of politics (good governance) or the economy (the achievement of macro-economic indicators), without any real relation to local concerns provokes a new crisis of the state wherein international sovereignty is not matched with internal legitimacy. This state of affairs is, for example, reflected in rural economic activity with the disengagement of the state and the multiplication of ineffective policies (see Yenshu Vubo 1998b).

In the social domain there are distortions at both vertical and horizontal level. At the horizontal level there is the resurfacing of ethnic and regional cleavages, as separatist tendencies constitute a real challenge to the nation-building project. For now, the balance sheet of the national unity or integration programme is far from illuminating (Nkwi and Nyamnjoh, op cit.). One can then ask the question whether it is possible for Cameroonians to feel Cameroonian and treat others as equal in terms of citizenship. Such a question implies that we examine the conditions of reciprocity: is this symmetrical or asymmetrical? Recent manifestations seem to put assumption of symmetry and integration into question. At the vertical level one may need to highlight the social dislocations evident in the social fabric: the poor handling of workers' social security by the monolithic state structures, the rise in the number of abandoned street children, peasant pauperisation with the withdrawal of state support and orientation, rising youth unemployment, juvenile delinquency, inter-generational conflicts, deterioration in workers' conditions and urban crime. These developments are exacerbated with the reorientation of social policy under pressure to conform to the neo-liberal model. Policies and strategies are incoherent and commitment half-hearted although good intentions are not lacking.

One may also question the state's response to the environmental crisis. Issues central to this concern are desertification, natural hazards and disasters (draught, earthquakes, gas explosions, landslides, floods), depletion of forests, soil erosion due to intense uncontrolled human activity, and massive destruction of crops by animals and insect pests. Subsidiary issues whose importance might not be very apparent are the questions of gas emissions, pollution, urban waste disposal and the emission of radioactive substances. Some of these concerns are specific to Cameroon but most of them transcend the national borders with some even directly linked to international or transnational phenomena (dumping, the uncontrolled importation of potentially dangerous equipment, the greenhouse effect, depletion of the ozone layer). The state, as erstwhile principal development agent, has not addressed the environmental question according to its manifestations but has simply acted according to the prevailing fashions or in response to international discourses and practices. At times the actions of the state have tended to contradict discourses at both national and transnational levels. This is principally the case with the issue of re-forestation that at certain moments did not match the rate of depletion. The exploitation of forest resources was largely uncontrolled by the state as the need to replenish state coffers tended to override the need to preserve the environment or to conform to international norms. Besides, the monitoring of natural hazards and the provision of social services to victims has not yet been the systematic concern of the state (Omboui-Bogui 1995:45-46). There is no concerted effort to forestall large-scale hazards like desertification, a phenomenon that is manageable. The failure of the state in the environmental sector implies a failure to provide a comfortable and sustainable framework for national existence.

The solutions proposed are varied and reflect the visions which they evoke. Two tendencies emerge. Conservative visions are basically sectional and are confined to specific university disciplines. This reflects the tendency of one-dimensional modernity to split reality into multiple fragmented facets (Marcuse 1967). Hence, economics would treat each of these problems as if the economic were the only or the major reality that underlies the causes of the multidimensional crisis. Political analysts would also tend to analyse the issues only in terms of the failure of the political system, in this case the pseudo-collectivist model inspired by the Cold War period or the post-Cold War fads such as good governance. As such, the solutions proposed all tend to stress the need to increase political participation at both the individual and community levels. Sociologists or anthropologists, who are also called in to propose their sociologism or humanism, insist almost entirely on the primacy of their conceptual frameworks. All these are inscribed within the liberal paradigm that is gaining new ground and which is propagated in the name of globalisation. It has to be noted that the ultra-liberal paradigm is gaining grounds not on intellectual (that is, on tested facts) but on ideological and political grounds (Amin 1994:15; 1998:39). It has to be borne in mind that the legitimacy of this model is derived from its success in the international competition with the communist model and should not therefore be confused with its operational value or treated as an indicator of its validity. This model leads to new openings but predominantly within the market-dominated model of economy, society and polity. As such, social groups, collective action and the state are considered as obstacles to the creation of the new society or the realisation of the only viable model of society. Proponents of this vision behave as if this was the only model or as if African societies were entrapped within it; in other words, we are informed that other models are doomed to failure even when there is no proof of the total success of the neo-liberal vision.

An alternative radical vision would transcend the present attempts at liberalisation that seem to situate the problems at the level of the state alone. In fact it operates a radical break with the traditional and extremist version of liberalism by situating the solution within the dynamics of the society. As such, the principal objective of the economy would be to promote and contribute to the well-being of all persons and not only prosperity for a few persons or an increase in global national indicators with regard to the economy. The economy should neither be determined exclusively by the private sector to the exclusion and subordination of large segments of society nor should it be driven by the search for surplus value or maximum growth without an impact on social welfare, with due regard to disadvantaged groups such as the poor, youth, women and peasants. Another threat to social conditions comprises the kind of industrialisation that leads to an imbalance in social groups, categories and regions within the national sphere. This certainly calls for a certain co-ordination role for the state and an active involvement of the society (or civil society) in the economy. There has been talk about a social economy but a radical vision would go beyond, to define new roles for economic, political and social actors (state, individuals, groups, communities) (cf. Yenshu Vubo 1997).

The Question of the Search for Development Alternatives

We choose to define development, in the context of this work, as a movement from a set of conditions (social, material, political, cultural) defined as undesirable or the cause of adverse effects to another set deemed necessary for promoting well-being. Such a simple operational definition will help us to overcome the hurdle of an absolutist judgmental end point. This is so because the definition of these sets of conditions has been changing with ideological shifts, for example, the movement from an economistic (material) to a humanistic perspective (witness the recent abandonment of the physical quality of life index in favour of the human development index).With the shifts, threshold levels also become a shaky issue. We are therefore not concerned with the question of surmounting threshold levels but with examining political projects (policies) aimed at facilitating the transition process within the development continuum, i.e. from the undesirable to the preferred or necessary set of conditions. Although there has however been no consensus on the modalities of transition from one state to another, each development effort has been accompanied by attempts at providing a conceptual framework to the understanding or interpretation of the problems, which serves to guide action.

Africa and the Development Concern

The changing mood in the theorisation of development has affected the African situation both in its intellectual climate and the strategies of development. Although situated in an internationalised environment, Africa's development problems are specific. In arguing for the uniqueness of the problematic of Africa's development in the Third World, Ekeh (1986) notes that, in the same way as in the Industrial Revolution, development thinking has oscillated between moods of optimism and pessimism, this situation following the oscillation between boom and depression that has characterised the world economy during the twentieth century. Historically, by the 1950s no efforts were made at conceptualising development in Africa - the latter still falling largely under the influence of colonial domination. Any concern with development was geared towards the study of involuntary social change in response to opportunities offered by contacts with the metropolitan centre of the colonial system with which the rest of the world was in contact. The theories, as elsewhere, were ahistorical and did not go beyond the colonial era, as was characteristic of modernisation theory which was built on the belief in the capacity of Africa and indeed all formerly colonised areas to follow in the path of European civilisation (cf. Long 1977). The influence of modernisation theory persisted into the period of independence and gained much official support. As a policy it was optimistic and at the ideological level it was prompted by Cold War rivalries. Modernisation theory failed in Africa, Ekeh argues, because the new states on which the hopes of 'modernisation-development' were founded were frail and fraught with the germs of disintegration.

This view was advanced much earlier from a Marxist perspective by Claude Ake (1978:66) when he argued that the African ruling classes 'pursue the task of economic development in the context of an ideological orientation which essentially accepts the developmental precepts of the metropolitan bourgeoisie', making of this ideology a hegemonic one. This bias was situated at the very core of the ideology that defined the development obstacles and the means of overcoming them. The obstacle advanced by this ideological orientation were the low levels of savings, limited achievement motivation, low propensity to invest, low productivity, inadequate technology, low wages, regional disparities, and inadequate manpower. As a status quo oriented ideology it served to conceal class distinctions by arguing that class structure and class struggle are irrelevant to the process of development and that there is no need to transform class relations. Such an ideology also serves to legitimise dependency by conceptualising 'development essentially as a process of becoming more like the bourgeois countries' (ibid.:67). In so doing economic dependence is presented as inevitable and thus no cause for alarm. The ideology also excuses the painfully slow pace of economic development in Africa characterised by a conservative thrust and the presentation of the development process as only possible through 'slow incremental change' (ibid.:68). The acceptance of this approach, he argues, would lead to the perpetuation of underdevelopment. Misconstruing and distorting problems, this ideology inhibited the solutions. It also masked the link between development and revolution. He therefore concluded that:

> Any approach, which makes the achievement of development in Africa compatible with the maintenance of the present exploitative relations of production and with the links to imperialism, can only hinder Africa (ibid.:69). Another major impediment to development is what Ake calls depoliticisation, or 'reducing the effective participation of the masses and non-hegemonic factions of the ruling class, and preventing some interests and points of view from finding political expression' (ibid.:78). The process reduces 'the prospect of overcoming underdevelopment by facilitating the ascending of elements of the ruling class associated with the coercive machinery of the state' (ibid.:79).

The disenchantment with modernisation theory led to a shift towards underdevelopment and structural dependency theory. This was both out of scepticism and of hostility to the dominant centre, and it encouraged the model of development proposed by Amin under the label of 'delinking', a theory of development advocating autonomous development out of the scope of the dominant world system. Samir Amin's analysis focused attention on the critique of the world system based on capitalist exploitation and inequality between nations (Amin 1974), a process he captured in the term 'polarisation' (1993; 2000a). This polarisation is presented as 'immanent to the global expansion of capital' (2000a:602). His analysis leads him to the conclusion that capitalism is fraught with three internal contradictions, namely commodity alienation (analysed in its incipient stages by Marx and Engels); global polarisation between nation-states and within segments of populations; within the nation-state and the destruction of the natural resource base of the planet, that is, ecological destruction (1993, 2000a:619, 1998:155-156, 2002b:340). Commodity or economic alienation is characterised by labour subordination as dictated by the rule of profit as against labour interests. Ecological destruction refers to the opposition between principles of economic calculation, which support a short-term vision, on the one hand, and the imperative of saving the future of the planet, that is, the inability of this economic rationality to take into account the fact that there are limits to the exploitation of the earth's resources. Polarisation points to the growing contrast between opulent centres and miserable peripheries, this situation being exacerbated by five monopolies that define the current phase of capitalism, considered by Amin as the third phase (2000a:618), and referred to as globalisation in neo-liberal terminology. This third phase is marked by the 'on-going scientific and technological revolution, computerization and robotics, decentralization of productive systems (delocalised production managed from a distance, sub-contracting, etc), tertiarization and quarterization of economic life and the decline of the share of industrial manufacturing' (2000a:618).

According to Amin (1993, 1994a:7, 1994b:21, 1996, 1998:137-138, 2000a, 2000b:5), the monopolies exercised by the capitalist centre are the control of the global financial system, control over science and technology, control over the management of natural resources, exclusive control over media instruments for the manipulation of the world's population, and monopoly over refined and state-of-the-art arms or weapons of mass destruction. The monopolies define the 'framework within which the law of value expresses itself' (2000b:5) and produce a hierarchy in the distribution of income on a world scale. While the law of value in the strict sense of the word would require that remuneration for work be at the same level for the same level of productivity, the globalised law of value dictates unequal remuneration for the same productivity level while the prices of goods tend to be the same world-wide (2002b:340).

These monopolies are also at the basis of distortions of a social, economic, cultural and political nature (1996). Economic distortions are characterised by growing inequality in the distribution of income at both the national and global level and the detachment of financial from productive activity and its constitution into an independent autonomous sphere (a process Amin calls 'financiarization') leading to a situation where a productive sector, operating on the basis of investments, exists side-by-side with an unused capital surplus. At the political level the distortions are reflected in the contradiction between the 'economic law of capitalism and globalization and the emancipatory democratic aspirations of the popular classes and nations victimized by capitalism', a situation that is 'increasingly barbarous' (2000a:621). There are also contradictions between 'markets and democracy and between liberal economic globalization and political-cultural universalism' (2003a). Distortions of a social and political nature are all derivatives of the economic distortions and constitute, according to Amin, 'the most serious obstacles to any project of sustainable development' (1996).

As concerns the periphery and Africa in particular, unequal development of the system leads to the emergence of two segments: an industrialised segment, which resembles a 'gigantic subcontracting enterprise controlled by countries of the centre and operating through the five monopolies', thus constituting the real periphery of the system or Third World; and another segment which faces the prospect of further marginalisation within the world system (1994a:21). The latter segment, which includes Africa, can be termed the Fourth World and belongs to the 'marginalized periphery' of the next generation (1994a:7). Amin holds that one of the most important consequences of globalisation is the creation of a labour reserve in the periphery. Faced with the drive to globalisation, the marginalised peripheries have no strategy or project of their own as the imperialist circles think and take the initiatives for them, they being merely 'passive subjects of globalization' (2000b:5).

In fact, the concepts of self-reliant development and African socialism fashionable in the decades following independence were actually meant to be self-supporting development paradigms following the direction charted by the delinking school. The mood of development thinking in the 1980s further shifted into one of despair with the series of crises that befell the continent, namely the Sahel drought, the food crises, generalised economic regression and the debt crisis. These crises caused not only the questioning of the feasibility of these models but also awakened Africans to their development problematic: how and by whom is development to take place in Africa?

The fluctuations in conceptual frameworks in African development thinking coincided almost totally with predominant modes of conceptualisation at the centre of the world system both in chronological succession and in nature. Development thinking in Africa has thus survived mostly as an intellectual colony of the centre of the system and has been dominated by economism, the rural-urban dichotomy (and the resultant relations of domination), and the external orientation of development. In the face of these pervading but frail approaches to development, alternative modes of conceptual analysis are constantly being proposed. In their practical content, they advocate a comprehensive societal approach to development while in their theoretical aspects they argue for a certain multi-disciplinary approach.

Calls for a revision of the development paradigm have, however, not often led to operational value, as the collapse of the former Soviet bloc has witnessed a triumphalist return to an unbridled neo-liberalism. It is in this context that we talk of post-developmentalism, defined as the discourses and practices related to development with a tendency towards their replacement (Yenshu Vubo and Fonchingong 2002). The calls and even the pressure for adjustment have been paving the way for a globalisation of a market economy presented as inevitable. It is also instructive to note that the development crisis has been accompanied by calls for the reorientation of conceptualisation and practice.

The question of alternatives has attracted attention in intellectual circles both in the centre of the current world hegemonic system and in the South (cf. Amin 1993, 1994 a & b, 1996, 1998 a, b, c & d, 2000 a, b & c, 2001 a & b, 2002 a & b, 2003, Houtart 1998, 2000, 2002, Mestrum 2002, Ekeh op cit., Van Nieuwenhuize 1983, Ake 1978, 1992, 1996, 1998, 2000) with the following convergence points. First, there is unanimity about the fact that the dominant model of development is a failure in terms of its content or orientation, operation (economism) and its actors, and that there is a need to transcend this model. It is in this regard that we can talk of an imperative of transcendence. While some critics limit their work to an academic discourse that would lamely call for the inclusion of certain parameters such as culture, environment and the social side of development, a more realistic view is careful to point out where the entry points are. Faced with the gigantic nature of the task at hand, the anti-globalisation school has even proposed a series of steps in the transcendence process, some short-term, some medium-term and some situated at the level of utopia. Second, there is a convergence of views about the need for alternatives that abandon the path of 'catching-up', whose latest disguised version, sponsored from the centre, is a diagnosis in terms of marginalisation and proposals in terms of adjustment to global conditions and internal measures which align with the neo-liberal gospel. That is why the imperative of transcendence may take the form of the search for indigenous pathways to development, the stress on the concept of autonomy (individual, communal, state) or the utopia of delinking, all operating at different levels. In this case, the imperative of transcendence is nurtured by the distortions of the current world-system or the shortcomings of the model of development that it has inspired as well as by the world time of development (Ekeh op cit.) and the constraints that it generates.

The crucial and central question that has not been adequately answered is that of actors or agents. Although the current state system has attracted a severe critique for its multiple flaws, no credible alternative seems to have emerged. Such a situation seems to be beneficial to the current neo-liberal attempts to construct a New World Order based on the dictates of the Market and Capital that animates it. Calls for a reform of the state in its present form and the elaboration of regional groupings outside the scope of the current order are lame, as the question of flag bearers still remains unanswered. Who will reform these states or will be the basis of radical regional blocs? An obvious answer will be a radical leadership responsive to the needs of local peoples. Although there are examples of such leaders who have emerged out of civil society (especially the labour movement), there is little in the literature about their performance as standard bearers of alternative projects. Moreover the mere mention of civil society is not enough to give assurance about credible alternatives. As has been underscored by many scholars, civil society could equally be a tool in the hands of the controllers of the current system, serving as it were as an instrument of systems maintenance (Houtart 1998; Founou-Tchuigoua and Kasanda 2002). It is in this regard that there is a need to undertake an in-depth analysis of the role of civil society in the search for alternatives, while highlighting its relation vis-à-vis the state and its relation to powerful radical forces world-wide. Alternatives cannot only come from a civil society evolving in a parallel manner to and as a marginal movement within the state system. This civil society must be in a position to effect political change or cooperate with radical political forces in the process of transforming existing conditions irrespective of the level at which such transformations are taking place. This analysis would inspire the current endeavour of research into the role the civil society has played in the search for alternatives as concerns the content of development practice, the organisation and structure of action and the actors.

The Promise of the Budding Civil Society

The Multiple Meanings of Civil Society

The concept of civil society has become a new fad, but is seems not to have the same meanings for everyone. Tostensen, Tvedten and Vaa (2001:11) remark that this concept is 'diverse and lacking in clarity. A multitude of terms is being used interchangeably and inconsistently, often without precise definition'. Since the term has become so prominent and fashionable, it has come to mean different things to different people: scholars, politicians and activists. As a result, definitions of civil society often reflect the function one set of actors intends it to perform (Bahmueller 1997). The principal bones of contention over the definition of civil society include whether the term should be primarily a normative or non-normative tool of social science, and whether we should consider the economic and religious and even the family as part of it. Michael Walzer defines civil society as 'the space of [politically] uncoerced human association and also the set of relational networks formed for the sake of family, faith, interest, and ideology that fill this space' (1990:293). It is not clear whether 'interest' in this definition includes economic interest. Jean Cohen and Andrew Arato explicitly eliminate the economic sphere from their 'working definition' of civil society as they limit it to 'a sphere of social interaction between economy and state, composed above all of the intimate sphere (especially the family), the sphere of associations (especially voluntary associations), social movement and forms of public communication' (1992:ix). In a similar vein, Narsoo (1991) argued that the concept of civil society is a contested terrain, insofar as the exact extent and limit of state intervention as against the integrity of civil society activity remains an open question. Civil society has been referred to as all that constitutes social relations, organisations and institutions that stand outside the state structures. Therefore the term 'organs' of civil society is often used with reference to these groups.

By contrast, Shils (1991:3) sees civil society as:

> ... composed of three parts. One is a 'complex of autonomous institutions' including economic ones, distinguishable from family, clan, locality, or state; a second is a portion of society that possesses 'a particular complex of relationships between itself and the state and a distinctive set of institutions which safeguard the separation of state and civil society and maintain effective ties between them'; and the third is a 'widespread pattern of refined or civil manners'.

Hefner, for his part, maintains that civil society is the arena of voluntary associations, including 'business associations' that extend 'beyond the household but outside the state' (Hefner 1998:6). While he confines local economic relationships to the civil society arena, he excludes large-scale, especially multinational corporations, as incompatible with the emergence of loyalty that face-to-face associations are capable of generating. Janoski applies an astute analytic hand in dividing the polity into state, public, private and market spheres, locating civil society as a sphere of public discourse among these four elements (Janoski 1998:13).

Offering a somewhat different interpretation of the term civil society, Salamon and Anheier (1997) restrict it to formally constituted 'non-profit' organisations. They describe these organisations as a significant economic 'sector' that contributes large-scale employment opportunities and expenditures to their respective national economies. They omit the family and highlight certain economic features of civil society. Benjamin Barber considers civil society as 'civic space' that 'occupies the middle ground between government and the private sector' (Barber 1996:27) and is distinctive in that it makes no claim to exercise a monopoly of legitimate coercion. Rather, work here is voluntary and, in this sense, inhabits a 'private' realm devoted to the cooperative domain and as such civil society shares with the private sector the trend towards the promotion of liberty: it is voluntary and it is constituted by freely associated individuals and groups. However, unlike the private sector, it is aimed at a common ground and at consensual (that is integrative and collaborative) modes of action. This idea contradicts Hegel's ground breaking concept of civil society as a competitive arena encompassing economic and other forms of social life lying between family and the state. In this view, followed by Marx and his adherents, civil society is a quasi-disorderly social realm where, among other things, the struggle for economic existence takes place. For Hegel, because civil society limits the forces inclining people to cooperate, the state must harmonise competing interests.

More recent definitions of civil society need to be considered in relation to the donor and so-called international development communities. Firstly, donors have had shifting perceptions of civil society. The main reason for donors to shift towards civil society was the increasing 'disillusionment on the side of the state as both the agent of economic development and locus of justice' (Howell 2002:118). These political assaults upon the state took place within the ideological context of neo-liberalism, which celebrated the allocative efficiencies of the market and derided the state as an agency for economic growth and management. Just like the arguments already mentioned, donor conceptions of civil society are also marked by complexity, especially in terms of a typology of civil society. By the late 1980s most bilateral donors channelled some of their funding principally through NGOs, regarding them in general as legitimate partners in development (Howell 2002:118).

The difficulty in situating civil society is illustrated in the way it was treated and integrated in its organisational structure. For instance donors tended to reduce civil society to NGOs. Howell remarks that 'from the mid 1990s onwards NGO units metamorphosed into civil society departments and donors sprouted civil society projects, civil society officers, civil society experts and civil society challenge funds' (ibid.:2002:119). While these are but a few of the formulations of the concepts of civil society, most of them illustrate the commonalities shared by nearly all definitions of the term.

Tostensen, Tvedten and Vaa (op cit.) identify some of the current multiple meanings associated with the concept of civil society. The first of these concepts considers civil society as the 'carrier of positive values' or the 'good society' (p. 12). A second regards it as the 'sum of organizations and activities that contribute to the civility of public life in one from or another'. A normative element is generally present, which includes the multiple functions Diamond (1994:11) attributes to civil society in the democratic dispensation (see also Barber, 1996). The third sees 'civil society as a sphere, a space or an arena for action by divergent interests, struggling against each other or against the state, or simple engaging in self-contained activities of various kinds', a view akin to Houtart's conception of civil society as the arena for social struggles (Houtart op cit.). A fourth connotation presents civil society 'as a specific product of historical and cultural conditions' (p. 12), while a fifth conception presents 'civil society as essentially an anti-hegemonic project against modern liberalism and capitalism... one strain puts the accent on the alternative visions of society, through quasi-clandestine forms that seek to dissociate from society considered to have derailed' (very much in line with Amin's vision of actors in the search for alternative) '[while another]... places civil society in direct opposition to a centralized or autocratic state as a countervailing power' (p. 13). This view is in reaction to the state's 'abysmal performance' in both development and democracy, necessitating as it were a need to roll back the state. This is the view held by the donor community.

They then consider the prevailing definitions based on the perception of civil society as a 'virtuous stereotype', a view which reflects 'wishful thinking on the part of the donor community, a favourable self-projection by sections of the civil society itself, or an ideologically tainted representation of segments of the academic community' (p. 13). After a critical analysis of these conceptions, they then propose a balanced definition which considers '[c]ivil society as the public realm of organized social activities located between the state and private household (on family) – regardless of normative orientation' (p. 13). They agree with the fact that civil society is the '... arena of diverse activity, some but by no means all of which [is] counterpoised to the state. Much associational life may be neutral vis-à-vis the state' (pp. 13-14).

This capacious concept of civil society – the whole range of civic action independent of formal political institutions – includes service associations, philanthropic groups, cultural groups, religious organisations, labour unions, athletic organisations, and youth groups, academia, the media, plus many more in every imaginable field of interest or endeavour. The concept also embraces economic relations, organisations, and activities not owned or directly controlled by the state.

The Historical Evolution of the Concept

In order to understand the dynamics related to the different meanings associated with the concept of civil society it is important to attempt a historical description of the analysis of the concept. We will base our reflections on contemporary scholars such as Houtart (1998), Tejada (1998), Santa Ana (1998) and Gallardo (1998), who are more or less agreed on the itinerary this concept has taken since the Enlightenment. As such it is generally agreed that civil society is a product of modernity with its roots traceable to the enlightenment social philosophers (Locke, Hobbes) who posited a dichotomy between a natural or savage or inferior society, and civil society, corresponding to the opposition between the state of nature and the state of civilisation. Rousseau and Hegel go further to make a distinction between three levels, natural society, civil society and political society. In this regard, civil society depends on political society. In these formulations civil society more or less takes the connotation of civilisation, a lawful society regulated by a government in contractual relations with citizens (the regulatory organ of so-called civilised society) in opposition to a state of lawlessness (natural or savage society). The concept of civil society thus limits itself to the part of the world considered as civilised and the rest of humanity considered as living in a state of nature. Marx and Engels offered a more restricted definition with the development of capitalist social relations, and define civil society as the set of social relations of the bourgeois society, making the two terms synonymous. It thus gives a class connotation to the term and even makes it a multi-class concept. Dogmatic Marxism even restricts this term to the set of economic relations of bourgeois society in opposition to the political society or set of regulatory institutions.

It is Gramsci who offered perhaps the most elaborate articulation of the concept. To him civil society is part of the superstructure in opposition to the structure or economic structure (what is referred to in classical Marxist thought as the 'base'). Civil society is understood here as the sphere of socially institutionalised action through which a social class achieves control or hegemony over other classes. Gramsci defines civil society therefore as 'l'ensemble des organismes vulgairement appelés privés... et qui correspondent à la fonction d'hégémonie que le groupe dominant exerce sur l'ensemble de la société' (in Tejada op cit.:29). In an attempt to clarify the Gramscian contribution to an understanding of the concept, Jose de Santa Ana (op cit) distinguishes five key concepts which, when articulated, bring out very clearly a full understanding of civil society. The first of these is the structure or the context in which economic interests are articulated, while the state corresponds to the set of organs through which the leadership class exercises hegemony and coercion over subordinate classes. Hegemony refers not only to the direction of preserving, defending and consolidating politico-economic interests but also the objective of elaborating educative strategies so as to obtain the consent of these subordinate classes in a manner that presents the interest of the dominant class as universally unchallengeable values. In this framework the civil society is the sphere within which individuals can associate with each other outside the scope of the economic structure and the state - i.e. the political structure (Santa Ana ibid.:42).

Santa Ana (ibid.:62) indicates that these organisations oscillate permanently between co-option by and resistance to the state, and function in an ambiguous situation where adaptation and resistance co-exist. This is because, in its hegemonic drive, the state tries to enlist or co-opt some of these organisations and transform them to serve the function of ideological legitimacy. This leads us to the concept of hegemony.

Hegemony, as we saw above, refers to the elaboration of educative strategies as a way of obtaining the social consensus of the dominant ideology (Santa Ana ibid.:64). In this process there is resistance from anti-hegemonic movements in the style of what Gramsci referred to as the hegemonic struggle, a real critique of common sense philosophies generated by the hegemonic drive of dominant classes and a certain type of education at popular level. To succeed in creating hegemony in society is to create the conditions for a cultural and moral orientation of society. Santa Ana therefore concludes by saying that there is a need to respect the autonomy of processes characteristic of civil society, since the potential thrust for social transformation is situated within it.

Houtart (op cit.), for his part, indicates that Gramsci does not take civil society to mean the space of organisations working independent of the state and the economy (most currently captured in the concept of the market), but the structuring of social relations through associations and cultural institutions. Civil society has relative autonomy vis-à-vis the state and the market because it is made up of organisations and actions which either facilitate the hegemonic practices of the ruling classes ('classes dirigeantes') or provide marginalised and exploited groups with the space to confront political institutions and the market with their claims and grievances. Houtart therefore concludes that civil society is the arena for social struggles, and the differentials observed in the meanings that the term takes are symptomatic of the ideological differences surrounding the concept. Gallardo (1998) proposes other conceptual refinements to the concept, such as the opposition between civil and military society, lay (and hence civil) and religious society, civil or urban and countryside, private (individual) and public, and lastly current vulgar distinctions between civil society and the state, a distinction which has its origins in the Marxist discussions on the concept. The last connotation associated with the concept owes much to the current context of globalisation that transforms the meanings associated with the concept (Vilas 1998, Tejada op cit., Houtart op cit.).

Tejada (op cit.) has indicated that the context of globalisation in which civil society has witnessed a new lease of life is characterised amongst others by polarisation (see also Amin 1998, 2000), exclusion from the formal economy, the intensification of real and relative poverty, the increase in migratory trends, and a precarious situation in employment. He describes this situation as one in which classical social forces (the labour movement, political parties of the left) have succumbed to a pitiless capitalist transition and where the world is divided into spheres of influence with international political and economic organisations becoming increasingly used as instruments of the northern countries in their domination over countries of the south, legitimising in a way the capitalist project at international level.

Santa Ana (op cit.:46-49) has also highlighted the rise in individualism as reflected in individual behaviour and practices in the dominant ideological precepts and in popular literature and folklore. There is therefore a tension between the process of globalisation, which imposes itself, and different and essentially new resistance movements that contradict the system (Santa Ana ibid.:55, Vilas op cit.:70). Although there are systemic movements that finally get entrapped in the system's hegemonic drive (for example, nationalist movements, labour, the great social movement of the nineteenth century), anti-systemic movements are at the heart of the most protracted social conflicts (human rights defence movements, feminist movements, movements fighting for the rights of oppressed ethnic and cultural groups, ecological movements and certain religious movements. Although the short-term outcome of this confrontation is favourable to the system, the long-term gains are a modification of the system under pressure from popular anti-systemic forces (Santa Ana op cit.).

It is in this regard that Vilas (op cit.:76-78) considers civil society as mostly an affair of the poor and an expression of the popular dimension of social dynamics. This leads him to think that the term corresponds to or tends to replace what used to be referred to as the 'People'. Vilas (ibid.:69) also remarks that the most important element in the revival of interest in civil society is the resort to the identity dimension of collective action.

This arena for popular manifestation, according to Vilas, is now more varied and more complex than it was four decades ago, as the context of globalisation has transformed it. In a similar vein, Gallardo (op cit.:93-97) describes this civil society as: the arena of economic, social, ideological and cultural conflicts that the state has to resolve – either by stepping in or by suppressing them; the base from which demands are made on the state; the arena for different forms of activism, mobilisation, associational life and the organisation of actors and social movements who do not directly wish to control power. It becomes in this context the domain of relations between individuals, groups and classes whose existence is independent of state institutions as well as the space for the popular exercise of de facto power in opposition to the political structure that is constantly in search of legitimacy. Treating civil society as a third sector, Gallardo (op cit.:97) thinks that it has the potential of serving as the arena in which social movements and actors can contest political legitimacy and engender new forms of legitimacy or even a new civic culture.

Moving in a similar direction, Houtart (op cit.:13-19), proposes a typology of civil society made up of three dimensions that abound in the current context but which are the products of the historical situation: a non-analytical or angelic vision, a pre-analytic bourgeois connotation, and a popular analytic conception. The non-analytical angelic vision considers civil society as the whole set of organisations or initiatives undertaken by all types of groups which constitute a third sector alongside the state. This sector is perceived as the playground of anti-state, interclass, utopian ideologies, which, although hoping to change the society, end up achieving very little. The bourgeois conception of civil society is one of a world of free enterprise and all that contributes to economic growth. This is the scope of the ideological apparatus of the state in the sense Gramsci would give the term: the school, health, mass communication institutions, cultural and religious organisations, professional organisations and, indeed, every other institution that operates in the direction of reproducing the social relations of the market. Voluntary associations are often added to this category as proof of the creativity of citizens or those organisations that are often co-opted in the direction of the dominant hegemonic drive and are subordinated to the market, which is presented as a natural structure (see also Santa Ana op cit.). Instead of being a third sector as is presented by the non-analytical vision, this pre-analytical bourgeois conception treats civil society as a simple third hand situated between the invisible hand of the economy and the visible regulatory hand of the state. The pre-analytical conception is non-critical in its presentation of the current order as untouchable, that is, it cannot be reformed. It is in this regard that Houtart treats this conception as situated within the perspective of the current ideology of a world without an alternative.

The analytical or critical perspective starts from the observation that the market – unequal class relations – determines civil society in its present connotation. Its heuristic value is that it enables one to see the civil society as multidimensional, comprising, according to Houtart, four dimensions:

- Institutions produced by social actors who monopolise rights and privileges because of their position in the economic field;
- Institutions produced by the popular classes, which the dominant classes co-opt depending on their interests and hegemonic designs;
- Social and cultural resistance movements, emptied of any vitality by way of fragmentation as well as atomistic, and hence harmless, struggles often tolerated or ignored by the system;
- Resistance movements searching for alternatives. In this category one would find not only the traditional categories of the proletariat and organic intellectuals but also social movements supported by other intellectuals in the process of articulating popular interests in a comprehensive manner.

In this regard, civil society is defined as the space for social struggles, resistance and the articulation of alternatives. It is the arena for the organisation of popular movements in their quest for the democratisation of society and the building of new economic, social and political relations, which imply confronting the state. The struggles of the popular classes for a place within the civil society is presented as nothing else than the expression of a social struggle for justice and the transformation of social relations.

Civil Society in the African Context

For the past almost two decades, civil society and especially the association spirit has emerged as a force within the African milieu, constituting as it were a massive collective fact of contemporary Africa that cannot be overlooked or underestimated (Jacob and Lavigne-Delville 1994). In fact, it has a life cycle of growth, blossoming and disappearance. Jacob and Lavigne-Delville (ibid.) argue that it is both the product of change and a catalyst of change itself, and demonstrate a link between the organisational effervescence characteristic of the emergence of civil society, on the one hand, and the social and political restructuring of the African rural world, on the other. They therefore proceed to wonder whether they cannot form the basis of local development. Founou-Tchuigoua and Kassanda (2002) identify four important components of what would constitute civil society and social movements in sub-Saharan African: civil society organisations (CSOs), trade unions, women's organisations, and the student and peasant movement. They argue that civil society in this context takes the connotation of associations with a non-political and non-ideological content, excluding in this regard all forms of expression and organisation through which the popular classes struggle towards transforming social relations. Such a conception, they posit, reduces civil society to a set of harmless and powerless associations that exclude from their agenda the task of transforming the world in the direction of adjusting to the demands of the dominant self-perpetuating system. The main actors in this regard are NGOs, who are providers of amenities for the so-called 'fight against poverty', development orientated associations and human rights defence activists. They indicate that their weak financial capacity exposes them to both a financial and ideological dependency vis-à-vis donor agencies. One can also add that very often NGOs or third sector activities operate as an underground economy and the source of embourgeoisement for their local promoters (Yenshu Vubo 1998b), even if there is a fall-out in terms of predominantly service jobs for a few employees. Founou-Tchuigoua and Kasanda (op cit.) also point out that both local governments and donor organisations and governments alike are concerned with ridding civil society organisations of any political substance and role that they are likely to play.

They also trace the history of the trade unions, and student and peasant movements back to the colonial period when they were closely associated with the nationalist struggle for independence. They observe that these three movements follow an identical itinerary as they were quickly associated to and later became adjuncts of the structure of political monolithism of the post-independence era, either through repression or peaceful acquiescence. All movements are reported to have benefited only from the spate of political liberalisation of the 1990s, as they could once more recover their vibrant nature. Special mention is made of the South African workers' movement as an active force at the forefront of the struggles that led to the transition to majority rule in that country (Founou-Tchuigoua and Kasanda ibid.:131-133). The student union, for its part, has come to face new challenges, namely globalisation, ecology, equity, population movements, brain drain and the reform of the school system. The balance sheet of the peasant movement is one of a movement suffering from state authoritarianism, the burden of financial constraints, and warped legislation with regard to the land. Even the new lease of life of the 1990s was only instrumental in projecting the peasant movement within a context of neo-liberal adjustment. As such, this movement is passing through a critical period in its history where factors such as population movements, civil wars, political manipulation, discrimination and the poor education of the leadership are unfavourable to its development as a force capable of making alternative proposal in coping with current challenges.

The women's movement is presented as one characterised by a proliferation of organisations working towards improving women's condition within a variety of ideological or programmatic frames: women in development (WID), anti-poverty, efficiency and empowerment. Beyond these, women are also involved in various forms of activism of either a spontaneous and circumstantial nature or of a systemic nature, with long-term implications. In the first case, Founou-Tchuigoua and Kasanda (ibid.) affirm that women have always been at the forefront of popular protest, although such action did not either target political structures or aim at a radical structural transformation of society. This would explain the phase of demobilisation that soon set in. The second case is made up of organisations which are involved in designing strategies towards a long-term transformation of society in the direction of gender equity and equality. The authors identify the neo-liberal reforms of the Washington Consensus, religious traditions and customs, and dependency vis-à-vis the state and international orga-nisations, as major constraints to this movement. They argue that one cannot conceptualise Africa's development without the women's movement (Founou-Tchuigoua and Kasanda ibid.:137). Finally they conclude that there is an imbalance between forces, which is unfavo)urable to radical social movements and results in a critical situation which is not hopeless but calls for new reflections on the strategies and the bases of struggle.

Other analyses of the civil society in Africa are equally critical and argue for giving an Africanist tinge to the varying definitions. Osaghae (1998b) analyses the dislocating effects of Structural Adjustment Programmes on national cohesion and regrets that the civil society has not been called into the search for solutions to the question of national cohesion. Political liberalisation and economic adjustment are presented as propelling 'contradictory forces... a conjunction of both processes [being] mutually destructive' (ibid.:6). He argues that 'although a reformed state, better governance and democratization are germane to the World Bank's concern with civil society, they are secondary to its pre-occupation with economic growth and development' (ibid.:8). He indicates that 'the point is forgotten that civil society functions as the engine room or theatre of national cohesion, the place where contesting and opposing forces (which tend to increase under adjustment) are played out and resolved' (ibid.). Concerning civil society itself he points out that the concept should not be restricted to its Western meanings, but that 'the process, structures and functions it entails are to be found everywhere there is a public realm and/or state' (ibid.:9). This implies that there was a civil society in pre-colonial or indigenous African society as in the colonial and post-colonial period. He then situates civil society in 'contradistinction to the state, as both of them occupy the public realm' (ibid.:13). Three notions therefore emerge from the widespread usages with which the concept has come to be associated: it is essentially a 'non-state space of the public realm' with the function of defending 'society against the intrusions of the state' (ibid.); it is a repository of 'common good, collective will and solidarity as well as public opinion, and acting on these bases, civil society sets the rules governing the functioning of the state and its operators' (ibid.:14); and it is not homogeneous, that is, it is the arena of contending social forces which are competing for 'dominance'(ibid.). It is not synonymous with associational life because not all associations qualify to be included under the umbrella of civil society. In fact, only those associations which are self conscious of opposition to the state need to be included in this category (ibid.:15). It would, however, be useful to include ethnic and other primary associations which are part of what Osaghae calls 'positive ethnicity', as they 'command the loyalties of the vast majority of the ordinary peoples from civil society' (ibid.:16). Osaghae also proposes that this concept be seen as a process rather than as mere structures (ibid.:17). In his comprehensive definition Osaghae includes formal and informal organisations as well as social movements. Elsewhere he also argues that the civil society has to play an important role in restructuring state-society relations in a context where such relations have been distorted by the alienating practices of the colonial and post-colonial state (Osaghae 1998b).

An analysis of the state's relation to civil society shows the monolithic one-party state as totalising and attempting to achieve unrestricted domination over civil society by claiming a monopoly of the public realm. In the period marked by democratisation in the 1990s, the emergence of civil society elements of various shades led to a confrontation between some of these elements and the state which was largely responsible for opening up public space. These groups did not only seek to articulate the interests of particular segments of society, they were particularly critical of SAPs which were responsible for both deteriorating social conditions and their dislocating effect on the common man. Working on the premise that civil society is an arena wherein social conflicts at the national level can be resolved, Osaghae argues that civil society has to be given greater attention in terms of its political functions and the influence of adjustment, if national cohesion has to be given the place it deserves on the adjustment agenda (pp. 30-31).

According to Mercer, although non-governmental organisations have come to be considered within the New Policy Agenda of Development as the panacea, they may be unable to live up to the hopes that have been placed on them. She argues that 'the nature of state-society relations as played out between governments and NGOs must be seen as a central issue' (Mercer 1999:248). She goes on to show that, in the case of Tanzania, the state's attitude has been characterised by an ambivalence which treats 'NGOs as an unknown quantity, yet they are a resource that needs to be brought under control... government is well aware of the contri-bution that NGOs can make to "civil society", and the government's policy is laced with references to this virtue of NGOs. Despite such rhetoric of participa-tion, however, it is evident that the government's overarching objective is to co-opt the NGO sector in social service provision' (ibid.:251). She points to an increasing attempt by the state to control and regulate the NGO sector, but masked by the 'language of participation and empowering development', which replaces the state control model of the 1960s and 1970s which had been 'facilitated overtly by the rigidity of the authoritarian state structures, and covertly by the Ujamaa language of self-help and modernization' (ibid.:252.) She also points to differential levels of participation in NGO activities among local peoples, demonstrating that participation has been restricted to 'middle-income families' (ibid.:254) with the richer categories showing little interest while the poor are simply excluded. The conclusion is that the space that has been offered by liberalisation has not resulted in greater participation for the poor. It has rather resulted in a 'new mechanism for the reproduction of inequality' (ibid.:255) and the exclusion of the poor.

Cameron argues that the failure of pastoralist NGOs in Tanzania was due to their inability to address themselves to wider political agenda closely related to their own programmes - the land question and socio-economic development. His article claims that these NGOs were doomed to failure from inception, 'given the broader force at play' (Cameron 2001:57). He argues that although 'democratization has opened up new spaces for civil organizing, embracing free market economics poses dangers to all Tanzanian communities' (ibid.:67). Cameron also points to the 'over- determining influence' of donors (see also Mohan) in the short history of a Tanzanian federation of NGOs.

Hearn (2001) argues that the current vision of civil society in Africa serves to stabilise rather than challenge 'the social and political status quo'. In a study in three African countries (South Africa, Ghana and Uganda), she shows that there are limits to the concept of partnership that is central to the usage associated with civil society, because it 'erodes the potential for civil society organizations to fundamentally challenge the status quo' (Hearn ibid.:52). In the case of Ghana, Hearn demonstrates how CSOs were used to facilitate rather than question market-driven reforms, while in South Africa they were the handmaiden for diverting attention from 'socialist, redistributionist paradigms aimed at directly redressing the gross material inequality left by apartheid' (ibid.:48) towards a liberal democratic form ('procedural democracy') (ibid.:49) in the manner which Samir Amin calls 'low-intensity democracy'. In the process, the concept of democracy was redefined and the new regime's control was enhanced over the 'same intensely exploitative economic system, but this time without heavily mobilized opposition [as in the anti-apartheid campaign period]... It has ensured that democracy in the new South Africa is not about reconstructing the social order but about effective system maintenance' (ibid.).

Mohan (2002) reveals the tensions that exist between northern NGOs and local partners, the tendency for local NGOs to create fiefdoms in their area of operation, and the propensity for NGO officials to exploit their organisations for personal benefit. He concludes that the third sector facilitates the neo-liberal agenda that leads to a factionalism that undermines development itself. It 'covertly promotes social divisions, promotes factionalism and marginalizes some groups' (see also Mercer op cit.). He also indicates that 'the current paradigm is based on a particular vision which sees civil society as an autonomous realm of associational life in which "interests" can be pursued collectively' (p.128). He then advances five points for an analytical understanding of civil society. He sees it as an entity constituted across local, national, and international boundaries. Second, it is not an unproblematic entity between state and family but is 'shaped by economic forces'. Third, there is a need to examine the 'shifting processes of rule operating in the "hybrid" interstices' between state and society. Fourth, generalisations about CSOs should be avoided given their varied nature. Finally, there is a need to interpret the CSO in Africa 'through locally relevant cultural norms and practices' (p.135) as Osaghae has proposed (op cit.). He reveals that some of the disappointments of civil society, as exemplified in the study of northern Ghana, are the external determination of the local agenda by foreign NGOs, the tendency to use NGOs in enforcing neo-liberal economic programmes where they should have acted as watchdogs (see also Hearn op cit), the tendency for local NGOs to exploit local culture as a defence mechanism against the external control of the agenda, the erosion of local autonomy with the external determination of agenda, the tendency for the state to control funding through the state via state-centred legislation, and the tendency for local elites to use NGOs for private ends. In addition, legislation may selectively favour one type of NGO over another (p.148; see also Temngah in this volume). Although there is no synergy between 'state and civil society... in more subtle ways the state and NGOs are mutually implicated' (ibid.:149; see also Mercer op cit.).

He demonstrates that, in the main, NGO activities, as with those of civil society, are generally an adjunct and an underside to the neo-liberal framework, working more as a facilitator than as a constructive agent with an autonomous agenda. The political implications are a new form of imperialism and an attempt to use civil society as an 'element in the struggle to contain the Third World and police its policies' (ibid.:150). There is therefore a need to 'link' participatory approaches to the wider, more difficult, processes of democratisation, anti-imperialism and feminism in order to achieve 'long-term changes' (ibid.:151, see also Founou-Tchigoua and Kasanda op cit.).

Civil Society in Cameroon: Towards a Situational Analysis

Social movements of the civil society have blossomed alongside or in consonance with the movement for democratic reform. The term 'civil society' became part of official discourses as early as 1991 with the so called Tripartite Talks that were convened by the regime to seek solutions to the crisis generated by the transition to democratic rule in Cameroon. The regime convened a meeting bringing together public authorities ('pouvoirs publics'), political parties, and civil society. While the opposition parties thought the political future of the country was an issue to be negotiated between only two parties in a long drawn-out confrontation – government and opposition – they were surprised to see a third actor, civil society. From the look of things the regime was enlarging the spectrum of political debate and action. However, by so doing they were also diluting the voices of protest by designating a chosen civil society. It seemed like the regime was recognising the civil society occasioned by the liberation of public space with the enactment of the liberty laws of December 1990. But this was not the case because the choice was arbitrary, and those representing civil society were carefully chosen to avoid troublesome elements where voices were identical with those of the opposition parties. This selective attitude was not only going to be representative of the regime's attitude towards the budding civil society, but the cleavage within the political class between opposition and regime became a constant feature of a dichotomy within civil society. This was all the more so as some associations had allied themselves to the platform known as the National Coordination of Opposition Parties and Associations, which avowedly had the same goals. This selective attitude had the effect of also essentially limiting the field of civil society to officially approved voices. In such a way, the regime either refused to grant recognition to associational forms suspected of harbouring hostile attitudes towards the state, or enacted legislative instruments that confined civil society organisations to benign forms of activity (law of association, law on religious organisation, law on non-governmental organisations, law on common initiative groups, law on economic initiative groups, law on international organisations). The inflation of civil society organisations also served the function of further diluting the voices of dissent. The legislation itself kept out a sizeable proportion of organisations that could not find a place in the restricted definition of civil society due to the selective attitude of the state. This is the case with the civil society organisations that are either based on age-old traditions (see Fonchingong et al. in this volume) or the related forms linked to identity manifestations that go under the name of cultural and development associations. We have not followed this path in the several papers that follow.

The number of civil society organisations has risen considerably following the passing of law No. 90/053 of 19 December, 1990 to define freedom of association in Cameroon (Civic Agenda 1998). Although originally linked to political movements, they have come to be apolitical or rarely political after the 1990-93 crisis years. According to Ballo (1995) they have shown a tendency to work towards the collective good of its members, finding solutions to some collective or individual problems and arousing a new consciousness or dynamics. Women, the youth and the poor are the most attracted to what are likely to improve the lives of members (Ballo 1995; ASPPA and OCISCA 1996). Associational activity has thus been given a new lease of life and pervades all facets of the national scene (Yenshu Vubo 1997a). The potential of these associations for the mobilisation of local peoples in the development process in a spirit of self-reliance and in a context where the state is unable to look after the needs of these constituencies has been highlighted (Nkwi 1997; Nagel 1987; Yenshu Vubo 1997a, 1998a), although not assessed. Specific associations such as credit and thrift organisations, Parent-Teacher Associations, and women's organisations have also been instrumental in articulating the interests of their members (Nagel 1987; Essombe-Edimu 1993). The trade union movement, once captured by the one-party state, has instead capitulated to political manipulation and internecine disputes to the extent that it is in shambles and can hardly mobilise workers (see Temngah in this volume). Some of the associations which emerged claim development to be their raison d'être, although the recurrent theme in the objectives of cultural and development associations in Cameroon closely links them to the identity question. The implication is that the question of development has followed the ethno-regional drift that has characterised Cameroonian politics in the past decade and a half (Takougang and Krieger 1998; Nyamnjoh 1999; Yenshu Vubo 2003). The locus of national life in politics as in development has thus shifted from the nation-in-the-making to the home village, which either has to rely on its own initiative and resources, or lobby for state intervention in a paternalistic manner. Global national development policies are thus relegated to the background in favour of trade-offs which involve the provision of amenities by a regime in exchange for support from local, supposedly loyal, peoples or tribes. This contractual politics is essentially flawed because of the drastically dwindled financial resource base of the state due to constraints on social investments placed on it by the World Bank and the IMF. This results in a perverted version of local politics which is equated with deceit – where politicians knowingly make promises which they know they cannot keep as a way of winning the battle. The other assumption that the community based on local primordial affinities can be the locus of development is assessed later (see Yenshu Vubo in a separate study in the present volume).

Challenges and Opportunities for Civil Society in Cameroon

Despite the apparent vitality of these organisations, they suffer from weak mobilisation, a narrow territorial base (few are national in scope), the absence of an adequate legislative framework (Civic Agenda 1998; Temngah in the present volume), and the fluctuating attitude of the state (Yenshu Vubo 1998). Moreover they are inscribed within a type of 'piecemeal collectivism' that is incapable of initiating change within the peripheral capitalist framework (Yenshu Vubo 1997b). What is lacking therefore is the organisation of the association movement into a national network capable of presenting an alternative framework for managing the crisis. One need not follow the road of extreme pessimism, as some scholars are wont to do (Nyamnjoh 1999:15). What is absent is an assessment of the potential of these movements often presented in a non-critical, euphoric (Tostensen, Tvedten and Vaa op cit.) or angelic manner (Houtart op cit.). The enthusiasm within the association movement is real, but the orientation is problematic. Both an assessment of the potential and orientation were therefore deemed necessary. In other words, little is known of their scope, content and functioning, that is, their potential for generating real involvement or participation in public life and genuine development (the possibility for the greatest number of people to achieve satisfactory levels of survival and self-fulfilment).

This boils down to the central question of whether the new civil society or social movements can provide viable alternatives for both development and a participatory framework within the state. This is the substance of the multi-disciplinary investigation that resulted in this volume. Initially we set out to explore the following themes: the quality of non-governmental organisations; the civil rights movement; trade unionism in the post-one party era; alternative strategies to the social integration of the youth; semi-formal and informal financial markets; the legal framework of civil society and social movements; and autonomous associations in the light of Osaghae's 'positive ethnicity' and the concept of self-reliant development. Other issues that we intended to investigate included the role of the religious component of civil society; the women's movement, environmentalism, which is largely an echo of transnational concerns; and the value of traditional associational life in development. We felt that a critical study of these movements could go a long way in enabling us to understand their potential in generating alternative visions and strategies with regard to the crisis. We have covered all these aspects except that of the issue of the civil rights movement.

The general objective of the study was to evaluate the nature and potential of civil society organisations and the role they could play in searching for alternatives to the current impasse around development. The study was conceived first and foremost as a multi-disciplinary endeavour bringing together competences in several disciplines of the social sciences (anthropology, communication, economics, geography and environmental science, political science, sociology, gender studies) and legal studies. Although it draws from the wealth of these disciplines, it humbly restricts itself to an evaluative methodology essentially qualitative in nature, with only an occasional resort to quantification. As can be observed, the project does not nurture an excessive ambition to cover all aspect of civil society, nor to evaluate all forms of development. We restrict ourselves to some key elements of civil society (trade unionism, women's movement, religious groups, home-based associations, NGOs, traditional associational life in the rural areas, and youth), and consider only what they might contribute to development (the social side of development and the environment). Our choices with regard to civil society combine three domains: first, organisations operating as it were in the Gramscian tradition of hegemony and culture, as echoed by the school of alternative society (Houtart, Santa Ana, Gallardo, Vilas) – the church, education, and trade unions. Second, we opted to consider the newer forms promoted by donor concerns with alternative funding outside the state (NGOs). Third, we look at organisations that command the loyalties of the 'vast majority of the ordinary peoples', in cases reflecting the notion of 'positive ethnicity' – home-based associations, local communities, traditional associational life, informal financial institutions, and local women's mobilisation movement. This third domain is a much forgotten dimension, which has been eclipsed in favour of the fashionable visions of civil society although it constitutes the real foundation on which modern society tries to constitute itself and dominate cultural life in both rural and urban spaces. These organisations stand clearly outside the state and are above the family as the intermediaries through which interests are articulated. In the present context of Africa in general and Cameroon in particular, the three facets of civil society under study constitute the essential tissue of what Vilas calls the expression of the popular dimension of social dynamics, in both modernising and traditional forms, and corresponds to what used to be referred to as the 'People'. These study areas are also the locus of a new civic culture that not only replaces the dilapidated fashions and corroded ethics of a corrupt and unjust regime, but also secretes alternative ethics and practices that are pointers to new directions.

With reference to methodology, we combine a post-facto (historical) analysis and a study of contemporary events. In this way we do not only arrive at an evaluation of achievements over time; we also attempt to capture on-going events within the unending dimension of history. We are therefore arguing that social science, legal studies and allied disciplines, are based on established historical fact, but that this history is an unfinished, open-ended process. This is the more so as we are dealing with the concept of development that is essentially turned towards the future, and with a civil society that is both rooted in the past and provides prospects for a new vision of society.

At the horizontal level, some studies have been regional in scope but some too have attempted to cover as wide a scope of the national territory as possible. We did not attempt to cover all of the national territory or all possible themes related to the domain under investigation. All the studies were conducted by English-speaking social scientists - a fact which by no means implies that there is an Anglophone bias to the work. The four empirical case studies (Fonchingong, Enoh Tanjong, Yenshu Vubo and Ndenecho) that focus on the Anglophone provinces are rather a personal choice of the authors. They do not claim to be able to extrapolate to the whole country. These studies are complemented by other studies that cut across the linguistic divide (Yenshu Vubo, Awung, Akoko, Temngah), and by reflections that cover the whole country (Ntangsi, Forje, Fongot-Kinni). Of course, in this study the policy background and balance sheet of development performance are global in nature. Our achievement has been, we consider, to have been able to touch on almost all the themes we set out to study. The studies have gained from discussions among the researchers, whose ideas have thereby tended to cross-fertilise one another. We acknowledge the three workshops and the process of peer critique that have, we trust, contributed to the quality of this work.

The work is divided into three sections. Section I deals with the development policy and legal background. Chapter One situates development experience in Cameroon as a background to the study in general. Chapter Two examines the legal and institutional framework for the operation of civil society and social movements in Cameroon. This Chapter provides us with the contextual parameters within which to evaluate the action of civil society. Section II presents an evaluation of some of the key actors, with chapters involving trade unions and religious organisations. Section III explores the interface between tradition and modernity as found in associations in traditional society, home-based associations and informal financial institutions functioning in the wake of institutional reforms and women's protest movements. Section IV is devoted to the study of non-governmental organisations as the most projected form of civil society organisations (CSOs). The authors not only explore the public appreciation of their effectiveness, they also evaluate their impact in certain specific domains (watershed management and environmental protection). A last section is made up of two chapters. One chapter explores the complex relationship between state and civil society and proposes ways forward within the current dispensation. The last chapter examines the place of the youth in the reorientation of the educational system as a basis for alternative strategies towards development. A synthesis provides a final conclusion to the work.

References

Ake, Claude, 1978, *Revolutionary Pressures in Africa*, London: Zed Books.

Ake, Claude, 1992, 'The Feasibility of Democracy in Africa', Keynote address at the Symposium on Democratic Transition in Africa, organised by the Centre for Research, Documentation and University Exchange (CREDU), University of Ibadan, 16-19 June.

Ake, Claude, 1996, *The Marginalisation of Africa: Notes on a Productive Confusion*, Lagos: Malthouse Press Ltd.

Ake, Claude, 2000, *The Feasibility of Democracy in Africa*, Dakar: CODESRIA.

Amin, S., 1974, *Accumulation on a World Scale. A Critique of the Theory of Underdevelopment*, 2 volumes, Translated by B. Pierce, New York: Monthly Review Press.

Amin, S., 1993, '1492: La polarisation des mondes. Entretien avec Samir Amin', *Cahiers des Sciences Humaines: trente ans (1963-1992)*, Numéro hors série.

Amin, S., 1994a, 'Africa: Beyond Crisis and Adjustment', *CODESRIA Bulletin*, No 1, 1994.

Amin, S., 1994b, 'Ideology and Social Thought: The Intelligentsia and the Development Crisis', *CODESRIA Bulletin*, No 3, 1994.

Amin, S., 1996, 'Economic and Political Distortions in the Modern World', http://www.geocities.com/combusem/Amin.HTM

Amin, S., 1998a, 'Regulating Markets to Promote Democracy', *The Courier*, No. 171, September-October, (Interview).

Amin, S., 1998b, *Africa and the Challenge of Development: Essays by Samir Amin*, edited by Chris Uroh, Ibadan: Hope Publications.

Amin, S., 1998c, 'How to Liberate Africa. On Intellectuals, Grassroots and the Media', Inter Radio, December.

Amin, S., 1998c, 'La Couleur du logarithme', *Bulletin du CODESRIA*. No. 3/4, 1998.

Amin, S., 2000a, 'Economic Globalisation and Political Universalism: Conflicting Issues', *Journal of World-Systems Research*, Vol.1, No 3, Fall/Winter.

Amin, S., 2000b, 'The Political Economy of the Twentieth Century', *Monthly Review*, Vol. 52, No. 2, June.

Amin, S., 2000c, 'Multipolar Globalization: The Condition for a Social Development for All', CETIM, AAJ, LIDLIP and WILPF, eds., *Globalization and Alternatives*, Text by Samir Amin and François Houtart, Geneva: CETIM, AAJ, LIDLIP and WILPF.

Amin, S., 2001a, 'Imperialism and Globalization', *Monthly Review*, Vol. 53, No. 2, June. http://www.monthlyreview.org/601amin.htm.

Amin, S., 2001b, 'Une radicalité démocratique', http://humanité.fr/journal/2001-01-29/2001-01-29-238694.

Amin, S., 2002a, 'Convergence dans la diversité', *Pensamiento Critico*,

http//www.pensamientocritico.org/samami0602.htm (9 février 2002) ; tradition libre La Gauche.

Amin, S., 2002b, 'Le Paradigme de Développement', Samir Amin and François Houtart, *Mondialisation et Résistances. Etat de Luttes*, Paris, Budapest, Torino: L'Harmattan.

Amin, S., 2003, 'For Struggles Global and National. An interview with Samir Amin', Znet, January31,2003.http:www.zmag.org/contents/showarticle.cfm?

Amin, S., n.d., 'Neoliberal Globalization and U.S. Hegemony', http://www.southcentreorg/southletter/sl36-13htm

Amin, S., 'Economic Globalization: Doomed to Break Down', http:www.brettowoodsproject.org/topic/environment/growth/ter7Samin.htm.

ASPPA and OCISCA, 1996, 'Projet d'appui aux stratégies paysannes et à la professionalisation de l'agriculture: Les organisations rurales du Sud-Ouest; Cameroun', Yaoundé: ASPPA/OCISCA.

Bahmueller, C., 1997, 'Civil Society in Africa: The Good, the Bad, the Ugly', *Civnet's Journal of Civil Society*, Vol. 1 No. 1.

Ballo, Jean Marie, B., 1995, *Les Associations Volontaires civiles d'intérêt collectif dans les quartiers de Yaoundé*, Institut Catholique de Yaoundé.

Banock, Michel, 1992, *Le processus de democratisation en Afrique*. (Le cas du Cameroun), Paris: L'Harmattan.

Barber, B., 1996, 'Jihad vs. McWorld', Sondra, M., (ed.), *Democracy is a Discussion Handbook*, Connecticut College: A joint publication of the US information Agency and Connecticut College.

Ben Hammouda, Hakim, 1998, 'The Third World in a Post-liberal Era', *CODESRIA Bulletin* No 2.

Burnham, P., 1996, *The Politics of Cultural Difference in Northern Cameroon*, Edinburgh: Edinburgh University Press.

Cameron, Greg, 2001, 'Taking Stock of Pastoralist NGOs in Tanzania', *Review of African Political Economy*, No. 87, March.

Chabal, P., 1992, *Power in Africa. An Essay in Political Interpretation*, Basingstoke and London: The Macmillan Press.

Civic Agenda, 1998, No. 1, September.

Chomsky, Noam, 1997, 'The Passion for Free Markets', *Scandinavian Journal of Development Alternatives and Area Studies*, Vol. 16, No. 3 & 4, September and December.

Cohen, Jean, and Andrew Arato, 1992, *Civil Society and Political Theory*, Cambridge: MIT Press.

Dembele, Moussa Demba, 1998, 'Africa in the Twenty-first Century', *CODESRIA Bulletin*, No. 1.

Diamond, Larry, 1997, 'Civil Society and Democratic Development: Why the Public Matters', Paper presented originally to the University of Iowa Lecture Series, 'Democratization: Does the Public Matter?', 16 September, 1996.

Ekeh, P., 1986, 'Development Theory and the African Predicament', *Africa Development*, Vol. XIII, No. 2.

Founou-Tchuigoua, B. and A. Kasanda, 2002, 'L'Afrique subsaharienne', in Amin, S. and F. Houtart,. (eds), *Mondialisation des Résistances: L'Etat des Luttes*, Paris, Budapest, Torino: L'Harmattan.

Essombe-Edimu, J. R., 1993, 'Contribution à l'analyse essentielle de la tontine africaine', *Africa Development*, Vol. XVIII, No. 2.

Gallardo, Helio, 1998, 'Notes sur la société civile: l'évolution du concept', *Les Cahiers Alternatives Sud*, Vol. V, No. 1.

Hearn, Julie, 2001, 'The "Uses and Abuses" of Civil society in Africa', *Review of African Political Economy*, No. 87, March.

Hefner, Robert W., 1998, *Democratic Civility: The History and Cross-Cultural Possibility of a Modern Political Ideal*, New Brunswick, NJ and London: Transactions Press.

Howell, J., 2002, 'In their Own Image: Donor Assistance to Civil Society', in Janoski, Thomas, (ed.), Citizenship and Civil Society: A Framework of Rights and Obligations in Liberal, Traditional and Social Democratic Regimes, Cambridge: Cambridge University Press.

Houtart, F., 1998, 'Editorial', *Les Cahiers Alternatives Sud*, Vol. V, No. 1.

Houtart, F., 2000, 'Social Development Alternatives to Contemporary Globalisation', in AAJ, CETIM, LIDLIP, WILPF, Globalisation and Alternatives, Geneva: AAJ, CETIM, LIDLIP, WILPF.

Houtart, F., 2002, 'Les Projets et les niveau d'alternatives', in Samir Amin et François Houtart, (eds.), *Mondialisation et Résistances. Etat de Luttes*, Paris, Budapest, Torino: L'Harmattan.

Jacob, J.-P. and P. Lavigne-Delville, 1994, 'Introduction', in Jacob, J.-P. and P. Lavigne-Delville, (eds.), *Les Associations paysannes en Afrique: Organisation et dynamiques*, Marseille: APAD; Paris: Karthala; Geneva: IUED.

Kaplan, A., 1994, 'NGOs, Civil Society and Capacity-Building: Toward the Development of Strategy', Cape Town: CDRA.

Konings, P., 1999, 'The "anglophone problem" and chieftaincy in Anglophone Cameroon', in E. Adriaan, B. Van Rouveroy, Van Niewaal and Rijk Van Dijk, eds., *African Chieftaincy in a New Socio-political Landscape*, Hamburg: Lit Verlag, pp. 181-206.

Konings, P. and F. B. Nyamnjoh, 1997, 'The Anglophone Problem in Cameroon', *The Journal of Modern African Studies*, 35, 2.

Konings, P. and F. B. Nyamnjoh, 2000, 'Construction and Deconstruction: Anglophones or Autochthones', *The African Anthropologist*, Vol. 7, No 1.

Long, Norman, 1977, *Introduction to the Sociology of Rural Development*, London: English Language Book Society and Tavistock Publications.

March, K. and Taqqu, K., 1986, *Women's Informal Associations in Developing Countries: Catalysts for Change*, London: Westview Press.

McNamara, R. S., 1991, 'La crise du développement de l'Afrique: Stagnation agricole, explosion démographique et dégradation de l'environnement', Washington: Coalition Mondiale pour l'Afrique.

Marcuse, H., 1967, *One Dimensional Man. Studies in the Ideology of Advanced Industrial Society*, London: Routledge and Kegan Paul.

Mercer, Claire, 1999, 'Reconceptualising State-society Relations in Tanzania: Are NGOs Making a Difference?', *Area*, 31, 3.

Mestrum, Francine, 2002, 'La lutte contre la pauvreté: utilité d'un discours dans un nouvel ordre mondial', in Samir Amin and François Houtart, *Mondialisation et Résistances. Etat de Luttes*, Paris, Budapest, Torino: L'Harmattan.

Mohan, Giles, 2002, 'The Disappointments of Civil Society: The Politics of NGO Intervention in Northern Ghana', *Political Geography*, 21.

Nagel, Inga, 1987, 'La femme au Cameroun et sa participation au développement du pays. Une étude sur la promotion féminine', Yaoundé/Berlin: DED.

Narsoo, M. 1991, 'Civil Society: A Contested Terrain', *Debating Socialism*, 76:24 - 27.

Ndulu, B., Gyekye, K., Mbembe, A., Aboyade, O., and Ouattara, B., 1998, 'Towards Defining a New Vision for Africa for the 21st Century', *CODESRIA Bulletin*, No. 1.

Nkwi, N., 1997, 'Rethinking the Role of Elites in Rural Development: a Case Study from Cameroon', *Journal of Contemporary African Studies*, 15/1, pp 82-84.

Nkwi, P. N. and Nyamnjoh, F. B., 1997, *Regional Balance and National Integration in Cameroon, Lessons Learnt and the uncertain Future*, Leiden: African Studies Centre/Yaoundé: ICASSRT. ICASSRT, Monograph No. 1.

Nyamnjoh, F. B., 1999, 'Cameroon: A Country United by Ethnic Ambition and Differences', *African Affairs*, Vol. 98, No. 390, January.

Omboui-Bogui, G., 1995, *Profil-Pays*, Yaoundé: Ministère de la Santé Publique/Organisation Mondiale de la Santé.

Osaghae, Eghosa E., 1998a, 'Structural Adjustment, Civil Society and National Cohesion in Africa', AAPS Occasional Paper Series, Vol. 2, No. 2.

Osaghae, Eghosa E., 1998b, 'Rescuing the Postcolonial State in Africa: A Reconceptualisation of the Role of Civil Society', QUEST, Vol. XII, No. 1, Special Issue: Proceedings of the Interdisciplinary Colloquium on State and Civil Society in Africa, Abidjan, 13-18 July.

Rosandar, E. E., (ed.), 'Transforming Female Identities: Women's Organizational Forms in West Africa', Uppsala: Nordiska Afrikainstitut Research Report.

Sachs, Ignacy, 1995, 'Searching for New Development Strategies. The Challenges of the Social Summit', World Summit on Social Development, Copenhagen, 6-12 March.

Salamon, Lester M., and Helmut K. Anheier, 1997, 'The Civil Society Sector', *Society*, 34.

Santa Ana, Julio de, 1998, 'Eléments théoriques pour comprendre la société la civile', *Les Cahiers Alternatives Sud*. Vol. V, No.1.

Shils, Edward, 1991, 'The Virtue of Civil Society', *Government and Opposition*, 26, Winter.

Takougang, J. and M. Krieger, 1998, *African State and Society in the 1990s*, Boulder; Colorado: Westview Press.

Tejada, Aurelio Alonso, 1998, 'Le Concept de société civile dans le débat contemporain: les contextes', *Les Cahiers Alternatives Sud*, Vol. V, No. 1.

Tocqueville, Alexis de, 1990, *Democracy in America*, 2 Vols., New York: Vintage Classics.

Tostensen, A., Inge Tvedten and Mariken Vaa, 2001, 'The Urban Crisis, Governance and Associational Life', in Tostensen, A., Inge Tvedten and Mariken Vaa, eds., *Associational Life in African Cities. Popular Responses to the Urban Crisis*, Uppsala: Nordic Africa Institute.

Van Nieuwenhuize, C. A.O., 1983, 'Culture and Development: The Prospects of an Afterthought', *Civilisations: Revue Internationale de Sciences Humaines sur le Tiers Monde*, XXXVIII, (2).

Vilas, Carlos V., 1998, 'L'heure de la société civile', *Les Cahiers Alternatives Sud*, Vol. V, No. 1.

Walzer, Michael, 1990, 'The Civil Society Argument', Gunnar Myrdal Lecture, University of Stockholm.

Yenshu Vubo, Emmanuel, 1997, 'Democratizing Development in Sub-Saharan Africa: Imperative and Possibilities', *Scandinavian Journal of Development Alternatives and Area Studies*, Vol. 16, No 2, June.

Yenshu Vubo, Emmanuel, 1997, 'Balanced Rural Development in Cameroon within a Democratic Context', in Nkwi P. N. and Nyamnjoh, F. B., *Regional Balance and National Integration in Cameroon: Lessons Learnt and the uncertain Future*, Leiden: Africa Studies Centre/Yaoundé: International Centre for Applied Social Science and Training (ICASSRT). ICASSRT Monograph No. 1.

Yenshu Vubo, Emmanuel, 1998a, 'The Discourse and Politics of Indigenous/Minority People Rights in Some Metropolitan Areas of Cameroon', *Journal of Applied Social Sciences* (JASS), Vol. 1, No 1, October.

Yenshu Vubo, Emmanuel, 1998b, 'The Evolution of Official Attitude to Grassroots Initiatives in Cameroon', *Community Development Journal*, Vol. 33, No 1, January.

Yenshu Vubo, E., and Che C. Fonchingong, 2002, 'The Rural Communities of Cameroon and its Development in the Era of Post-Developmentalism', Paper Presented at the 10th General Assembly Conference of the Council for the Development of Social Science Research in Africa, December.

I

Policy Background

1

A Balance Sheet of Economic Development Experience since Independence

Ntangsi Max Memfih

Introduction

Cameroon is a country blessed with tantalising potential: favourable vegetation, alluring topography, vast deposits of mineral resources, and a large, hard-working and resourceful human power. These factors suggest that the country has the ability to sustain high growth. Compared with other sub-Saharan African countries, Cameroon has one of the most diversified production and resource bases, as it produces and exports a broad range of raw material commodities including oil, coffee, cocoa, bananas, palm oil, natural rubber, timber and aluminium. It is a net exporter of oil, and although oil production has been declining steadily since 1986, it still amounted to above 37 million metric tons in 2002, representing about 13 per cent of GDP. Agriculture has remained the mainstay of the economy and employs over 70 per cent of the labour force. Industrial development has largely been rudimentary and confined to affiliates of transnational corporations. Government attempts to enter this sector through parastatal companies have been a dismal failure, to the extent that most of the companies have been privatised during Structural Adjustment Programmes. The population of the country as of 2003 was estimated at 15.5 million people with an annual growth rate estimated at 2.8 per cent, while the per capita GDP for the same year stood at $610 with an annual growth rate of 4.5 per cent (World Bank 2005). The inflation rate, which stood at 3.9 per cent in 1997/1998, fell to 3.1 per cent in 1998/1999. It has been maintained at that level since then.

Cameroon's development efforts were managed since independence through a series of five-year Development Plans until the implementation of the Structural Adjustment Programme during the late 1980s. Six successive plans were implemented between 1961 and 1990. Economic policy objectives as well as specific strategies that were pursued during the course of each plan fell within a general development ideology. Nevertheless, during the course of each plan, policy initiatives were undertaken and changes in strategies that were not initially envisaged in the plan as well as emergency changes were introduced. Thus, almost invariably at the National Assembly Budget Sessions on the occasion of national agricultural shows (that were held every two years), and on other occasions, the President of the Republic announced new policy initiatives.

The underlying principles of Cameroon's economic policy changed very little during the course of all six plans. Firstly, all plans continued to underscore agriculture as the priority sector in national development and emphasised the direct and indirect contributions of this sector to overall economic development. Secondly, all continued to assign the same policy objectives to this sector, and, thirdly, they all continued to identify the same basic constraints and problems limiting the sector's development. Nevertheless, in view of the complex nature of certain constraints, the interaction between them, the ineffectiveness or failure of existing strategies and the accentuation of certain problems through time, various plans pursued different approaches and adopted different solutions and strategies. Apart from a state presence via the establishment of parastatal companies in key sectors (for example, air, sea, railway and urban transport; aluminium transformation; electricity and water; cement production; paper pulp), indigenous involvement in industrial development was virtually absent. Industrial development was more or less left to free market forces dominated by transnational companies. The same is true of the commercial sector for finished goods in which local economic operators featured only as distributors (retail and wholesale) of products produced in the centre of the capitalist system. The services and financial sectors also continued to be dominated by external economic interests.

However, as expected growth in the economy was not achieved, the unfavourable international economic climate in the mid-1980s plunged the country into a devastating economic recession. This led to the institution of the World Bank and International Monetary Fund Structural Adjustment and Stabilisation Programmes (SAPs). The immediate effect of the policy was a rise in poverty and mounting debts, leading to Cameroon becoming a Highly Indebted Poor Country (HIPC). To qualify for external funding, the Cameroon government needed to establish a Poverty Reduction Strategy inspired by policies of the Bretton Woods institutions. Thus, during the period from the late 1980s to the present, development has been externally managed; initially through SAPs and, later on, through the Highly Indebted Poor Country Initiative (HIPCI) and the Poverty Reduction Strategy Papers (PRSPs).

This chapter builds on the above foundation. Its main objective is to examine the balance sheet of economic development experience in Cameroon since independence. The analysis concentrates on policy changes with regard to the extent of government intervention in the economy, and the centralisation of decision-making in relation to the allocation of resources between the private and public sectors. This perspective enables us to consider how policy affected efficiency in resource use, and thus the performance of the economy. The following are some specific objectives of the study:

- Identifying the various policies and their shortcomings;
- Assessing the performance of the economy during the period of study; and
- Making recommendations on how to target development policies in Cameroon in order to achieve any meaningful and sustainable development.

Development Policies and Economic Performance since Independence

Cameroon's development efforts were managed since independence through a series of five-year development plans until the implementation of Structural Adjustment during the late 1980s. Six successive plans were implemented between 1961 and 1990. Five phases can be identified in the evolution of economic policy in Cameroon.

The first phase, which runs roughly from independence to the end of the 1960s was marked by the continuation of French and British colonial economic policies and institutions, with rather limited government intervention in the economy. The second phase, covering the period from the late 1960s to the late 1970s, was one of institutional proliferation with the creation of an astonishingly large number of institutions with widely varying structures. The third phase, initiated roughly since the late 1970s and covering the preparation and launching of the fifth and sixth plans may be called a reflective phase because it marked the beginning of an effort to undertake major economic policy reforms that were well overdue, particularly in the face of the stagnation in the economic export sector and the poor performance of the economy. The fourth phase began during the late 1980s with the implementation of the Structural Adjustment and Stabilisation Programmes following continuous imbalances in the economy. The fifth phase runs from the late 1990s to the present, covering the Heavily Indebted Poor Countries' Initiative (HIPCI) and the Poverty Reduction Strategy (PRS).

First Phase: Prolongation of Colonial Policies

This period which extends from 1960 to the late 1960s saw continuity in the French and British policies and institutional structures, reflecting the country's dual colonial heritage. The main concern during this period was the agricultural sector, which provided a livelihood for virtually the entire population. Cameroon was ruled under a federal system until 1972, with two federated states (East and West Cameroon), each with its own Secretariat of State for Development. In the Francophone East, basic extension services continued to be carried out by the 'Secteurs des Modernisations' (SEM), the marketing of export crops by the Caisse de Stabilisation (Stabilisation Fund), and research largely by French institutions. In the Anglophone West, extension services continued to be provided by the Department of Agriculture, Cooperatives and Community Development, the marketing of export crops by the Marketing Board and research by the Department of Agriculture. To coordinate the development efforts of the two states, the Department of Agriculture and Rural Animation was created in 1964 and placed under the Federal Ministry of Planning.

The two colonial systems presented significant differences in their organisational structure. For example, the French system provided a tighter network of extension services and research than the British. Furthermore, while the Marketing Board enjoyed a monopoly over the export of products, in the case of the Caisse de Stabilisation this role was entrusted to private licensed buyers. Despite these differences, the development models of both were based on the diffusion/modernisation model. The model presented three main features. Firstly, it was centred on the peasantry as the primary agent of development. Secondly, it involved the transformation of peasants through progressive diffusion and adoption of innovations with the assistance of extension agents. Thirdly, it relied on limited government intervention through research, extension, provision of inputs at subsidised rates, and so on.

This approach was pursued to a lesser extent in the second plan (1966–1970) although government showed signs of dissatisfaction with the approach. Indeed, it was noted that, notwithstanding the satisfactory performance of the economy during this period, growth in output had come essentially from increase in the volume of inputs and not from productivity gains. Accordingly, while not completely abandoning the diffusion/modernisation approach, government envisaged experimentation with other forms of intervention structures and new forms of production aimed at inducing technical change/productivity gains in the economy.

Second Phase: State-Centred Developmentalism

This phase covered the period between the late 1960s and the late 1970s and was characterised by three main features: increased government intervention in the economy and centralisation of decision-making; the concentration of government expenditures in state corporations and the parastatal sector; and the virtual neglect of the peasant sector that was responsible for about 90 per cent of total economic activity; and the increased indirect taxation of the peasantry and small enterprises through withdrawals by the National Produce Marketing Board (in the case of peasant farmers).

This phase witnessed a multiplication of new intervention structures and new production institutions. The second plan recommended the expansion of the estate sector, rural settlement schemes or projects to move people from densely populated areas to sparsely populated areas, specialised development agencies (sociétés de développement spécialisées) charged with organising and supervising the production of specific activities undertaken by peasants, and integrated rural development projects stimulating production as well as providing social services. By the late 1960s, more than ten development agencies were created. During the third plan (1971-1975), fourteen more were created. The fourth plan (1976-1980) in addition to continuing the projects of the third plan, attempted a further expansion of the modern sector. Twenty new projects were enshrined in the plan, most of which were never implemented due to the lack of donor interest and support.

Despite their structural and organisational complexities, the development agencies could be broadly classified under five categories. Category one covered Integrated Rural Development (IRD) projects (such as WADA, ZAPI-Est, ZAPI-Centre, SODENKAM), which were among the earliest development agencies to be created. IRD projects reflected third world and donor wisdom at the time, and combined in one project elements to increase agricultural production, to improve health, education, infrastructure, and other social services. A second category covered large-scale plantation projects. On the basis of the positive and encouraging results obtained by some private large-scale plantations that survived from the colonial period, the government sought to establish a significant modern agricultural sector by creating large-scale state-owned estates. The Commonwealth Development Corporation (COMDEV) was thus nationalised in 1973 and its name was changed to the Cameroon Development Corporation (CDC). This body was expanded, and a number of new estates were created with the aim of diversifying agricultural production and in the long run, serving as pilot centres for associated peasant growers and therefore, as a nucleus for the spread of modern farming methods.

A third category included development agencies that operated at the national level and offered certain vital services in the form of inputs (credits, agricultural chemicals, fertilizers and small equipment) at concessionary or subsidised terms through a rural bank, the Fonds National de Développement Rural (FONADER), in the form of marketing services (MIDIVEV up to 1984), in the form of cooperative services (CENADEC in the Centre and South, UCCAO in the West, NWCA in the North West), or in the form of the development of small machinery (CENEEMA). A fourth category included specialised sectoral agencies that organised and supervised peasant activities like SODECOTON for cotton, SODECAO for Cocoa, SEMRY, UNVDA and SODERIM for rice, etc. During the fourth, fifth and sixth plans, a fifth category of development structures emerged in the form of regional or provincial development agencies. This step reflected a change from centralisation towards a regionalisation in development planning. These bodies were either newly created institutions like the Hauts Plateaux de l'Ouest, MIDENO, MEAVSB, MEAL, or existing institutions whose functions were redefined and broadened, as was the case with SODECAO.

The donor community initially endorsed the government's interventionist policy. This support explains why government was able to create such a vast number of development agencies. Donor interest could be explained by the fact that these agencies were run as parastatal enterprises (with administrative, technical, and financial autonomy and therefore potentially efficient) but also by the fact that most of the projects aimed to combine marketable output with basic peasant needs. This idea fitted very well within the basic needs approach to rural development widely adopted by donors and the international intellectual community during this period.

This second phase in the evolution of economic policy in Cameroon had three central features. Firstly, the government sought to increase productivity, particularly in agriculture, through the establishment of a sizeable modern sector. Secondly, there was increasing dissatisfaction with the diffusion/modernisation approach as a development model. Thirdly, economic policy became more interventionist.

By the mid 1970s it was evident that the interventionist approach had not produced the results expected. The attempt to create a modern sector proved to be too costly, with only a marginal impact on total output. Furthermore, the proliferation of new institutions and structures while still maintaining the old ones resulted in the widespread overlapping of institutional functions and competences. Consequently, the various bodies often worked at cross-purposes, power conflicts arose, and above all there was a general confusion among stakeholders. The situation was exacerbated by the fact that the agencies were supervised by different government ministries with little or no provision for the coordination of activities. The poor performance of this strategy led finally to donor retreat. Thus many projects proposed under the fourth plan were not financed.

Third Phase: Revision of State-Centred Policies

The third phase comprised the period from the late 1970s to the mid-1980s. The fragmented institutional situation, the high cost and rather marginal impact on the economy, the neglect of the peasant sector in favour of the estate sector, and above all, the generally poor performance of the economy during the 1970s as compared to the 1960s, resulted in the need for an in-depth review of policies. This phase was a time for reflection in which new solutions and new dimensions in economic policy were sought.

The need for an overall policy review became clear following the steady decline in general economic performance, although Cameroon was frequently cited as one of the few countries in sub-Saharan Africa to have achieved satisfactory economic growth because of its agricultural potential, and one of the few to have attained virtual food self-sufficiency.

The decline in economic performance necessitated a search for new directions in economic policy orientation. However, because of the discovery of oil, which became a major economic activity providing enormous funds to the government in the late 1970s, reform was delayed. As in many oil producing countries, the 'Dutch disease syndrome' set in. All attention was shifted to oil production, but the revenue allowed government to postpone necessary reforms. Government policy continued to expand the public service with resulting increases in expenditure on the civil service, subsidies to inefficient public enterprises and parastatal companies, and a low return on capital-intensive investment. This only contributed to the deterioration of the economy which completely collapsed during the mid 1980s when international market conditions were unfavourable. Thus, the third phase was virtually that of reflection with no particular policy initiative being put in place except the continuation of the five-year development plans. The change in leadership in 1982, when Paul Biya took over from Ahmadou Ahidjo, contributed to the stagnation in reform and aggravated the decline of the economy.

Fourth Phase: Crisis and Structural Adjustment

The fourth phase covered the period from the mid-1980s to the early 1990s. During the mid-1980s, the drop in the dollar prices of Cameroon's major exports (oil and agricultural products) and the depreciation in the dollar itself exposed major structural weaknesses, plunging the country into a deep crisis. The government responded by launching the IMF/World Bank austerity and structural adjustment programmes. These programmes were instituted by the Bretton Woods institutions as recovery measures for countries that were not able to service their debts in a sustainable manner. Hence, economic policy making during this phase was externally propelled.

The Cameroon government embarked on these programmes by reducing salaries and cutting subsidies in order to bring down government budgetary deficits in the short-run. Public enterprises and parastatals were restructured and rationalised. The government undertook to liberalise its external trade policies while improving the exchange rate and providing incentives for the export sector. These policy objectives and instruments were acompanied by a number of immediate social and long-term economic costs. These costs included a reduced expenditure on social infrastructure and services (public utilities, health, and education), increased unemployment, the deterioration in real per capita incomes, and an inequitable distribution of income.

Between late 1988 and early 1994, economic policy was directed primarily towards the objective of internal adjustment by internal measures. This implied forcing down wages through fiscal policies of austerity, while at the same time seeking to raise productivity through structural reforms. For an economy that had been dominated by the public sector since independence, the choice of an internal adjustment strategy and the way it was implemented resulted in increased poverty and its unpalatable consequences.

The first point to note about the poverty impact of this strategy was that it failed in its main economic objective of restoring competitiveness. Agricultural export markets continued to be lost while domestic food crops and industrial goods systematically rose in price relative to import competition. The loss of product markets was reflected in the lower demand for labour. This limited the employment and income possibilities of Cameroonians.

The second point was that internal measures consisted of a combination of demand compression and fiscal austerity to reduce inflation, coupled with structural measures to lower production costs. The effort to compress wages and prices sufficiently to make up the gap in competitiveness resulted in a protracted deep recession. The austere monetary policy including tight ceilings on aggregate credit from the banking system led to the contraction of domestic credit from around 900 billion FCFA to less than 750 billion between 1985 and 1993 (World Bank 1994). The combined effects of these policies weighed heavily on the poor through the trickle-down effect of reduced economic activity and unemployment. These programmes continued to be unpopular in almost all countries that implemented them in sub-Saharan Africa. In Cameroon, the efficiency of government services was lowered as reduced circumstances led to demoralisation among civil servants. In general, SAPs failed in Africa as a whole and in Cameroon in particular, and the process has been perceived to be all pain with no gain.

Indeed, one area in which the failure of SAPs has gravely affected the Cameroonian economy is the aggravation of the poverty burden. There are more poor people in Cameroon today than in 1985. Since the adoption of SAPs necessitated the retrenchment of workers, the removal of subsidies, salary cuts, currency devaluation, trade liberalisation, and the privatisation of public utilities, the burden of poverty was greatly aggravated. SAPs, which were intended to increase economic growth and to lead to a trickle down of income to lower income groups, instead led to a trickle up effect, through which most of the resources intended for the poor actually benefited the small middle-class and the very rich.

Thus, poverty has manifested itself in many ways, including high rates of infant mortality, low levels of literacy, the reduction in life expectancy, limited access to medical facilities and the propagation of the deadly HIV/AIDS. The burden of poverty has increased over the years because more than 73 per cent of internal fiscal revenue was oriented towards external debt servicing, thus drawing investment away from the social sector.

The immediate results of SAPs were that during the period 1987 to the late 1990s, Cameroon's debt burden indicators deteriorated very rapidly. Overall, the stock of debt grew on average by about 17 per cent per year while export growth virtually stopped. As a result, debt-to-export and debt-to-GDP ratios rose from 219 per cent and 32 percent in 1987 to 369 per cent and 113 per cent in 1997 respectively. By 1996, the country was classified as a heavily indebted poor country (HIPC), with a net present value (NPV) of debt equivalent to 353 per cent of exports of goods and services.

Fifth Phase: Heavily Indebted Poor Country Initiative (HIPCI) and the Poverty Reduction Strategy (PRS)

The fifth phase saw the introduction of the Heavily Indebted Poor Country Initiative (HIPCI) and the Poverty Reduction Strategy (PRS). These measures correspond to the period after the mid 1990s. Development policy during this period in Cameroon was likewise externally managed as in the fourth phase, since the end result was virtually the continuation of structural adjustment. The main difference, however, was that policies were more focussed on short and medium term poverty alleviation as more emphasis was placed on the social sector pro-grammes, particularly education, health and basic infrastructure.

The HIPCI was proposed by the World Bank and the IMF to governments around the world in 1996 as the first comprehensive approach to reducing the external debt of the world's poorest, most indebted countries, and represented an important step in placing debt relief within an overall framework of poverty reduction. While the initiative yielded significant early progress, multilateral orga-nisations, bilateral creditors, HIPCI governments, and civil society have engaged in intense dialogue on the strengths and weaknesses of the new programme. A major review in 1999 resulted in a significant enhancement of the original framework, and produced a HIPCI which entails deeper, broader and faster debt relief. It also focuses on strengthening the links between debt relief, poverty reduction and social policies. It is central to the enhanced HIPCI that countries continue to show commitment to macroeconomic adjustment and structural and social policy reforms. But it does mean that there is higher spending on social sector programmes like basic health care, education and infrastructure.

Indeed, there has been a general consensus among creditors, debtors and the civil society that the HIPC initiative is, for now, the only way out of the debt problem. This is because, unlike the other debt relief strategies, it engages both bilateral and multilateral debt cancellation. With a net present value (NPV) of debt of 353 per cent of export of goods and services, a scheduled debt ratio of debt-service to government revenue of 94 per cent, Cameroon gained admission into the HIPCI-2 alongside many other African countries. If the country reached the 'decision point' it was to benefit from debt cancellation of up to about 90 percent of its debts. The effect of the HIPC Initiative in Cameroon on poverty alleviation at present is rather ambiguous. If the funds saved through this initiative are well used in the social sector, poverty will be significantly reduced. On the other hand, if the funds end up in the pockets of the small middle-class or the very rich, then the poverty burden will even be heavier. Cameroon has embarked on a Poverty Reduction Strategy (PRS), which is described by the World Bank and the IMF as one of the best in the world, but the real effect on poverty reduction is still controversial. Although highly rated by the World Bank and the IMF, Cameroon's PRS displays some weaknesses which if not adjusted will fail to bring about poverty alleviation in the country even if the 'completion point' is reached.

After Cameroon's debt has been reduced under the framework of the HIPC Initiative, the country will have much less debt service (interest and repayments) owed to its creditors. The prognoses of the World Bank and the International Monetary Fund envisage that Cameroon will pay its creditors between 70 and 150 million US dollars less than before the Initiative. About 30 per cent of the money thus saved is to be paid into a poverty alleviation fund. Debt relief is conditional on the Cameroon government's adoption of a Poverty Reduction Strategy Paper (PRSP). The World Bank stipulates that the PRSP be prepared and implemented through a broad-based participatory process. This was hardly the case in the past, as the government had little interest in the participation of civil society organisations, who in turn expected nothing positive from a fund administered by the government.

The IMF must be criticised for its negative effect in the past on the self-determination of indebted countries. Due to the required adoption of IMF economic reform or stabilisation programmes, governments must take steps which are partly contrary to their national economic interests. Many see a failure in local 'ownership' of the measures, with policies for the most part developed externally. With the new concept of allowing indebted countries to develop their own poverty reduction strategies, these countries are, at least theoretically, given more freedom to decide on the pace and quality of reforms.

The Cameroon government has been reluctant to embrace cooperation with NGOs, and the latter's proposals for poverty reduction strategies have not received proper attention. There was, as part of the PRSP process, a consultation, or rather a survey, on the subject of poverty and poverty reduction, but one can hardly speak of meaningful participation. NGOs lack extended networks and thus cannot easily unite in order to wield more influence. But as it becomes clearer that civil society must be able to speak with one voice, the beginnings of at least sectoral networks have sprung up.

Despite the above named difficulties, the participation of NGOs is important, not only for reasons of democratisation. Many NGOs have extensive knowledge of the circumstances and the problems of the poor. Daily work with grass-roots groups has strengthened NGOs in poor communities. Their ability to communicate in the language of the target groups has caused a strong identification of many people with the work of the NGOs. Since most NGOs in Cameroon see fighting poverty as the central priority of their work, they have, through different activities and projects, earned a certain competency in problem solving, particularly at the local level.

The three largest religious movements (Protestant and Catholic denominations of Christianity, and Islam) have played the most important role in the participatory process. As a large percentage of the population belongs to one of these faiths, they have true democratic legitimacy and are well suited to represent popular interests. They have at this point in time, however, barely been a part of the PRSP process. Only now are the first steps being taken in the health and education sectors to get all denominations working together to strengthen their hand and win influence in the participatory process for the development of a PRS. Thus, the fifth phase is characterised by a drastic change in development ideology with NGOs and civil society intended to play very vital roles in government-related economic policy issues.

Conclusion

From the above discussion, a number of conclusions are discernable. Firstly, development efforts in Cameroon have been characterised by a number of significant policy changes, although with very few achievements in real terms. Efforts to improve productivity and sustainability have lacked real commitment and political will, and thus have had a negligible impact. Secondly, economic development today in Cameroon continues to face the same problems as in the past with poor governance, weak institutions, and poor infrastructure topping the list. Thirdly, macroeconomic stability and a predictable policy direction remain essential to any attempt to foster sustainable development. Fourthly, productivity improvements cannot persist without the type of generalised capital accumulation associated with broad-based improvements in health, education, food security, and institutions that sustain social stability. Fifthly, a major stimulus to both productivity and sustained growth could be achieved relatively rapidly through concerted efforts to reduce waste and inefficiency. An obvious place to start is the government's own operations. Finally, there needs to be a renewed focus on improving management at all levels.

We have argued that in the present situation the government needs to work together with all components of the civil society (labour unions, religious organisations, federations of associations, consumer associations, students, farmers' movements, women's groups, professional associations, intellectuals, producer unions and the media) in seeking solutions to the problems that undermine development. It is significant that civil society has already been involved within the scope of the IMF-inspired reforms, albeit timidly or only as a token. Should this path be pursued in the spirit of fairness and with consensus on the common good, there is some possibility that it will lead to a significant improvement in the direction that development will take.

References

Fambon, S. and F. M. Baiye, 2002, 'Income Distribution and Poverty in Cameroon', Paper presented at the Conference on Spatial Inequality in Africa, University of Oxford, 21-22 September.

IMF, 1999, 'Modifications to the Heavily Indebted Poor Countries Initiative', Paper prepared by the staff of the IMF and World Bank. Washington DC: The World Bank.

Ngassam, A. and Roubaud, 1994, 'Cameroun: Un profile de pauvreté', A study for the World Bank (unpublished).

World Bank, 1998, 'Targeted Programs for the Poor during Structural Adjustment. A Summary of a Symposium on Poverty and Adjustment', Washington DC: The World Bank.

World Bank, 1994, 'Cameroon: Diversity, Growth and Poverty Reduction: Working Drafts', Human Resources and Poverty Division, African Region.

World Bank, 2005, *African Development Indicators*, Washington, DC: The World Bank.

2

The Legal Framework of Civil Society and Social Movements

Temngah Joseph Nyambo

Introduction

Law functions as a means of directing and imposing restraints on human activities and it must therefore seem something of a paradox that the idea of freedom can be embodied in the law (Lloyd 1964:138). There is the question of the right of various types of groups, whether social, political, or economic, or of any other kind, to organise themselves and to conduct their own affairs.

In Cameroon, as elsewhere, it is thus a common feature of daily life that people tend to constitute themselves into groups which may be permanent or transient. Such groups, when they become instituted are treated in law as persons possessing a separate identity and continuity from its members. The movements differ very markedly in size, character, composition, and purpose, so it by no means follows either as a matter of logic or even common sense that all should be accorded similar recognition on the doubtful analogy of the individual human person (op cit.:303).

Civil society and social movements in Cameroon reflect complexity and diversity. This is amply illustrated in the legal instruments governing their modes of creation, organisation, functioning and other details such as goals, and particularly, their sources of revenue. In the structuring of civil society in Africa therefore, Ekeh argues that care should be taken to include associations and institutions that possess not just a manifest but also a latent capacity to confront the state. On this basis, he identifies four categories of civil society organisations in Africa: civic public associations, for example, trade unions, student unions, mass media; deviant civic associations, for example, secret societies and fundamentalist religious movements; primordial public associations, for example, ethnic associations; and indigenous development associations, for example, farmers and traditional women's unions (Ekeh 1992).

It must be remembered that the end of the East-West conflict and the sudden breakdown of the socialist experiment in Eastern Europe are at the basis of the emergence of civil society organisations as is the adoption of neo-liberal market-led reforms and of political pluralism. Generally, it is believed the civil society movements in Africa constitute a fifth power. This explains why the good governance programme of Cameroon has designed a strategy which consists of strengthening civil society and social movements. Gradually, the state is disengaging from several key sectors of national life in favour of civil society by facilitating its legal framework (Temngah 2000:2).

The attitude adopted by the state in creating the legal space for civil society has been one of both caution and repression. For the purpose of this chapter, a sample of legal instruments regulating civil society and social movements will be presented. Our next task shall consist of analysing the adequacy of such legislation in an attempt to illustrate the state's attitude of caution and repression. Finally, the thesis that there is still the possibility of harnessing these groups into a total national network capable of presenting an alternative framework for managing the crisis-ridden state within the present legal context will be highlighted as a way forward.

Diversity of Legal Instruments

The legal framework of non-state actors is abundant and rich. Civil society organisations consist of groups of non-state actors representing a number of sectors with different, and possibly divergent, interests. Such diversity can constitute a valuable asset but it also constitutes a veritable obstacle to the sustainable and coherent organisation of the civil society (Mbaye 2003:24). Cameroon's legislation on associational life is regulated and controlled through legal instruments having drawback clauses intended to maintain a firm grip on associational life (Law No. 90/053, Law No. 99/Law No. 90/053, Law No. 99/014). The legal instruments confer on the groups a legal personality enabling them to act in their own name(s) within the ambit of the law as artificial persons separate from their founders (Salomon v. Salomon 1897). It is in affirming its attachment to fundamental freedoms contained in the universal declaration of human rights and other regional and international human rights instruments that the Cameroonian Constitution guarantees freedom of association as is the case with other freedoms (Republic of Cameroon 1990).

It is consequent on the liberalisation of public life in Cameroon that a 'baby boom' emerged in associational life in the context where the state had failed in both its governmental functions and developmentalist claims and where donor agency attention was tilting towards civil society organisations.

Table 1: Legal Instruments and their Domains of Applicability

No	Nature Of Group	Legal Instrument(s)	Competent Authority
1	NGOs	Law No 90/053 of 19 December 1990 Law No 99/014 of 22 December 1990 Decree No 2001/150/PM of 13 May 2001	Ministry of Territorial Administration and Decentralisation
2	Trade Unions	Law No 90-053 of 19 December 1990 Law No 92-007 of 14 August 1992 Decree No 93/574 of 15 July 1993 Decree No 93/576 of 15 July 1993 Convention No 87(1948) Convention No 98(1949)	Ministry of Labour, Employment and Social Welfare
3	Cooperative Movement	Law No 92/006 of 14 August 1992 Decree No 92/455/Pm of 23 November 1992	Ministry of Agriculture Ministry of Finance
4	Common Initiative Groups	Law No 92/006 of 14 August 1992 Decree No 92/455/Pm of 23 November 1992	Ministry of Agriculture Ministry of Finance
5	Mass Media	Law No 90-052 of 19 December 1990 Law on Trade Unions	Ministry of Communication Ministry of Territorial Administration
6	The Church	Law No 90/053 of 19 December 1990	Ministry of Territorial Administration and Decentralisation, Presidency of the Republic
7	Professional Associations	Law No 90/053 of 19 December 1990 C.f. Cameroon: Rights and Freedoms 1990	Ministry of Territorial Administration/MINREX (Ministry of External Relations)
8	Students Movements	Law No 90/053 of 19 December 1990	
9	Feminist Movements	Law No 90/053 of 19 December 1990	
10	Development	Law No 90/053 of 19 December 1990	
11	Separatist Movements	Not authorised; no legislation Sectarian Movement,	Ministry of Territorial Administration
12	Religious Fundamentalists	Not authorised; no legislation, deviant group	Ministry of Territorial Administration and Decentralisation
13	Ethnic Movements	Socio-cultural, may not need formal authorisation	May not need formal authorisation
14	Secret Societies	Operate clandestinely. Not allowed, considered as deviant structures	Legal instruments are lacking

Source: Constructed from Legislative Instruments of Republic of Cameroon.

The first legislation that inaugurated the new age of civil society in Cameroon is Law No. 90-053 which repealed Law No. 67/LF/19 of 12 June 1967. It is a law of general application (articles 1, 2) which reflects the organisations' diversity and alludes to specific laws (Art 5.4) for the likes of political parties and trade unions. A survey of the legal instruments in this domain reveals a concerted effort to contain it through system checks by curtailing its effect as a major partner or force in the development process. Though legislation gives the movement legitimacy, the attitude towards it is one of caution and repression through the various regulations in force. Table 1 illustrates the various legal instruments in force regulating civil society movements.

The Attitude of the State

In legislating on association life, the state has two complementary attitudes. On the one hand, there is an ambiguous approach guided by caution, which consists of granting rights and freedoms in the most of liberal terms and on the other hand issuing enabling instruments that tend to limit the freedom of association through repression. Law No. 90-053 of 19 December 1990 on the Freedom of Association proclaims that everyone is free to set up an association and has the right to belong to any association. One reading of this law is that it is a liberal piece of legislation which resulted in the emergence of various groups which had even been outlawed through the repressive law of 1967. Religious organisations, such as the Jehovah's Witnesses and secret societies like the Brotherhood of the Cross and Star (Olumba Olumba) (Calabar), outlawed some years ago, re-emerged and became free to conduct their activities within this new context. So far so good! However the same law as well as other relevant legislation limits the associational thirst of Cameroonians through drawback clauses in the various laws governing associations.

Caution

A reading of the aforesaid laws reveals that the state is acting with caution. With the exception of public utility associations, no declared association may obtain subventions, gifts and donations (art. 11) and the state has very wide powers as far as the dissolution of associations is concerned (articles 12-14). In effect, articles 12-14 deal with public order and policy. For one reason or the other the authority in charge of the maintenance of public order may dissolve an association which is deemed to be pursuing goals that are contrary to the constitution, laws and good morals, as well as acting in a way that tends to affect national integrity and unity and the security of the state (art. 4). It is the authority that qualifies the said act and once the association is dissolved, the only recourse is to the Administrative Bench of the Supreme Court within ten days, and while the matter is pending, the decision remains valid.

Article 15 which deals with foreign associations gives them the ample freedom to set up and function. Foreign associations here refer to groups having their headquarters abroad or in Cameroon whose leadership is composed of foreigners or a majority of them. In authorising their existence, the authorising body may issue a temporal legal status or may submit it to regular renewals on the basis of certain conditions and can withdraw their authorisation at anytime without the need to show cause for its decision (art. 17). Under this condition, the association shall proceed forthwith with the immediate cessation of activities and liquidate its assets within a time frame of three months. According to Chapter V (articles 22-31), which defines the parameters for religious associations, in as much as they can be freely set up, they may not receive subventions from the public in the form of gifts and grants.

The law is also subjected to enabling statutes (the textes d'application), which subvert the veneer of liberality enshrined in the statutes. For example, when it comes to granting the status of accredited association, there is Decree No. 2001/150/PM of 3 May 2003 setting up the functioning and organisation of a technical ministerial committee in charge of accrediting NGOs and the follow-up of their activities. This statute saw the light of day only three years after the law on NGOs entered into force. Secondly, the accreditation procedure is so tight that less than twenty groups received their accreditation three years after the law of application (Law No. 99/01, Law No. 90/053). This requirement is very strict since it leaves no room for transitory measures for existing groups before the enacting of the law.

Repression

In as much as there is freedom of association (Temngah 1995:178-205), this freedom has not gone unchecked. Generally, associations are expected to have rights and obligations. In the present context, the sanctions, which might either be civil or criminal, are more often than not repressive.

Civil Sanctions

Civil sanctions consist of the dissolution of the group by the Minister in charge of Territorial Administration for acts incompatible with public order and policy or activities that undermine the security of the state. Again, the group may be suspended by the competent authority on the recommendation of the follow-up committee for the duration of three months when members pursue objectives contrary to their statutes. The conditions for dissolving an association are arbitrary since the administrative authority alone may determine the degree of incompatibility with public order, policy or the security of the state. In this way the administrators have wide-ranging powers over a domain which is meant to ensure alternative forms of participation and liberties for the common man.

Criminal Sanctions

Criminal sanctions against leaders of groups may be inflicted on the basis of articles 184 and 225 of the Cameroonian Penal Code for embezzlement of public funds since these funds are considered public funds (Tchokomakoua 2000:18). The 1999 law proceeds to punish a person (founder, delegate, administrators of groups) with a jail sentence of three months to one year and a fine of 100,000 FCFA to 1,000,000 FCFA or one of the sanctions for the continuous activity of a dissolved or suspended group. The sanctions are very severe as they are doubled when the activities of the group(s) are considered inimical to national unity either in an armed or unarmed manner. The sanctions extend to persons who purportedly act as if the group was accredited pending outcome of the accreditation file and to someone who facilitates in any manner meetings of dissolved or suspended groups (Tchokomakoua 2000). Indeed, in these matters the powers of the administration are wide and discretionary.

Taking the example of the law on NGOs, there is a violation of the principle of non-retrospection. Existing groups have the same obligations to produce an application for accreditation in a similar manner to new ones, without considering their previous achievements. The law itself talks of an association, which for three years has contributed to development within its domain of interest. One would have logically expected that older groups should have benefited from transitory measures on the basis of their achievements within this minimum period and given accreditation automatically.

Another major aspect of repression is the fact that the judiciary cannot review a refusal of accreditation of any association. The wide discretionary powers of the competent authority are such that associations, which may not be to the taste of the system, can simply be outlawed. The 'baby boom' of associations can then be halted by the Minister of Territorial Administration for acts incompatible with their statutes and endangering public order and state security (Temngah 2000, Republic of Cameroon 1993, Mbu 1986:263-69). It may be recommended that the right attitude should be for the legislator to review the laws on associations in order to avoid the conflicts, inadequacies and the many pitfalls that impair the largely liberal spirit and may eventually defeat the purpose for which it was intended.

Recourse to the Courts of Law for Judicial Review

The powers of the judiciary to review a dissolution or suspension order are negligible. The judiciary is not an independent structure as it ought to be although the 1996 constitution nominally consecrates it as a power like the executive and the legislative. In practice it has not been possible for it to affirm this role of a power because the Ministry of Justice, which is the supervisory body of the judiciary, is paradoxically part of the executive arm of government (see Decree No. 84/353 of 28 May 1984). By this arrangement judges are placed under administrative structures which exercise wide powers that often undermine the independence of the judiciary (Temngah 1997:362-363). For instance, there are multiple pressures on the judiciary from the executive arm of government. Once a decision has been issued by the authority suspending or dissolving an organisation or structure, the judiciary is usually reluctant to interfere, especially given that grounds for dissolution or suspension usually consist of matters relating to public order, national security and territorial integrity. Under such circumstances, the courts will normally invoke laws relating to subversion and terrorism as was the case with the one-party days or the aftermath of 9/11.

Response of Potential Civil Society Actors in the Affirmation of Roles

In the face of caution and repression on the part of government, potential civil society actors have resorted to circumventing the laws and setting up spontaneous structures. The very existence of deviant groups and secret societies is a response to the state's refusal to give legal status to such organisations. The phenomenon of rebellious groups and other associations sprouting up with diverse interests and strategies is a response to the tight legislation (for example, the Southern Cameroons National Council). Moreover, some of the structures may not need formal recognition as their impact on the state will be minimal. In any case, recognition is necessary if funding has to be sought in the pursuit of their activities. This is the case of associations changing their denomination to become cooperative societies or common initiative groups and others ridding themselves of the political overtones of their objectives, activities and slogans.

This attitude is illustrative of the view that there is still ample legal space for civil society organisations in Cameroon. Despite severe sanctions and various administrative hurdles, associational life in Cameroon is promising. Of course, one should not lose sight of the fact that this all depends on the economies of the country concerned, given that development assistance is conditioned upon a minimum of stability and peace and the level of democratisation. In addition, there is the lack of experience due to the novelty of the phenomenon and the non-democratic nature of regimes in Africa. Institutional lapses and the high level of corruption do not augur well for the proper implementation of programmes for development that will benefit the masses. The diversity of civil society organisations also accounts for the low level of understanding and the nature of dialogue between the state and non-state actors. The overall picture is not so bleak, but from the Cotonou Agreement (2000) there is hope based on the strategies of setting up platforms at various levels (local, national, regional and international). The strategies employed, such as capacity building, advocacy and training, can only enhance this spirit of solidarity between the various stakeholders.

Legal Framework and Development Role of Civil Society

In order to examine the relationship between the legal framework of civil society and development, one can classify them into either organisations pursuing broad collective interests or those with specialised focus.

Organisations Fostering Broad Collective Interests

It is clear that there is a great diversity of organisations from the legislation regulating civil society in Cameroon. Groups such as 'Cercle des Amis du Cameroun (CERAC)', 'Association Mondiale de Défense des intérêts des Albinos' (ASMODISA), 'SOS Dialogue', and 'African Synergy against Aids and Suffering' present themselves as organisations taking up the general interests of their members or the community they seek to protect. These groups embrace almost everything and it can be said of them that they are generally focused as they embrace a variety of activities. This is usually by virtue of their funding capacity. For instance, CERAC (Cercle des Amis du Cameroun) is a prestigious group, headed by the wife of Cameroon's current President. Its membership is open to spouses of ministers and accredited ambassadors, a fact which enhances the funding capacity and is at the basis of the strength of the organisation. Table 2 presents NGOs as typical organisations with a broad focus.

It is worthy to note that only the seven organisations cited above were able to obtain the status of NGO from the Ministry of Territorial Administration (*Cameroon Tribune* 2003:8), and as of May, 2004, two others, namely 'Ligue pour l'Education de la Femme et de l'Enfant' (LEFE) (Yaoundé) and 'Association Ecole et Développement' (Yaoundé) equally received accreditation (*Cameroon Tribune* 2004:28).

Table 2: Examples of Non-Governmental Organisations with a Broad Focus

No	Name Of Group	Objectives
1	Centre d'Acceuil de l'Espoir (CAES)-Yaoundé	Contribute to the fight against HIV/AIDS, care for children and the girl child
2	Organisme de Développement d'Etude de formation et de Conseil (ODECO)- Yaoundé	Accompany partner organisations in the development process of professional training
3	Organisation des Jeunes pour la Santé, la Sécurité Alimentaire et le Développement	Contribute to the welfare of man particularly the woman and her offspring
4	Service d'Etudes et d'Appui aux Populations à la base (SEAPB)-Yaoundé	Promote development through the participation of individuals
5	Femme, Santé et Développement en Afrique Subsaharienne (FESADE) Yaoundé	Offer training to ameliorate the competencies of women for the resolution of their health problems, their families and their communities.
6	Rural Development Foundation-Buea	Offer training and assistance to projects in underdeveloped rural zones.
7	Mouvement International Contre la Pauvreté en Afrique-Cameroun (MIPACAM)-Yaoundé	Assistance to destitute local peoples.

Source: *Cameroon Tribune*, Friday, 7 November 2003, p. 8, Translation by the author.

The proliferation of associations with a broad focus is the fruit of liberalisation through which the media and civil society can thrive. This category of organisations pursue broad and often vague objectives giving them room for manoeuvre in the development process. Though the law purports to be liberal, the enabling act on NGOs is very severe on granting NGO status to existing associations in Cameroon. From 1952 to 1990, 301 associations of various types were legally operating in Cameroon (Temngah 2000:8) while in the period 1991–1993, 278 associations were declared and from 1990–1993, 16 foreign associations and three organisations operating as public utilities were authorised (Human Rights in Cameroon 1993:79, 81).

Organisations with a Specialised Focus

At the end of the Cold War, there were a number of UN Conferences on issues such as the environment (Rio Earth Summit 1992), health and population (Cairo Summit 1994), socio-economic Matters (Vienna 1993), and Women (Beijing 1995). It is in response to these international concerns that some Community-Based Organisation (CBOs) emerged as organisations with special focus around the new issues heralded by globalisation in domains such as social justice, meaningful employment, welfare, environmental rights and awareness, local empowerment, human rights, community development, natural resource management, poverty alleviation, the monitoring of environmental standards, and practice in the local oil industry and the impact on the local oil-producing communities (Obi 1999:24).

This focus is a direct result of donor impact on these groups. For instance, since Rio, environmental associations have fared well in issues such as land rights, peoples' rights to a clean environment, poverty alleviation with people living in dangerous zones (pollution, etc.). The preservation of the environment can be properly handled by specialised and focused groups of a given community. A shining example in Africa is the Movement for the Survival of Ogoni People (MOSOP) in the Delta Region of Nigeria (Obi 2000). In Cameroon, several groups are concerned with the environmental needs of the Cameroon Oil and Transportation Company (COTCO) of the Chad-Cameroon pipeline project. If the 1970s and 1980s were decades when the world was preoccupied with issues surrounding supply of security, the 1990s look set to be the decade of the environment. The present environmental discussions have their roots in the Brundtland Report of 1987. That report took a broad view of the problems facing mankind, including the Third World problem of poverty. Although the causes of pollution are the result of the industrialisation process in the developed world over the past two-and-a-half centuries, Third World countries too, are also experiencing the environmental challenge. From the many issues involving the decline in rural economies in developing countries, it is understandable that organisations with a narrow focus may be effective in tackling common questions of their livelihoods in their various communities.

Another key sector which has attracted groups is gender and empowerment, from which the women's movement has benefited greatly. The feminine or women's movement has benefited from the UN's emphasis on the gender question during the Cairo Summit and also during the Copenhagen Conference and then Beijing where these issues came up prominently. The Cameroonian public has taken advantage of this advocacy to set up groups responsive to specific rights. The 'Ligue pour l'Education de la Femme et de l'Enfant' (LEFE) is just one of such organisations pursuing specific questions dealing with gender and the empowerment of women. During the Beijing Conference of 1995, the leader of this group, Pauline Biyong, was part of the Cameroonian delegation for this major advocacy in favour of women's rights. Her movement is gaining ground in this fight for the empowerment of the Cameroonian woman. Many groups and NGOs were involved in this forum for the adoption of the Cameroonian platform and policies have been influenced in favour of women in Cameroon. Women are thus involved in the creation of micro-finance groups and other local community groups for the implementation of the Beijing platform for women. To this effect, laws have been changed in favour of women as pressure mounted from within and abroad. The Cameroon government, through the Ministry of Women Affairs, prepared the official documents that were adopted in April 1997 as the platform of action and policy for the empowerment of women in Cameroon. Many groups, thanks to the opening, are blossoming in this sector.

Another issue that has become the focus of specific groups is children's rights. These groups draw their force from instruments such as the UN Convention on the Rights of the Child (1979) and the ILO's Programme of Action for the elimination of the Exploitation of Child Labour of the Human Rights Commission. In Cameroon, some children live in absolute penury, malnutrition, disease, prostitution, and delinquency. No doubt, in this field, one can find groups militating against the sexual abuse of children and other related issues in partnership with UNICEF.

Our next concern is with the attitude of the state to this blossoming associational life.

Prospects for Building Civil Society Networks as an Alternative Framework for Development in Cameroon

Despite statutory and legislative drawbacks dealing with the administrative, institutional and legal framework in Cameroon, there is still enough legal, administrative and institutional space for a blossoming of associational life in Cameroon. If the central approach to development has failed, there is an acknowledgement that non-state actors can play a vital role in the development process. Despite legal hitches, the nature of the group is fundamental to this approach. Self-help and corporate associations and farmers' groups may not need any formal recognition. Sometimes, local government may be part of this process. The decentralisation process engaged through the 1996 constitutional reforms that imply certain forms of political disengagement on the part of the central government and liberalisation of public life constitute a major concern by central authority to allow local peoples the latitude to manage their own affairs.

In this regard, Cameroon may gain from the recommendations of Article 4 of the ACP-EU Partnership Agreement signed in Cotonou on 23 June 2000 (The Cotonou Agreement), which acknowledges and recognises the complementary role and potential for contributions by non-state actors in the development process. Article 6(1)(b)(2) of the same agreement defines non-state actors as the private sector, economic and social partners, including trade unions and the civil society in all its forms. One of the central objectives of the Cotonou Agreement is poverty reduction, democracy and the recognition of better structured and organised non-state actors in the entire process. Participation of non-state actors in all the sectors of society in the definition and formulation of policies and strategies according to the realities and needs of each country remains a major concern. This emphasis contributes to enhancing ownership of all development strategies by the beneficiaries, thereby consolidating their role as facilitators of public-private partnerships.

The Cotonou spirit lays further emphasis on dialogue in national development strategies, sectoral policies and programming. Pre-Cotonou agreements between the ACP and the EU have been the monopoly of governments, but today the partnership has been extended to non-state actors. To achieve the overall goals of the Agreement, national platforms of civil society organisations representing all its components have now become a necessity. For instance, it may cover a wide range of organisations such as NGOs, trade unions, women and youth organisa-tions as well as other movements that fall under the rubric of non-state actors within the meaning of article 6(1) (b) and (2) of the Cotonou Agreement.

National platforms are necessary for shaping policies and programmes within a given member country of the ACP-EU for the sake of sustainable development. These networks may not be sufficient. Participation requires partnership across regions, given that once organised, these groups are given consultative status with the UN Economic and Social Council (ECOSOC). During the negotiations leading to trade issues of the World Trade Organisation (WTO) at Seattle, non-state actors were very involved in contributing to the outcome of the Agreement. During the 1990s, several civil society organisations from all regions of the world, constituting themselves as national platforms and regional coalitions representing the civil society viewpoint were active at the various UN summit conferences (Rio 1992 on the Environment, Vienna 1993 on Socio-economic matters, Cairo 1994 on Population and Health, Beijing 1995 on women). Their force cannot therefore be underestimated. The successful setting up of the International Criminal Court (ICC), whose mandate is to prosecute and punish perpetrators of genocide, war crimes and crimes against humanity, was the brainchild of the NGO Coalition for an International Criminal Court and its contribution in the process of signing the ratification of the instruments of the court is immeasurable.

From this recognition and through their advocacy skills, non-state actors have played an important role in shaping, defining and formulating policies and development programmes according to the needs of their beneficiaries. Although they usually pursue diverse and even divergent interests, there is a need for platforms at national, regional, and international levels. This approach is feasible given that CSOs exist at local, national, regional and international levels. An examination of the modalities of building civil society networks at all levels in the quest for participation and action towards development is therefore necessary. At the close of the exercise, there should be sufficient evidence that such arrangements are capable of considerably influencing policy. For instance, in the case of Cameroon with supposedly liberal laws having drawback clauses, a lot of lobbying can be done at this level to ensure that legislation on civil society movements conforms to the spirit of civility and this can be done if we borrow wisely and integrate elements of international practice correctly. After all, human problems are universal with the only difference being that the world is divided into poor and rich segments. Since our exercise concerns the developing world, there is need to cooperate with others in order to share experiences. This can take the form of building national platforms, federating civil society organisations, working sector by sector or federating at regional level.

Conclusions

Cameroon's liberal and multifarious approach, as evidenced from the legal framework of associational life, must be reviewed as a matter of urgency. There is hope that this can happen in view of the prevailing international context of globalisation. In the search for alternatives, there is nothing that restrains a group from carrying out its development vision. The partnership existing between the various stakeholders in the definition and implementation of development objectives gives room for hope. As the fever for 'change' of the vibrant and turbulent period of the 1990s passes on, people are settling down to conceiving clear and achievable development goals. I will recommend that the various legal instruments be combined into one with two broad parts, namely, the general part that will cover all general provisions concerning the orientation and cardinal principles, and a special part dealing specifically with different groups. This will avoid repeating the same provisions from group to group. The competent authorities will also be limited to take into account only advisory opinions of the specific sector from which the group has to emerge. The Cotonou partnership and the existence of NEPAD have acknowledged the role of non-state actors in the development process and so it is hoped that any shortcomings in the legal framework of social groups in Cameroon can be made good and so there is still some legal space that civil society and social movements can capture and make much good of a bad situation.

References

Cameroon Tribune, Friday Nov. 7, 2003.

Cameroon Tribune, May 5, 2004.

Ekeh, P. P., 1992, 'The Constitution of Civil Society in African History and Politics', in B. Caron, E. Gboyega, and E. Osaghae, eds., *Democratic Ttransition in Africa*, Ibadan: CREDU, University of Ibadan.

Lloyd, D., 1964, *The Idea of Law*, London: Penguin Books.

Maurizo, C., 2003, 'The Role of Non-state Actors in Development Policy: Perspectives and Changing Practice', *The Courier*, the magazine of the ACP-EU Development Cooperation, no. 199, Brussels'.

Mbaye, B., 2003, 'Civil Society Participation and the Cotonou Process in West Africa', *The Courier*, The magazine of the ACP-EU Development Cooperation, no. 199.

Mbu, A. N. T., 1986, *The Mill of Justice*, Yaoundé: Cameroon Publishing and Production Centre for Teaching and Research (CEPER).

Obi, C., 1999, *The Crisis of Environmental Governance in the Niger Delta 1985-1986*, Harare: African Association of Political Science, Occasional Paper series, Vol. 3, no. 3.

Obi, C., 2000, 'Economic Adjustment and the Deepening Environmental Conflicts in Africa', in Adele Jinadu, ed., *The Political Economy of Peace and Security in Africa: Ethno-cultural and Economic Perspectives*. Harare: AAPS Books.

Osaghae, E. E., 1997, 'The Role of Civil Society in Consolidating Democracy: An African Comparative Perspective', *Africa Insight*, vol. 27, No. 1.

Osaghae, E. E., 1998, *Structural Adjustment, Civil Society and National Cohesion in Africa*, Harare: African Association of Political Science, Occasional Paper series, Vol.2, No. 2.

Republic of Cameroon, 1993, *Les Droits de l'Homme au Cameroun*, Livre Blanc publié par le gouvernement de la République du Cameroun, Yaoundé: Imprimerie Nationale.

Republic of Cameroon, 1996, Law Number 96/06 of 18 January 1996 to revise the 1972 Constitution of the Republic.

Tchokomakoua, V., 2000, *Analyse du cadre juridique des ONG au Cameroun*, Yaoundé: GTZ.

Temngah, J. N., 2000, 'Civil Society and Constructive Pluralism: The Case of Cameroon', Paper presented during the joint Francophonie-Commonwealth International Colloquium on the theme of democracy in pluralistic societies, Yaoundé, January 24-26.

Temngah, J. N., 1995, *The Protection of the Right to Work under Cameroonian Law*, Yaoundé: University of Yaoundé II, Unpublished Doctorat de Troisième Cycle Thesis in Law.

Temngah, J. N., 1997, 'The Independence of the Judiciary in Emerging Democracies in Africa: The Case of Cameroon', Conference Proceedings of the ASICL conference, Abidjan, 4-6 August.

Thibault, G., 1995, 'On the Diversity and role of NGOs', *The Courier*, the magazine of the ACP-EU Development Cooperation no. 152, Brussels'.

II

Classical Social Movements

3

The Evolution of Trade Unionism
and the Prospects for Alternatives
to the Labour Question

Temngah Joseph Nyambo

Introduction

The labour movement in Cameroon has a very rich and telling history. Pre- and post-independence Cameroon was characterised by a plurality of free and autonomous trade unions, particularly in the plantations (CDCWU) in West Cameroon and the union led by Ngom and Ruben Um Nyobe in East Cameroon, which was to become a political party known as the Union des Populations du Cameroun (UPC).

The immediate post-independence state of Cameroon, faced with the eagerness of these groups to occupy political space, thereby exceeding their original claims and objectives, adopted an attitude of repression through the emasculation of individual and group rights. This drive was prompted by the project of national unity and integration, which, according to post-colonial African leaders, was possible only under a one-party or authoritarian regime. The result was the kind of undemocratic and dictatorial regime which became fashionable all over the continent during the Cold War. Repression became the order of the day and all organisations, particularly labour movements, which had become critical of the state in its quest for development, were proscribed. This explains the genesis of the central labour movement known as the National Union of Cameroon Workers (NUCW), styled after the single party, the Cameroon National Union (CNU) and, later, the Cameroon Trade Union Congress (CTUC) under the Cameroon People's Democratic Movement (CPDM). Today, thanks to the re-emergence of multipartyism, the plurality of trade unions has returned (see also Founou-Tchuigoua and Kasanda 2002).

The purpose of this chapter is to examine the history of the labour movement in Cameroon and its impact on development. It is argued that the centralisation of the union movement and its eventual marriage with the one-party state did not augur well for its adherents in the quest for decent working conditions. I further argue that, instead of strengthening the state and reinforcing its capacity to be responsive to social interests, the link between state and labour movements rendered the political and social structures rather fragile and vulnerable, preparing the way for the collapse of the one-party state and the emergence of political pluralism as well as the resurgence of a new labour movement.

Furthermore, these groups, particularly vibrant in the early 1990s, witnessed a dramatic growth in number. Social unrest mounted with widespread protest against the state. The impetus behind the protest movements came from popular resistance to the Structural Adjustment Programme (SAP) to which Cameroon had subscribed and which affected all classes of workers as a result of the restructuring of state-owned companies. For example, the banking sector was hard hit and the privatisation of giant income-generating structures had a direct negative impact on the workers with the unions unable to protect them. The labour movement remained a lame dog. It lacked the necessary means to live up to the expectations of the workers in the face of a repressive government backed by capitalists for whose benefit SAPs were instituted.

Finally, although within a liberalised space, the trade union movement in Cameroon in the post- one party era is dwindling in importance and, given the growing unemployment rate, people are reverting to other forms of social orga-nisation. These associations often maintain direct links to foreign capital to fi-nance their objectives. The legal and institutional framework of social movements is marked by diversity and so one protest group under one denomination can easily be found under the umbrella of another.

The above notwithstanding, the trade union movement in Cameroon, as in other less democratic countries, is under government scrutiny. The present legal framework gives government the latitude to constrain all unions or associations which are not under its control, and even to outlaw some of them in case of alleged misdoing (Law No. 92/007: 1992, Decree No. 93/574: 1993, Decree No. 93/576: 1993, L. Kaptue 1994:64, Temngah 1995).

In this hostile legal environment, trade unions must still survive and protect their membership, and if necessary confront the state in the broader context of a globalised capitalism with the prevailing inequality where powerful economic and political giants are dominant (Temngah 2001, Kahn-Freund 1972).

The question to be answered is whether the trade union movement can play its role in the post-one party era. A question which is a corollary of the first is: under what legal conditions can trade unions function? If trade unions are failing to respond to the aspirations of their membership, what can be done in order to strengthen them in Cameroon so as to enable them to meet the challenges of sustainable development within a context of globalisation?

The purpose of this chapter therefore is to explore the nature and potential of trade unions in Cameroon. Specifically, the research explores the role of the trade union movement in democratic transformation and alternative development strategies. In addition, we shall evaluate the scope, objectives and functioning as well as the attempt at democratic participation and genuine autonomous development. Another specific objective is to discover the forces that have sustained trade union movements and enabled them to foster links with other groups in the search for alternative forms of participation.

The adoption by the United Nations Organisation of the Universal Declaration of Human Rights in 1948 gave a boost to trade union movements by advocating freedom of association. The International Labour Organisation for its part followed up very closely by adopting two fundamental conventions in 1948 and 1949 on trade unionism, namely Convention No. 87 concerning the freedom of association and the protection of the right to organise trade unions, and Convention No. 98 dealing with the application of the principles of the right to organise and to bargain collectively.

These principles were recognised in Cameroon before and after independence and reunification. The preambles to each of the successive constitutions (Federal Republic, United Republic and finally that of the Republic of Cameroon) allude to these ideals. We will trace the history of the trade union movement in Cameroon as a background to the present situation. This history is closely tied to the political history of the country.

The Emasculation of Trade Unions in the Immediate Post-Independence Era

After independence, many African leaders set out to re-model trade unions to serve the dominant party, the regime and the all-powerful state structures along the lines of the Soviet model of state organisation. Thus, a new model of trade unionism – state-controlled unionism – was intended to replace the autonomous unions. The post-independence period was characterised by instability and internal wrangling within the unions in Francophone Cameroon. Although the unions heeded to the call to set up a single union at the service of the state, problems of diversity of ideologies and goals rendered any genuine attempt at unification very difficult. Some of the unions were radical and pro-Marxist. For example, the Conseil National des Syndicats du Cameroun was affiliated to the Czechoslovakia-based World Federation of Trade Unions (WFTU) which appeared to some as a spring-board for the spread of Marxism-Leninism doctrine in Cameroon (Temngah 1995:251). This reasoning led to a split within the 'Conseil'. The Union Camerounaise (UC) took advantage of the conflict to intervene in its activities and launch an appeal for national trade union unity.

At the 1962 UC congress in Ebolowa the party appealed to all trade unions to fuse into one organisation. This appeal of the ruling party in East Cameroon affected trade union matters nationwide. The following year the FSC headed by Joseph Amougou and Jacques Ngom as Secretary General was created and expressed the desire to cooperate with the party and the government. This call was preceded by an earlier one to all parties to come together under a single political party.

As the internal squabbles continued unabated, the CDCWU remained autonomous, free and responsible. At the same time, the Southern Cameroons preserved the colonial trade union model inherited from the British. In the political blueprint of the ruling party in West Cameroon, the Kamerun National Democratic Party (KNDP), it was clear that it intended to subject unions to the partisan interests of the ruling party. Notwithstanding the position of the party on trade union unity, the party did not take any practical steps either to transform the unions into development partners, nor enter into any form of alliance with the various unions. The government had inherited the trade union model introduced during the trusteeship period that guaranteed trade union autonomy. However, there was always pressure from the government on the union leadership to join the party. The unions accepted collaboration with the party on condition that government would not interfere in trade union freedom or infringe on union autonomy. G. B. Fogam, the Secretary General of both the CDCWU and the West Cameroon Trade Union Congress, who had occupied a number of leading international functions both in the ILO and the ICFTU, had strong beliefs in the ideals of both institutions, making him an advocate of 'free but responsible trade unionism' and an opponent of state control over unions in Cameroon.

The KNDP government in West Cameroon stayed clear of any intervention in trade union matters and only supported moves to set up a Central Labour Organisation for West Cameroon. This move gave birth to the West Cameroon Trade Union Congress (WCTUC), independent of government. It never sought any alliance since its major preoccupation was the preservation of an autonomous trade union in West Cameroon.

While West Cameroon attempted to preserve trade union autonomy, the Cameroons under French Trusteeship was ready and willing to submit to state control, thereby sacrificing autonomy with the creation of an essentially state-controlled central trade union. This was achieved within a decade in the whole of Cameroon after independence.

The Movement towards the One-Party State and its Impact on the Development of Trade Unionism

President Ahidjo's 1962 appeal was repeated in Garoua in 1969 during the first congress of the Cameroon National Union (CNU) which he had set up in 1966, as a merger of the existing political parties from both federated states of West and East Cameroon. At the time the CNU was established, a bill (Law no. 67/ LF/6 of 12 June 1967) for the 1967 draft Labour Code was already before the Federal National Assembly for adoption. At this time, one can conveniently state that the Federal authorities used the 1967 Labour Code to control labour relations in the Federation. To further tighten the grip of the Federal authorities over the unions, the party appointed union leaders to top party positions while the President of the Confederal Bureau was a member of the Central Committee of the CNU. With this arrangement, the programmes of the unions were defined by the ruling party. In the Garoua first ordinary congress of the CNU Ahidjo spelt out the role of trade unions in the new dispensation and the relationship with the single party. He proceeded to invite trade unionists to settle their differences.

The Emergence of the National Union of Cameroon Workers (NUCW) as a State Controlled Entity

During the Garoua Congress, three central organisations (the FSC and USCC in East Cameroon and the WCTUC in West Cameroon) were more committed to the establishment of trade union unity than integrating trade unions into the party. Moreover, the USCC was against trade union unity since the Ebolowa appeal. The Secretary General of the WCTUC, who was invited, refused to sign a document accepting the appeal for unity on behalf of his union. He supported trade union unity; but wished to see an autonomous union which was free of government interference. The resistance notwithstanding, the WCTUC was to yield to the appeal, especially after numerous pressures from the government and party through the Labour Department. By 1971, all the unions had dissolved giving rise to the NUCW (National Union of Cameroon Workers) whose leadership was immediately co-opted into the ruling party. Its first President, Moïse Défith Satouglé, became a Central Committee member of the CNU.

The new Labour Code proceeded to declare all strikes illegal. This notwithstanding, illegal strikes took place, and it appeared to government that the Confederal Bureau of the NUCW was not adhering to the partnership. As a result, in August 1975 it was dissolved. However, the leadership of the NUCW – particularly its President Moise Défith Satouglé – continued to defend the workers and not the government during strikes (Taa Ngwa 1975:4).

Impact on Development of Worker Interests

During the late-1970s the NUCW was forced to evolve into an arm of the one-party structure. This relationship stripped the union of any independent action. It could not undertake strike action. Under this arrangement, Cameroonian workers suffered injustice from both the government and their respective employers. Although S.3 of the Labour Code prohibited political activities by the unions, in 1990 union leaders could be seen marching alongside party men and women to warn against the dangers of a precipitated multi-partyism. This cohabitation led to the loss of the right to work. All workers were automatically members of the NUCW and the party.

The relationship of the CTUC with the party made it difficult for the former to carry out any independent action in favour of its members. For example, when workers were laid off in major parastatal corporations in the name of structural adjustment, the relevant union failed to protest. Louis Sombès (in his 1990 May Day address) would be remembered in Cameroon for launching an indefinite nationwide strike on 28 November 1993. However, this strike was called off on 10 May 1994 following a Protocol Agreement signed between the state and the various trade unions by which the state promised to review its position vis-à-vis the grievances of the union. Since then, nothing has been done in advancing the interests of workers. The salary cuts of 1993 have not been reversed as requested by the striking workers. This inaction further led to a split within the union and the rise of independent trade union organisations and an assertion of trade union independence by the CCTU.

The dissolution of independent trade unions did a great disservice to the Cameroonian worker. First of all, the leadership of the union was appointed by the party (CNU and later CPDM) until very recently, when Salome Ntsogo launched the Confederation des Syndicats Libres du Cameroun (CSLC) during the first quarter of 1995. Once appointed, the leader became a member of the Central Committee of the ruling party with the result that the party's doctrine was passed down to the workers irrespective of their political preferences. By this arrangement, the workers had no possibility of questioning or controlling the manner in which their union was run, since they did not take part in electing their leader.

Secondly, the concept of tripartism, which is so dear to the ILO and central in all labour matters, was completely eroded through the cooptation of the union by the ruling party. Thirdly, the state ignored the role unions could play in nation building. Fourthly, the union's programmes, as well as its operation strategies, were regulated by the state. Lastly, although the unions were free to make their own rules, the latter had to be approved by the Ministry of Labour and Social Insurance. The single workers' union in the light of the developments above failed to carry out its duty of defending workers' rights after its subordination to and incorporation in the former one-party-state structure.

The Post-One-Party Era

The most important development during the period of political liberalisation was the emergence of several autonomous trade unions in the civil and public services, especially the educational sector (Konings 2003:465). This period was marked by state repression against these new unions which stood out against existing ones for their inaction in the defence of workers' interests. For example in 1994, Louis Sombès, one-time Secretary General of the CCTU, was forcibly removed from office and jailed. Within the educational sector, the pioneer President of SYNES, Jongwane Dipoko, was attacked by unidentified armed men at his residence and had his fingers cut off. As if that was not enough, he and the Secretary General Isidore Noumba were tried by the Disciplinary Council of the University of Yaoundé and heavy sanctions were meted out to them, namely two years without pay (FUC 1997:34). Some organisations such as the Teachers' Association of Cameroon (TAC), which had met initial successes when its request for a General Certificate of Education (GCE) Board was finally granted, have since sunk into oblivion. In an open letter to the President of the Republic of Cameroon, the confederation of Anglophone Parents petitioned the Head of State on the GCE Crisis on 19 September 1993 calling on him to use his wide powers to stop this cultural genocide.

A chronology of some of the crises that rocked the CCTU during this period may be helpful in appraising trade unionism at this time. On 1 December 1997, Bakot Ndjock Emmanuel and Essiga Benoit emerged after the second ordinary congress of the CCTU held from 28 November to 1 December as President and Secretary General respectively. From the same congress emerged another bureau with Mbappe Ndoumbe Jacques and Louis Sombès as President and Secretary General. At this point a media battle between the two factions ensued. Two days after, both factions appeared at the headquarters in a bid to install their various bureaus. The first group attempted to break in and take control of the offices, the second were accompanied by a bailiff to assess the level of damage done by the first group.

This atmosphere within the leadership of the CCTU could not be helpful to its members. It instead weakened the union as each faction used all the measures to forestall the actions of the other. They then became entangled in a protracted legal and administrative battle for the control of the confederation. It must be mentioned straight away that the crisis was a fall-out of the 1995 elections led by Etame Ndedi and Louis Sombès. In the face of these happenings, both factions agreed to bury the hatchet by convening an extraordinary congress between 7 to 9 April 1999 which was later boycotted by the Sombès-led faction. After its boycott, the Sombès faction refused to recognise the election won by Benoit Essiga. The presence of representatives of the Kenya-based Pan African Trade Union Movement during the elections could not dissuade Sombès from dropping his claims to the leadership of the organisation. This is the picture of the post-one-party union movement in Cameroon. Another meeting was planned for 25-26 August 2000 at the conference centre in Yaoundé, but did not settle the leadership question. The absence of Louis Sombès on a union assignment in Kenya did not dissuade his following from laying claim to the leadership of the CCTU. On May Day 2000 Zambou Amougou, the leader of the CCTU, attributed the present imbroglio that exists between the trade unions to the 1993 salary cuts and then called for the restoration of workers' purchasing power to the level of the salary index of 1992 for workers in the public sector and the level of 1988 for workers in the private sector.

In the educational sector there has been a protracted dispute between the Cameroon Teachers' Trade Union (CATTU) led by Simon Nkwenti Aziah and the authorities of the private lay educational sector. The dispute is linked to the economic situation in which teachers had to endure salary cuts followed by the immediate devaluation of the CFA in 1994 and the consequent loss of workers' rights.

The law now authorises independent trade unions, but some of these unions have very little means to pursue their objectives in a significant way. In this present context, the unions can be classified into two broad categories: those that are pro-government and those that are vocal and anti-government. Leadership also affiliates these unions with international trade unions only for the purpose of their personal gains and not for any lobbying or advocacy for its group interests. Though there has been a rise in the number of trade unions thanks to the 1990 'liberty laws', there has been a decline of working class militancy as workers are searching for alternative survival strategies. During this period the labour movement has been marked by schism rather than by unity. As these unions operate, already enfeebled by repression and the constant internal wrangling, they do so under the watchful eyes of state security. Notwithstanding the problems, the trade union movement has the organisational continuity, the experience, and the vocational capacity to express a consistent agenda (Adesina 2000:497).

Fragmentation of Trade Unions, Proliferation of Professional Associations and Decline of Trade Union Vitality

Following the return to multiparty democracy in 1990, two union leaders, C.P.N. Vewessee and Emmanuel Etame Ndedi, launched an appeal for the return to independent and free trade unions in Cameroon (Temngah 1995:281). The emergence of several independent trade unions in 1993 may herald a labour movement that is free and independent. The post-one-party period has been marked by the promulgation of laws on various freedoms and liberties in all domains of social life (associations, unions, private press, multiparty democracy, NGOs, etc.). Nevertheless, the autonomy and freedom of trade unions are far from assured. The powers-that-be fear the role that trade unions can play in an emerging democracy.

The spirit of the 1990s regarding trade union freedom has been enshrined in various legal instruments. These instruments have painted a very liberal picture of trade union activity in Cameroon. But it appears in the post-one-party era that the reality is that the state still aspires to control union activity. Convention no. 87 requires unions be set up freely without the need for any external pressure being placed on them. But in Cameroon, there is a de facto tutelage of the state over union activities. Despite the emergence of independent unions such as the Syndicate of Teachers of Higher Education (SYNES), the Syndicat National Autonome de l'Enseignement Secondaire (SNAES), the Teachers' Association of Cameroon (TAC), the Cameroon Public Service Union (CAPSU) and l'Association Nationale Autonome des Chauffeurs d'Autobus, des Taxis et des Cars du Cameroun etc., there is a downward trend in union activities. Civil servants and the opposition parties have failed to assert themselves against government. The Anglophone community, through the Teachers' Association of Cameroon, the Confederation of Anglophone Parent-Teachers Associations (CAPTAC) and the churches, fought very hard to have an independent general certificate of education examinations Board granted to them in 1993, but have done little to consolidate this victory. Since 1990, journalists of the private press have been victims of the selective application of a repressive press law; yet they have been unable to organise themselves into a strong union capable of defending and promoting their interests. What today passes for a Union of Cameroonian Journalists is unrecognised by many journalists (including an impressive number of veterans). It lost credibility when its president Amadou Vamoulke became a member of the ruling CPDM party central committee and recently was later appointed as General Manager of the state audio-visual media corporation, CRTV. Teachers, tutors and university lecturers are similarly disorganised, preferring to go in for sinecures rather than fight for professional interests. In general, attempts to empower civil society have yielded little fruit. This is true regardless of which aspect of society we look at (Nyamnjoh 1999:104).

Although there are signs that the 1990 Law on Associations and the 1992 Labour Code paved the way for the revitalisation of union activities, there has been a decline in union growth in the country as a whole. The Cotonou Agreement of the ACP-EU has placed emphasis on the role trade unions can play in national development. The employment programme of the ILO recommends employment as socially beneficial in terms of the production of goods and services which, in turn, generate income. It calls for the establishment of specific programmes in the interest of workers. The attitude of the state in the post-one-party era reflects a colonial mentality which was once expressed by Tom Mboya, the prominent Kenyan unionist turned minister, as follows: private wars between labour and management cannot be permitted in poor developing countries. According to this logic, the cost of strikes may be bearable to labour and management but the social costs are unbearable. Following this logic all governments have placed restrictions on trade union freedom. The post-1990 laws seem to have been concerned more with protecting the old regime than with the furtherance of democracy and the strengthening of worker freedoms and rights.

The Role of the Administration

Trade unions are not allowed to operate if they have not obtained their certificate of registration from the Registrar of trade unions. In terms of article 6(1) of the 1992 Labour Code, anyone who violates this provision runs the risk of criminal sanctions. Under article 11(1) of the same Code, the Registrar of trade unions has a period of one month to issue this certificate of registration, failing which state acquiescence in the existence of the union is assumed. This apparently liberal provision does not apply in practice since the administration will usually not issue an acknowledgement receipt of the application. In addition, applications for trade union registration have to take cognisance of a range of other laws. Why not put all the laws in one code or piece of legislation so as to avoid confusion and misinterpretation? It would seem here that the administration retains the monopoly of interpreting the laws, which it often does in its favour.

A Weak and Dependent Judiciary

Judicial review of administrative acts usually follows the letter and not the spirit of the law. The result is the supremacy of the legislature as the judiciary fails to assert an independent stance in interpreting the law. The judiciary is highly dependent on the executive which restricts its latitude to act.

Conclusion

Trade unionism during the post-one-party era has dwindled and the unemployment crisis and structural adjustment programmes have weakened the unions. The exis-tence of independent trade unions on paper is a only a token sign that associational life is flourishing in Cameroon since the 1990s. Unfortunately, the practice regarding trade union matters is far from being liberal. The laws on freedom of association and on trade unions still contain clauses that undermine real trade union autonomy. In trade union matters, much has to be done and only proper consultation between the various stakeholders with a view to producing truly and genuinely acceptable liberal laws on the matter seems a viable solution. Under the colonial governments, restrictions were not placed on trade unions, but today, ambiguous laws and the personal ambitions of union leaders seeking lucrative appointments override general interests, leading to continuing trade union weakness.

References

Adesina, J., 2000, 'Workers, Politics and the State', in Okwudiba Nnoli, ed., *Government and Politics in Africa: A Reader*, Harare: AAPS Books.

ILO, Conventions No. 87 and 98 concerning the freedom of Association and the Protection of the Right to Organise Trade Unions and to Bargain Collectively.

Kahn-Freund, O., 1972, *Labour and the Law*, London: Stevens & Sons.

Kaptue, L., 1990, 'De la clandestinité à la légalité: Protosyndicats et syndicalisme. institution-nel au Cameroun de 1919 à 1944', *Annals of the Faculty of Arts Letters and Social Sciences*, University of Yaoundé, Vol. VI, No. 1 & 2, January-July.

Kaptue, L., 1994, 'Droit et syndicalisme au Cameroun', *Revue Juridique Africaine*, No. 4.

Konings, P., 1993, 'Labour Resistance in Cameroon: Managerial Strategies of Labour Resistance in the Agro-Industrial Plantations of the Cameroon Development Corporation', Leiden: ASC.

Konings, P., 2003, 'Organised Labour and Neo-Liberal Economic and Political Reforms in West and Central Africa', *Journal of Contemporary African Studies*, 21, 3.

Ngwa, S. Taa, 1975, 'Coup d'œil sur le syndicalisme au Cameroun', Yaoundé: Ecole Supérieure International de Journalisme du Yaoundé (ESIJY), Unpublished diploma dissertation.

Republic of Cameroon, 1990, Law No. 90/053 of 19 December 1990 on the Freedom of Association.

Republic of Cameroon, 1990, Law No. 90/056 of 19 December 1990 on multipartyism.

Republic of Cameroon, 1992, Law No. 92/007 of 14 August 1992 to institute the labour code and its instruments of application.

Temngah, J. N., 1995, 'The Protection of the Right to Work under Cameroonian law', Yaoundé: University of Yaoundé II, Unpublished Doctorat de 3e Cycle in Law.

4

Religious Organisations and Differential Responses to the Economic Crisis: The Roman Catholic Church and the Full Gospel Mission

Akoko Robert Mbe

Introduction

In its 1990 *World Development Report*, the World Bank recorded that the number of individuals living below the poverty level was on the decrease. Latin America, East and South Asia all showed substantial success in reducing poverty. The exception was sub-Saharan Africa. The numbers living below the poverty level in this region were projected to rise well into the present century, and indeed this has been the case. Other indicators of social welfare all show that Africa is on a different trajectory from much of the rest of the less developed world. When South Africa is excluded, the region's average income is the lowest in the World – just $315 per capita. With about 460 million inhabitants, sub-Saharan Africa's total income is just over that of Belgium, which has only about eleven million inhabitants. But this income is divided among 48 countries with median GDP of barely $2 billion, about the output of a town of 60,000 in a rich country. In Africa, unlike other developing regions, where the average output per capita had risen by the end of the 1990s, it has fallen by more than half. And at thirteen per cent of GDP, the region's average savings rate has been the lowest in the world (*World Development Report* 1990). According to the head of the United Nations Programme of Action for Africa's Economic Recovery and Development (1986-90), Africans were generally 40 per cent worse off in 1990 than in 1980. Per capita consumption in sub-Saharan Africa fell by one-fifth in the 1980s. Spending on health care declined by 50 per cent and on education by 25 per cent. Since the mid-1990s as many as 10,000 African children die each day from the effects of malnutrition and the lack of rudimentary health care.[1] However, some gains were recorded towards the close of the 1990s. Despite this trend, the region entered the twenty-first century with most of the world's poorest countries (average income per capita still lower than at the end of the 1960s). The declining exports shares in traditional primary products, little diversification into new lines of business, massive capital flight and loss of skills to other regions, have made matters worse because these have eroded the place of the African in the global market. For these reasons, it is fair to say that Africa faces an economic crisis, with falling standards of living, increased exposure to epidemics, famine and progressive marginalisation from the world economy. Moreover, political instability has impeded the creation of social, political and economic institutions, thereby retarding progress towards even limited self-sufficiency. A continued tendency towards authoritarian regimes has reflected another dimension of the crisis–that of the legitimacy of the state (Kennet and Lumumba-Kasongo 1992, World Bank Report 2000).

In Cameroon, the economic crisis has affected almost everybody and has retarded progress significantly since the mid-1980s. It has exacerbated poverty, misery and unemployment in the country. Public and private institutions continuously retrench workers and, worse still, the recruitment of new workers has drastically reduced. Salaries of workers have been slashed both in the private and public sectors several times, with immeasurable hardship for many families. Government efforts over the years to tackle the crisis have yielded little dividends.

Also worried about the crisis have been Christian bodies. The crisis has affected each religious group to a point where they cannot effectively accomplish their objectives. Some have taken it as a duty to make their own spiritual contribution (praying to God) to bring the crisis to an end. They have also expressed their views on the crisis in the form of pastoral letters, sermons and media interviews. For instance, the Episcopal conference of the Roman Catholic Church in Cameroon met in Yaoundé in 1990 and deliberated on the economic crisis. In the pastoral letter issued at the end of the deliberations, the prelates expressed their view on its causes, effects and how it could be solved (cf. Pastoral Letter of the Episcopal Conference of Cameroon 1990). On the causes, the prelates attributed the crisis to the 'structures of sin', which they believe dominate the world of today. They argued that the 'structures of sin' are deep-rooted in personal wrong-doing, and thus always linked to the behaviour of the individuals (referring here to political leaders) who introduce these structures, consolidate them and render them difficult to be removed. They argued that the 'structures of sin' emanate from the world economic order, which is based solely on profit, egoism, exploitation of the poor, and the defenceless of the latter in the face of the rich and powerful nations of the world. This order has imposed new models of economic, political, cultural and financial dependency on the weak countries and has impoverished them. They believed that it is not in compliance with the spirit of the Gospel or the special teachings of the church for the rich nations to recuperate, at excessive interests, their loans to the poor nations. The Bishops then argued that:

> the consequences of this anti-Gospel spirit are immeasurable in Cameroon. In public life, the absence of the spirit of citizenship, promotes amongst civil servants of all classes, corruption, laissez-faire, absenteeism, mercenary spirit and notorious embezzlement of public funds, which defy all vigilance. Custom fraud, tax evasion and misuse of public property are the habits that one observes right through the vital sectors of the economy of our country. Such behaviour constitutes, for a Christian, grave faults, which are contrary not only to citizenship but again to morality in the Christian sense of the word.

At its 1993 meeting in Bamenda, the Synod of the Presbyterian Church in Cameroon (PCC) also expressed worry about the crisis. The Committee felt disturbed that the crisis had caused a majority of Cameroonians to wallow in misery and poverty while a few could still afford to live in affluence. It was its view that any policy conceived to recover from the crisis should be aimed at reducing the prices of goods and services in order to boost production and consumption. The Committee advocated a more efficient management of the economy and expressed its concern on how all calls for more transparency seemed to be undermined and that poor accountability, embezzlement and capital flight remain the reality. It equally expressed the fear that if the crisis were not checked, the future of the Cameroonian children and their grandchildren would be mortgaged indefinitely for temporary comforts and conveniences of the moment. It gravely lamented the rising crime wave in the country, which has destabilised production and argued that increasing banditry frustrated all efforts by honest Cameroonians to engage in gainful economic activity. It called on the government to step up its fight against this ill to enable a secure business atmosphere (Nyansako-Ni-Nku 1993).

The aim of this chapter is to make a comparative analysis of the reactions of the Roman Catholic Church (RCC) and Full Gospel Mission Cameroon (FGMC) to the crisis. Regarding the RCC, a special focus is on the Bamenda ecclesiastical province, which is believed to be the most organised (Gifford 1997). The two churches are selected for the study because they differ from each other on liberation theology and in explaining the causes of the crisis, although they converge on practical solutions (Akoko and Mbuagbo, forthcoming). Secondly, this comparison is particularly important because Pentecostalism claims to bring prosperity. Thirdly, the RCC is the largest mainline church in Cameroon and it could be taken to represent the mainline churches, while FGMC, the biggest Pentecostal church, could be said to represent the Pentecostal groups (Gifford 1997, Knorr 2001). Such a selection is useful because it covers a considerable proportion, both mainstream Christianity and Pentecostalism, of the Christian church in Cameroon, and makes for less time-consuming research than a general overview. The article starts by providing a general picture of the economic crisis, then looks at the churches and how each has been affected. It then brings out how each interprets the crisis and the measures it proposes to combat it.

The Churches and the Crisis: A Comparative Analysis

The Roman Catholic Church

The Roman Catholic Church is undoubtedly the largest Christian group in Cameroon, although it was only introduced into the country in 1890, much later than the other mainline churches (the Baptists in 1844 and the Presbyterian Church founded by the Basel Mission in 1884). It is truly a national church because others have tended to be geographically limited – for example, the Presbyterian Church in Cameroon (PCC) is an Anglophone church, the Eglise Presbytérienne Came-rounaise has its base among the Bulus to the south of the country, the Union des Eglise Baptistes Camerounaises (UEBC) around the Littoral province and the Lutheran Church around the Adamawa province. However, this trend is slowly changing for a number of reasons, among which is the determination of each group to plant churches in other areas. The churches also follow when functionaries and businessmen are transferred to another region. Most of the major churches can now be found in nearly all the provinces, although this does not cancel the fact that each church has a centre of gravity in the area where it took root. About 30 per cent of the country's population identifies itself as Catholic, but the distribution is not uniform. In the southern provinces over 50 per cent claim to be Catholic, while the densely populated provinces account for only about 25 per cent. In the vast Muslim northern provinces Catholics account for a mere five per cent of the population.

The Catholic Church in Cameroon is divided into five ecclesiastical provinces (Bamenda, Yaoundé, Douala, Garoua and Bertoua) with twenty-three dioceses. The Ecclesiastical province of Bamenda covers four dioceses (Buea, Mamfe, Kumbo and Bamenda). The province corresponds with the South West and North West civil administrative provinces of Cameroon, otherwise known as the Anglophone Cameroon. It comprises thirteen civil administrative divisions: six from the South West and seven from the North West province. This section of the country, which used to be known as Southern Cameroons, was part of the United Nations trust territory placed under British rule until 1961 when the world body gave it (including the Northern section called Northern Cameroon) two alternatives: either to join the Federal Republic of Nigeria or to become part of French Cameroon. A plebiscite was conducted to this effect on 11 February, 1961 and the northern section opted to join the Federal Republic of Nigeria while the southern section voted to join the Republic of Cameron (Levine 1964, Eyongetah and Brain 1974, Ngoh 1990, Chiabi 1997). Although this area is part of the Republic of Cameroon, it retains the Anglo-Saxon tradition in most of its institutions, while the rest of the country maintains the French tradition.

The Bamenda ecclesiastical province, like others, has been severely affected by the economic crisis. In his concern over the situation, the archbishop has on several occasions addressed the issue to his priests and faithful in letters and sermons. This problem has also been aggravated because the church authorities did little to encourage the local churches to be financially self-supporting. The reason was that much financial and missionary assistance used to be provided by external benefactors and donors abroad. While these contributions were frequent in the past, today they are a rare phenomenon.[2] Rare, because most connections for assistance were made by the Western missionaries working with the church. Now most of them are retiring and they are not being replaced because the church is becoming self-governing and local priests are being trained. Moreover, foreign bodies are not interested anymore in providing aid because they want the church to be self-supporting, except as regards special projects, which have been evaluated to be very important but too costly. The crisis has become so severe that for the first time (1999), the ecclesiastical province had to include a Finance Commission in its convention. The convention, which took place in Bamenda, established a Finance Commission which was charged with deliberating on how the diocese and parishes could achieve material and financial self-sufficiency.[3]

Among the services provided by the church that have suffered from the crisis is education at all levels (nursery, primary and secondary). Financial difficulties have made the future of this service, to which the church attaches great importance, a matter of concern. The education crisis has its genesis partly from government's inconsistent policies regarding subventions to private schools. Apart from external assistance from other mission bodies, it used to be the policy of the state when the economy was in a boom to make Grants-in-Aid to religious bodies. These grants were for the running of vital services such as schools and hospitals, since they were delivering services that the state would have been obliged to provide unaided had the churches not done so. Up until 1976, the school system in the British tradition, which prevailed in the present ecclesiastical province of Bamenda, made it a legal obligation on the part of the state to pay Grants-in-Aid to approved voluntary agencies (Baptists, Basel Mission [now Presbyterian] and Catholic Schools). The actual amount of Grants-in-Aid payable was calculated by deducting the assumed local contribution (a figure which represented the expected income from school fees, and varied according to the ability of the community to pay) from the recognised expenses of a school, this latter figure being made up of the total salary bill together with an allowance for other expenses. The Grants-in-Aid regulations in the British Cameroon were spelt out in the Education Ordinance No. 17 of 1952. The provisions of that ordinance in the matter of Grants-in-Aid were substantially retained in Law No. 69/LW/ 11 of September 1969 'to regulate the conduct of Primary Education in West

Cameroon'. In the system, all the teachers' salaries and insurance contributions, and the cost of improvements and repairs to buildings were provided by the state. The state equally provided medical help to the schools and grants to Teacher Training Colleges were awarded by the state depending on the size of their personnel. Teachers were paid according to the same scale, taking into account their qualifications and length of service, and not whether they belonged to confessional or government schools.[4]

On 8 July 1976, the Cameroon Government passed a new Law (No. 76-15 of July 1976) to reorganise private education in Cameroon. This Law abolished the legislative texts which had governed the conduct of education in Anglophone Cameroon up to that date. In so doing, it retained nothing of value in the legislation underlying the educational system in the former West Cameroon. The Grants-in Aid regulations, as spelt out in the 1952 Ordinance and in the 1969 Law, were abolished and replaced by what is known as 'Government Subvention'. The notion of approved voluntary agencies as enshrined in the legislative texts of West Cameroon was abandoned and all private agencies, confessional and non-confessional alike, were lumped together under the title 'Private Education'.

As from 1976 onwards, confessional schools began to experience a new situation in which government's participation in the financing of confessional schools was not governed by any principled criteria. Agents of the Ministry or Ministries concerned unilaterally and arbitrarily decided the amount of subventions which the government paid to these schools annually. The chancy, problematical and uncertain nature of this system of government subventions starkly stands out in Law no 87/022 of 17 December 1987 whose section 16 is couched in the following terms:

(a) The funds of a private educational establishment shall be derived from;
  - The proprietor's own funds,
  - School fees (tuition, board, canteen),
  - Proceeds from the various activities of the establishment or agency,
  - Donations or legacies obtained in accordance with the laws in force,
  - Assistance from parent-teacher associations.

(b) Taking into account the available resources, the state or local authorities may, if necessary, grant subsidies to the proprietor of a given establishment.

(c) Government Grants-in-Aid shall be given on the basis of criteria laid down by Decree.

According to the Catholic Education Secretary in Buea, government subventions to Catholic schools began to register a significant and regular decline from 1985. For instance, for the year 1990/1991, the government decided to allocate only two-thirds of the amount of subvention it had allocated for the previous financial year. The following year, (1991/1992), the same two-thirds were allocated as subvention but the money was disbursed in three irregular instalments. For 1992/1993, the amount dropped and has persistently been dropping and irregular, as payments are made in some years and not in others.

Faced with this precarious situation, the National Episcopal Conference met in 1989 to deliberate on the problems of Catholic Education. At the end of the conference, they came out with a pastoral letter, which, however, did not provide any practical or concrete solution to the crisis. In the letter, the Bishops only drew the attention of Christians and all people of good will to the serious problem of Catholic education. After presenting the church's educational philosophy and a short historical reminder in the letter regarding how the state used to give maximum support to approved voluntary agencies, the Bishops lamented the situation at the time. They called on the government and every Christian to help rescue the schools from collapsing.[5]

The situation worsened as the economic crisis persisted. The state became poorer and poorer and could no longer fulfil its obligation of enabling these schools to survive. The Roman Catholic Church, just like the other churches, felt the effects more than the non-confessional schools because they had relied on state subventions for long and had provided good working conditions to their teachers, which they could no longer afford to do. Within a short time the mission accumulated many debts in providing education. A report from the Catholic Education Secretariat, Buea, reveals that the accumulated arrears of salaries, social security contributions and taxes for Catholic teachers of the Buea diocese alone had reached 283,626,277 francs CFA in 1993. This brought incalculable suffering to the teachers, as they had to stay for more than fourteen months without receiving salaries. Without money, some of the teachers who stayed in rented houses were evicted because they could not pay their rents, others were unable to travel either to go home on holidays or to return from their homes to their schools, some could not adequately feed their families, others could not pay school fees for their own children and some were unable to provide medical care for their families. The church authorities also found it increasingly difficult to employ new teachers.[6] This appalling situation of course brought about adverse effects on the performance of the pupils and students because most of the teachers had to involve themselves in other activities to raise additional income. In addition, there were frequent strikes and threats of strikes from the teachers to press for better working conditions, which hampered the smooth running of the school year. In the Buea diocese between 1993 and 1998, enrolment in most of the rural schools dropped drastically as those communities fought to open free government schools as their own way to survive the economic crisis. Despite this development, the mission did not close any of its schools.

Since the National Episcopal Conference could not come up with any practical solution and the situation was deteriorating further, the Bishops of the Bamenda ecclesiastical province decided to take some practical measures aimed at putting an end to any further increase in arrears of salaries owed to teachers. The measures taken by the Bishops stated that:

- Teachers of the church who had attained the age of sixty years were advised to take retirement. This measure equally applied to those who had attained this age but had fraudulently reduced their real ages. People do this either to stay longer in service or to obtain jobs which prescribe a maximum age limit.
- Teachers who had attained the age of fifty-five and had already put in fifteen years or more in service were strongly advised to take anticipated retirement.
- The salaries of all serving teachers were reduced by fifty per cent so as to enable the schools to function within the income that the Catholic Education Authority itself could collect, mindful of the ominous silence of the Cameroon Government on the question of subventions.

The Bishops then directed their Education Secretaries to begin implementing the above measures from 1 July 1993. As a reaction, the church was dragged to the courts by some of the teachers who did not support the measures (Ngoh 2000).

Apart from schools, many projects which were started by some parishes or local churches have been halted or are being carried out sporadically whenever a little money becomes available. This is the case with projects which do not have external funding. A majority of members find it difficult to fulfil their financial obligations toward the church because of poverty. For example, in an interview with the parish priest of the Molyko Catholic Church of Buea on a church hall project of the Parish, whose construction work is very slow, the priest asserted that although the project is so vital for the parish, the work is slow because of financial difficulties. He revealed that before the crisis, any project of that magnitude took a short time to realise because the financial sources were available. Regular Sunday offering has dropped drastically and the only period when a relatively substantial amount of money could be raised is during harvest thanksgiving, which is once a year.

Also affected by the crisis are the priests because the church has drastically curtailed the facilities which it used to provide them. For instance, each parish priest was entitled to a car, food and a cook, and free medical care, in addition to their monthly stipend. Now some parish priests must get by without these facilities. No doubt, the performance of the priests has been affected and impacts negatively on the church. For instance, as a solution to the shortages in cars, the archbishop of the diocese of Bamenda instituted a car-pool system in which no one owned a car individually. All now belonged to the diocese, for the work of the diocese. So if a priest's congregation, relatives or friends buy him a car, it belongs to the diocese and remains at its disposal. Also the user of the car pays so much per kilometre to the diocese (the rate increases for trips outside the diocese in order to discourage private travel), with the result that by the time the car needs replacing, the diocese has built up a sizable sum towards its replacement. This arrangement not only ensures judicious use of the cars but also enables every priest to have access to a car (Gifford 1997).

The Full Gospel Mission

The Full Gospel Mission Cameroon is the second oldest Pentecostal church in Cameroon after the Apostolic Church, and is the biggest in terms of adherents and establishments. Reverend Werner Knorr introduced the church, which is of German origin, into Cameroon in 1961 under the sponsorship of the United Missions Friends Inc. of Germany (Knorr 2001). According to the 2000 statistics from the office of the National Superintendent of the church, it has a membership of roughly 59,062 with 518 assemblies (local churches) located in all provinces of the country. Membership has been increasing rapidly and the Mission has penetrated all nooks and crannies of the country and beyond. The high rate of growth can be attributed to some of its doctrines and practices such as divine healing and protection, good leadership, political liberalisation, evangelisation strategies, its caring traditions towards the needy, and a shift from complete asceticism to a gospel of prosperity.[7] The church has gone down in record as the first in Cameroon which has extended its activities beyond the national frontiers. Its presence is felt in Chad, the Central African Republic, Nigeria, and in its future projects plan, 2001-2005, it intends to move into the Republics of Congo and Gabon. It also goes down on record as the first Pentecostal church to have been introduced into Nigeria from Cameroon. This development is interesting because recent Pentecostal churches are in the main introduced into Cameroon from Nigeria and a majority of the existing Pentecostal groups in the country were founded by Nigerians (Knorr 2001, Akoko 2002).

The Mission has equally been affected by the economic crisis in that members find it difficult to meet their financial obligations, such as tithes to the church, making it difficult for it to run its activities successfully. Even if members were to pay their tithes, the total amount received by the church would definitely be smaller than when the economy was prospering. This short-fall is because tithes are supposed to be an obligatory one-tenth of an individual's income as prescribed by the Bible and as such, the lower the income the lower the amount that is raised. Compared to the mainline churches, members of Pentecostal groups take this financial obligation to the church seriously and all do pay, thereby making it a major source of income for the Pentecostal churches. If members are unable to pay or can pay only a little, the church will be unable to run its activities.

The Mission has been receiving financial assistance from foreign bodies for specific projects. For instance, the Assemblies of God from America joined other European Mission bodies to purchase building plots and erect church buildings (Njemo 2001). This kind of assistance is not on a regular basis and it is usually directed to specific projects when solicited. The bodies giving the assistance cannot shoulder the whole financial burden for the diverse needs of the churches – building plots and putting up the structures, paying salaries of workers and taking care of rallies and crusades. The Mission relies heavily on its own members to raise money for such undertakings rather than on external assistance. At national level, some vital projects of the church, such as the main building of the national headquarters in Douala, have been slowed down or suspended. At the local level, the Molyko assembly of the church is facing difficulty in raising money to build a library and guest house project, for which it had long acquired a plot.

The Full Gospel Mission is characterised by frequent evangelisation campaigns, rallies and crusades. These activities have been reduced in most districts because they require too much money. The church's ambition of penetrating the Republic of Congo and Gabon before 2005 seems to be very uncertain because there is no money to send missionaries to these countries. The ambition was included in their five-year project planning in 2001, but barely a few months thereafter it was certain that it would not be realised. Compared to Catholic education, Full Gospel Mission schools have not faced the type of educational crisis which the Catholic Church experienced because all of its schools were started during the economic downturn. The schools have been opened taking into consideration the economic crisis and everything is planned within that context, for instance, low salaries for teachers and the provision of low cost and basic infrastructure.

Reactions to the Crisis

The Roman Catholic Church

In its Fourth Enugu Diocesan Priests' Annual Seminar held in 1991 on Human Rights, Human Dignity and Catholic Social Teachings, the Catholic Priests of the Diocese expressed their grief at witnessing the misery and suffering in which an increasing majority of Africans were condemned to live, in particular because of the implementation of structural adjustment programmes by various African governments. They argued that although these economic reform programmes might appeal to foreign businessmen and to the London and Paris Clubs, the IMF and World Bank, etc., they were unacceptable because they subordinated the human person to economic goals. They thus contradicted one basic principle of Catholic social teachings, namely that all economic and socio-political programmes find their justification as a service to man. In other words, the sufferings are completely unacceptable because they lack a comparable justification. The priests also felt scandalised that the suffering poor are taunted and their sensibilities insulted by what they called the *nouveaux riches* who make a senseless and extravagant display of their often ill-gotten wealth. They appealed to the conscience of these people to show mercy and compassion towards those suffering by sharing their wealth and fortunes (Obiora and Ugonna 1992).

In line with the above social teachings of the church, the RCC, as discussed in the introduction of this work, has been vocal on political and economic issues in Cameroon which inflict suffering on the masses. This quest for a society free of suffering has always been a source of conflict between the church and the state in Cameroon. The Pastoral Letter of the Episcopal Conference of Cameroon of 1990 states clearly that the church also attributes the economic crisis to political mismanagement, which does not auger well for the politicians (Titi Nwel 1995, Akoko and Mbuagbo, forthcoming).

The archbishop of Bamenda made a further pronouncement in September 1993 when it was clear that the crisis would persist. This pronouncement was in a special address to the priests of his diocese entitled 'Some Special Thoughts on Cameroon's Economic Crisis'. In the address, the bishop called the attention of his clergy to the realities of the economic difficulties faced by church members of the diocese. To illustrate the gravity of the situation, he quoted the *Wall Street Journal* and reports of the World Bank, which revealed that the economy of Cameroon had declined over the previous six years. He called on his priests to be in full solidarity with those Christians hard hit and impoverished by the catastrophic economic crisis. He cited the plight of Catholic teachers and called on the priests to reflect on ways in which the local church could live within its meagre means. He invited them to self and collective scrutiny of their lifestyles so that they reflected true solidarity with their people. Agreeing that foreign involvement in Cameroon's economy has worked to the detriment of the country, he then stated that the economic situation could only be resolved if the political scene was not characterised by the exclusion of some groups from meaningful participation in national life while other groups held a monopoly of power (referring to the ruling party and the president's ethnic group in particular). In several other addresses the Archbishop has sought to sensitise the priests and Christians of the diocese to the seriousness of the crisis.

Such statements clearly reveal that the RCC and the PCC hold that bad governance has contributed greatly to the economic crisis. This view is explicit in the declaration of the PCC synod committee of 1993 in Bamenda on the economic crisis. The PCC had been fighting to minimise the crisis among its members right from the beginning in various ways: firstly, when mission bodies started facing financial difficulties arising from the reduction and irregularity of state subventions some schools were closed down. For instance, the PCC had to close down some ninety primary schools in 1992. The result was that the teachers were retrenched and their conditions became severe.[8] The RCC did not close any of its establishments but instead more were opened. One of the reasons given for this decision by the Catholic Education Secretary in Buea was that the mission did not believe in retrenching its workers because of the difficulties these people faced in picking up other jobs. Alternatively, the mission reduced salaries by 50 per cent, and older teachers were asked to consider retirement. In reaction, serving teachers of the church have formed the Catholic Teachers Association (CATA), with its most important objective being to press for good working conditions of members. The union has been putting pressure on the authorities of the church to increase salaries because of the rising cost of living.[9]

The Catholic Women Association (CWA) has been encouraged by the church to alleviate poverty amongst women. The CWA is a movement which started as a non-profit, apostolic group in 1960 in Buea with the sole objective of building a spiritual path among women of the Roman Catholic church (Atabong 2000). With the coming of the economic crisis, the association included, as one of its objectives, the alleviation of poverty among members and this step has enabled it to engage in profit-making ventures. It reduces poverty by providing and promoting education and training for the social and economic welfare of women.

The women have adopted two methods to alleviate poverty among members. One is embarking on joint economic ventures which enable branches to carry out income-generating projects. Profits from the projects are used to assist the members who are in difficulty and to carry out charitable works among the poor and needy. In the Buea diocese, the Bishop has introduced a loan scheme which enables various groups to obtain interest-free loans from the coffers of the diocese for any project of their choice. Repayment of a loan begins after twelve months (Barr 2003). To enhance the functioning of this scheme, the Bishop selected a CWA animator from each division of his diocese. The women selected were sent to the Buea regional Pan-African Institute for Development (PAID), West Africa to undergo training on project management. The animator evaluates a proposed project and makes her recommendation to the Bishop. If it is accepted for funding, she monitors it to make sure the objectives are met. Some of the projects which the groups in Fako Division of the Buea diocese have carried out within the last three years include corn and cassava grinding mills, purchase of chairs and canopies for hiring, pig and tomato farms, and the sale of palm oil (See Fako Division project animator reports from 2001-2003). All these and many other projects have generated income for the various branches.

A further method is to invite experts to teach the women different income-generating skills to enable them to become self-supporting. In the last three years, the project animator for Fako Division has organised seminars through which the women have learnt basic skills on the making of milk, doughnut and powder from Soya bean; washing, medicated and powder soaps; pepper in oil, tomato paste, body lotions, pies and rolls, fruit juice and wine, birthday and graduation cakes; dyeing and stitching of cloths, designing and cutting of envelopes, cough syrup and baking using local methods (locally called three-stone fire side) (see also the above reports). Some of the women who have benefited from these seminars can be seen selling some of the items they produce on Sundays in church and at other church gatherings.

A third method, which was recently adopted by the authorities of the church to alleviate poverty was the reinvigoration of the service of charity (caritas). In the Episcopal Conference of the Bishops of Cameroon, which was held in Ngaoundere in January 2004, the prelates decided to institute a special Lenten collection in all its parishes. In a pastoral letter issued after the conference, the Bishops urged each Christian to put in a small amount each month or when able. Although not compulsory, the bishops in the letter have used various biblical citations to appeal to the conscience of every member on the necessity to make this gift. Caritas is meant to support the poor, the jobless young who have no parents, and the destitute and the aged who are confined to their homes. Any amount collected by a parish is channelled to the national body, which shares it out in the following manner: 25 per cent for parish caritas, 50 per cent for diocesan caritas, and 25 per cent for national caritas. The Bishops in their letter pointed out that caritas is a traditional Christian practice which the church had neglected and therefore has now seen the need to reinvigorate (Cameroon Panorama No. 557 of March 2004). Before this initiative, the Bishop of the Kumbo diocese had created in the late 1980s a caritas organ in his diocese known as the 'Diocesan Social Welfare Committee'. However, this committee remained very weak and little was known of its activities. In July 1994, the bishop decided to make it stronger and functional by converting it into a department called the Social Welfare Department of the diocese. He then appointed new officials (secretary, accountant, coordinator, animator) to manage it.

The 1990s was the period when the economic crisis was at its peak and the poverty level was rising. This period started with the inability of the government to pay civil servants for two months (September and October 1990). Shortly afterwards, salaries were twice slashed by 50 per cent while the devaluation of the CFA franc in 1994 further aggravated poverty. The private sector is not very strong in Cameroon and many people rely on the civil service for a living. When this sector is paralysed, many families suffer. That is why this period was particularly rough for many Cameroonians. The situation must have prompted the Bishop of Kumbo to strengthen the work of his caritas initiative. In an interview with the secretary of the department he argued that 'it is the duty of the church to take into consideration the life problems, suffering, joy and pain of every woman and man so that mankind should be liberated. The social pastoral care is out to let mankind live as witness to the gospel, thus the exercise of charity by all women and men to all women and men. It is also the witnessing of God's love for all so that by action of solidarity, sharing of justice and love, God's love can easily be felt by each and everyone'. The secretary said that the following were the objectives of the department:

- Sensitisation and organisation of communities in community charity and development;
- Identifying community needs, problems and solutions with the community;
- Organising artisan and home training programmes in various communities, in order to enable beneficiaries to earn a living;

- Raising funds for development projects in various communities; and
- Executing, monitoring and evaluating projects.

The Full Gospel Mission

Pentecostal groups in a number of countries have criticised governments for their unpopular policies which inflict suffering on the masses. For instance, the Pentecostal Fellowship of Nigeria (PFN) through its President in 1998 decried the deplorable state of the Nigerian economy and called for a probe into the accounts of those believed to have looted public funds. The association regretted that following the death of General Abacha in June 1998 shocking revelations were emerging about how the national treasury was massively looted by Abacha's and the preceding Babangida regime. They reiterated their call on the Federal Military Government of Abdulsalam Abubakar to respond publicly to the allegations of fraud aired in the media. Should the allegations be shown to be correct, then the government should institute fearless probes to investigate and bring to book all that were actually involved in plundering the national treasury (Afe 1999).

Unlike these groups, the Full Gospel Mission Cameroon shuns liberation theology,[10] and it does not link the crisis to political mismanagement. Unlike the PCC and RCC, it has never come out with a position on any burning political issue because it fears it may be interpreted as the church involving itself in politics. This church attributes the crisis more to the refusal of a majority of Cameroonians to 'accept Jesus Christ as their saviour' or become 'born again', the result being sanctions from God in the form of economic difficulties. This implies that when an individual truly becomes 'born-again', God takes care of all his economic problems. 'Born-again' is derived from the cornerstone of Christianity, which requires every individual to repent and 'give their life to Christ'. When it comes to practical solutions to solve the crisis, while pleading to God to act and appealing to individuals to become 'born-again', the Church has in the last decade embraced accumulation as a solution.

Initially, the church had adopted an ascetic doctrine, which did not make room for private accumulation. But in the last decade with the economic crisis it has to a large extent also embraced a gospel of prosperity, which has cleared the way for members and the church itself to accumulate (Akoko 2002, 2004).[11] As I have argued elsewhere (see Akoko 2004), one of the reasons for this shift in doctrine has been the economic crisis affecting Cameroon. The Mission previously did not need to embrace the gospel of prosperity, because the economy of Cameroon was booming. As with the other churches, it was rich because members were able to make substantial financial contributions to running the church. In addition, many sources of funding from Western missionary bodies were available to various churches as compared to the current situation. In addition to these sources, the mainline churches in Cameroon engaged in business ventures in order to raise additional money for their activities, for example in the areas of education, health, printing, agriculture, etc. Like the other Pentecostal churches, Full Gospel Mission avoided involvement in business ventures for doctrinal reasons. However, there was pressure on the church authorities from the state government and even some of its members for the church to engage in the provision of social services along the lines provided by the mainline churches. The leaders of Full Gospel Mission long resisted this step because they believed it was going to be an impediment to the growth of the church. Members were not encouraged to go into business because the church feared that they could fall victim to the temptations of materialism.[12]

However, institutions managed by other churches were highly valued by the public, which considered them to be of a higher quality than state services.[19] These church-managed activities generated considerable income. Moreover, the policy of the state in subsidising schools and hospitals in the form of duty-free imported drugs also increased church income.

It could be argued that the availability of various sources of funding to Full Gospel Mission contributed to its adopting an ascetic doctrine from the outset. With the economic crisis, contributions from members and external financial support dropped drastically. In order to survive, the alternative has been to embrace the Gospel of prosperity, which could help to raise the income level of members and the church.

The Gospel, as practised now, allows members or the church as a body to engage in business or profit-making activities. From my own observations, this shift has had a tremendous impact on members, and has re-oriented their lifestyle from asceticism to accumulation. There are no restrictions on dressing, nor is wealth seen as ungodly. On the contrary, fine clothes, nice cars, foreign goods are common currency. The pastors themselves foster this image through their lifestyles. The church itself within the last decade has followed the path of the mainline churches in providing income-generating services in the areas of education, health, and printing.

The church runs six nursery and primary schools, and according to the Education Secretary there are prospects of opening more in many other towns in the country in the near future. The church operates a bilingual teacher training college in Mbengwi, a technical college in Muyuka, and a secondary school in Bamenda (Nwancha 2001). In the area of health, the church runs health centres in Garoua and Yaoundé, which according to the Secretary of the Medical Department would be upgraded to hospitals soon. It has two other health centres in Mbakeng and Banteng (Shu 2001). In Bamenda, it operates a printing press (Gospel Press), which went into operation in 1986 with the intention of printing exclusively gospel materials distributed free of charge or at moderate price. But with the crisis, the technical manager of the press noted that they now print work on a commercial basis. It owns five Christian literature centres in Bamenda, Muyuka, Yaoundé,

Douala and Kumba. Each contains Christian literature including audio and video cassettes, calendars, diaries, stickers, T-shirts, key holders and almanacs for sale. These establishments of the church have been of tremendous importance in alleviating poverty because they provide employment opportunities to many who would otherwise have been jobless. Government officials have acknowledged this positive influence, for instance, during the 2004 convocation ceremony of the Teachers' Training College Mbengwi, the Divisional Officer for Momo Division hailed the church for helping the government in alleviating poverty by providing Cameroonian youth with the required education to enter a highly competitive job market (*The Herald,* 17 April 2004).

In the same way as the Roman Catholic Church, the Full Gospel Mission is deeply concerned with poverty alleviation among women. Unlike the RCC, which undertakes this task through the CWA, the FGM has a Women's Ministry (a strong organ in the administrative organisation of the church) charged with organising the women and mobilising them to fight the crisis. According to its national coordinator, the main objective of this department is to unite all women of the Full Gospel Mission in a common effort to help spread the teachings of the church. Besides this activity, it aims at encouraging the women to lead a Christian life in their homes and at times provides practical tuition in such occupations as needlework and house craft which could help them earn a living (Kankeur 2001). The objective of empowering women economically dates back to 1971 when the mission started a social centre for home economics in Muyuka where girls were trained in subjects such as house craft, mother and child care, health care and Christian marriage (Nwancha 2001). However, this programme seems not to have yielded the expected results because the centre did not function for very long, and it was converted into a co-education technical college in 1995.

Within some Assemblies, for instance Buea town, the women have, in collaboration with the Women's Department, improved the economic condition of the women despite the generally low income of many. In a seminar paper presented by one of the women of Buea town assembly on 'Women in Poverty Alleviation', Mary Kamara, using a biblical quotation, argues that a virtuous woman uses her hands, head and talent to perform great exploits for her family and becomes a blessing to her family and community. She reveals that the women of the assembly have adopted this approach and are able to pay school fees for their children, and afford to pay for health and social demands of the family. The Women's Department of the church provides experts who teach the women of the assembly various income-generating skills with which they can raise income to alleviate poverty. They are taught how to make soap, neckties and dye cloths, the production and sale of palm oil, fish pies, body lotions, cakes, scotch eggs and mayonnaise (Kamara 2004). Unlike the CWA, the Women's Department of Full Gospel Mission runs a thrift-and-loan scheme (locally known as 'tontines' or 'njangi') through which members can take a loan at very low interest rates to operate a business. This system does not only provide the women with the skills but also the necessary business capital. What is important for the survival and success of such a scheme is putting in place a mechanism through which defaulting, for instance, inability to pay back the loan or interest, or the intestate death of a debtor, could be held in check. According to Kamara, all the necessary security measures, such as having collateral, are taken into consideration before awarding any loan.

One beneficiary of the scheme is Helen who said that life had become so difficult for her and her family because her retired husband had not been receiving his retirement benefits and she was unemployed. She said her situation had greatly improved with the church's help. Kamara claimed that the women of the assembly also organise afternoon classes for candidates intending to write public examinations. The candidates pay for the classes and any profit is used in the interests of the women. The money in their bank account is at the disposal of any member who wants to borrow part of it. When the need arises, some of this money may go the church for any project.

Conclusion

The discussion has indicated that the two churches have been seriously affected by the economic crisis and each is working to rise above it. While the RCC education department has suffered because of its long reliance on government subsidies, the FGM seems not to be in a similar predicament. The authorities of the church made the decision to operate schools during the period of the economic crisis and took the necessary measures to avoid running into financial difficulties. Catholic Mission teachers find it difficult to accept their present working conditions when compared to the past and this has been a bone of contention between the authorities of the church and the teachers. The Full Gospel Mission does not face this problem because the teachers were recruited during the crisis on terms that they accepted. Moreover, most of them are young people who feel contented with whatever is given to them given the high rate of unemployment.

In support of Nash's contention that if a people are poor therefore the church must be a church of the poor (Nash 1984), the two churches are preoccupied with reducing poverty among its members. Given that each is becoming self-financing, contributions from members make up a sizeable source of income. Unfortunately, the crisis has handicapped many people in providing financial support to the churches and this accounts for why each church, in order to succeed, tries to alleviate poverty among its members. This has created a reciprocal relationship in which the church overcomes the crisis by alleviating poverty among members, who in turn provide the necessary finance for running the church. The success of the church is therefore determined by the ability and degree to which it reduces poverty among its members. The higher the number of members raised out of poverty, the more the financial assistance provided to the church.

Providing employment to members in the establishments (schools, hospitals, etc.) run by the church is a method used to enable members to gain a source of income. While the PCC and other churches closed down schools because of the crisis, the RCC did not take this move in a bid to avoid creating unemployment. Instead, more schools were opened (creating more employment opportunities), although salaries of serving teachers were slashed by fifty per cent. The FGM for its part embarked on providing these services during the crisis. These have provided employment opportunities for members of the church. One of the reasons which I have argued elsewhere as being a contributory factor to the rapid growth of the church in the last decade is the decision to operate these services. The establish-ments are run on a trust basis, and only members of the church or those ready to be converted may be employed in them. Many people have been converted to the church because of this (Akoko 2002).

The two churches have shown a special interest in alleviating poverty among women. It is very likely that one of the reasons behind this is to liberate women economically because it had been a tradition for women (especially the majority who do not have a regular source of income and are full-time housewives) to rely on their husbands' earnings. The intention here would not only be to empower the women financially but enable them to assist their husbands in running the home since it is increasingly becoming difficult for one person to do. Also, as argued by Kamara, the mismanagement of money by some men, for instance, in drinking, running after women, or playing the lottery makes it worthwhile for women to engage in income-generating activities to meet the financial commitments of these men (Kamara 2004).

Both churches also believe that helping the needy is important during this period of economic crisis. The reinvigoration of the service of charity by the Catholic Church is indicative of the interest the church has in helping the needy. Unlike the Catholic Church, which has institutionalised this service and prescribed the methods for raising its funds, FGM has not institutionalised charity. It follows another way of taking care of needy members. When a member deserves assis-tance, a special appeal is launched during a service of worship for members to make a financial contribution, which is then handed over to the person.

Notes

1. For more World Bank publications on Africa, portraying the changing situation: *Sub-Saharan Africa: From Crisis to Sustainable Growth: a Long Term Perspective Study* (1989); *The Social Dimensions of Adjustment in Africa: a Political Agenda* (1990); *Sub-Saharan Africa: From Crisis to Sustainable Growth* (1993); *A Continent in Transition: Sub-Saharan Africa in the Mid 1990s* (1995); and *Can Africa Claim the 21st Century? Overview* (2000).

2. See Maimo's presentation during the Seventh Bamenda Ecclesiastic Province Annual Convention in Bamenda in 1999, entitled 'Financial Self-sufficiency in our Local Church'.

3. Report of the Bamenda Ecclesiastic Province Seventh Catholic Convention, Mankon, 1999, and the pastoral plan, which was a follow-up of this convention.

4. Ministry of Education and Social Welfare (1963); *West Cameroon Educational Policy - Investment in Education*, Buea, West Cameroon Government Press.

5. More details in 'The National Episcopal Conference of Cameroon: Pastoral Letter of the Bishops of Cameroon about Catholic Education', January 1989, SOPECAM, Yaoundé.

6. Letter of the Catholic Education Secretary, Buea, August 1993, to the Provincial Delegate of Labour South West on the plight of Catholic teachers and measures adopted for the survival of Catholic schools.

7. A detailed explanation of the factors which have accounted for the rapid growth of the church is contained in Akoko R., (Unpublished), 'An Overview of Full Gospel Mission Cameroon and the Factors Accounting for its Rapid Growth'.

8. Memorandum presented to President Paul Biya by the Moderator of the PCC in Buea on 27 September 1991 in which he elaborated on the plight of mission schools and also his address on the occasion of the 35th Presbyterian Church day, 15 November 1992.

9. *The Herald*, 17 April 2004, on the confrontation between the executive members of CATA of the Bamenda diocese and the Education Secretary on the rejection of low salaries by CATA.

10. Liberation theology calls for the church to combine preaching the gospel and administering the sacraments with a deep commitment to social justice. According to this theology, the church should announce in words and action an integral form of salvation, or liberation, from all manifestation of sin, and not merely offer individuals the means of personal salvation through the sacraments.

11. Knorr, W., 'Full Gospel Mission Cameroon: What does the Bible say? Our Position on Prosperity'.

12. Nwancha, E., (2001), 'Our Social and Educational Involvement', in W. Knorr, ed., *Full Gospel Mission on its 40th Anniversary*, Gospel Press, Bamenda, pp. 54-58.

13. Chiabi, E., 1997, *The making of modern Cameroon. A history of sub-state, nationalism and desperate unions, 1914-1961*, New York, University Press of America; Keller, W., (1969), 'The history of the Presbyterian Church in West Cameroon', Presbook, Limbe, pp. 65-73 and 101-102; Kubuo, J., (2000), 'An overview of the Buea Diocese, 1890-1990', in Njeuma, M., ed., *Pilgrimage of Faith. A History of the Buea Diocese*, Copy Technology, Bamenda, pp. 11-51; Weber, C. W., (1993), *International Influences and Baptist Missions in West Cameroon: German-American Missionary Endeavour under International Mandates and British Colonialism*, Leiden, E. J. Brill, pp. 87-133.

References

Afe, A., 1999, 'Religion and Economic Development in Nigeria', *The Nigerian Journal of Economic History*, No. 2, September.

Akoko, R., 2002, 'New Pentecostalism in the Wake of the Economic Crisis in Cameroon', *Nordic Journal of African Studies*, Vol. 11, No. 2, pp. 359-376.

Akoko, R., 2004, 'From Asceticism to a Gospel of Prosperity: Case of Full Gospel Mission Cameroon', *Journal for the Study of Religion*, Vol. 17, No. 4.

Akoko, R. and T. Mbuagbo, (forthcoming), 'The Christian Church and the Democratisation Conundrum in Cameroon'.

Atabong, D., 2000, 'The Catholic Women Association', in Njeuma, M., ed., *A Pilgrimage of Faith. A History of the Buea Diocese*, Bamenda: Copy Printing Technology.

Atabong, D., 2004, 'The Catholic Women Association and Poverty Alleviation', in Endeley, J., S., Ardener, R., Gooderidge & Nalova Lyonga, eds., *Issues in Gender and Development: Vol. I. New Gender Studies from Cameroon and the Caribbean*, Buea: Department of Women and Gender Studies, University of Buea.

Chiabi, E., 1997, *The Making of Modern Cameroon: A History of Sub-state Nationalism and Desperate Unions, 1914-1996*, New York: University Press of America.

Eyongetah, T. and Brain, R., 1994, *A History of Cameroon*, Essex: Longmans.

Gifford, P., 1997, *African Christianity: Its Public Role*, London: Hurst & Co.

Kamara, M., 2004, 'Full Gospel Women and Poverty Alleviation', in Endeley, J. S., Ardener, R., Gooderidge & Nalova Lyonga, eds., *Issues in Gender and Development: Vol. I. New Gender Studies from Cameroon and the Caribbean*, Buea: Department of Women and Gender Studies, University of Buea.

Kankeur, E., 2001, 'Work among the Women', in W. Knorr, ed., *Full Gospel Mission on Its 40th Anniversary*, Bamenda: Gospel Press, pp. 41-53.

Keller, W., 1969, *The History of the Presbyterian Church in West Cameroon*, Victoria: Presbook.

Kennett, David and Tukumbi Lumumba-Kasongo,.1992, 'Introduction', in David Kennett and Tukumbi Lumumba-Kasongo, eds., *Structural Adjustment and the Crisis in Africa: Economic and Political Perspectives*, Lewiston: The Edwin Mellen Press.

Knorr, W., n.d., 'Full Gospel Mission Cameroon. What does the Bible say? Our Position on Prosperity', Unpublished privately circulated mimeograph.

Knorr, W., 2001, 'As it was at the beginning', W. Knorr, ed., *Full Gospel Mission on its 40th Anniversary*, Bamenda, Gospel Press, pp. 8-15.

Konings, P., 1996, 'Post-Colonial State and Economic and Political Reforms in Cameroon', in A.E. Fernandez Jilberto and A. Mommen, eds., *Liberalization in the Developing World: Institutional and Economic changes in Latin America, Africa, and Asia*, London/New York: Routledge, pp. 244-265.

Kubuo, J., 2000, 'An Overview of the Buea Diocese', in Njeuma, M., ed., *A Pilgrimage of Faith. A history of the Buea Diocese*, Bamenda: Copy Printing Technology.

Levine, V. T., 1964, *The Cameroons: From Mandate to Independence*, Berkeley and Los Angeles: University of California Press.

Maimo, M. M., 1999, 'Financial Self-Sufficiency in our local Church', in Ateh, J. et al., 'Report on the Seventh Catholic Convention: Ecclesiastical Province of Bamenda', Bamenda: Copy Printing Technology.

Ministry of Education and Social Welfare, 1963, *West Cameroon Educational Policy - Investment in Education*, Buea: West Cameroon Government Press.

Nantang, Jua, 1991, 'Cameroon: Jump-Starting an Economic Crisis', *Africa Insight*, Vol. 21, No. 3, pp. 162-170.

Nash, M., 1984, 'Church, Poverty and Development in Southern Africa', Cape Town, Carnegie Conference Paper No. 242.

Ngoh, V. J., 1990, *Constitutional Developments in Southern Cameroon, 1946-1961: From Trusteeship to Independence*, Yaoundé: CEPER.

Ngoh, J., 2000, 'The period of Bishop Pius Suh Awah 1973', in Njeuma, M., ed., *A Pilgrimage of Faith. A History of the Buea Diocese*, Bamenda: Copy Printing Technology.

Njemo, D., 2001, 'Preface', in W. Knorr, ed., *Full Gospel Mission on its 40th Anniversary*, Bamenda: Gospel Press.

Nwancha, E., 2001, 'Our Social and Educational Involvement', in W. Knorr, ed., *Full Gospel Mission on its 40th anniversary*, Bamenda: Gospel Press, pp. 54-58.

Nyansako-Ni-Nku, 1993, *Cry Justice: The Church in a Changing Cameroon*, Limbe: Presprint.

Obiora, F. and Ugonna, I., 1992, 'Human Rights, Human Dignity and Catholic Social Teachings: Lessons for the Church in Nigeria', Uwani: CIDJAP.

Obiora, F. and Ugonna, I., 1999, 'Pastoral Plan: Ecclesiastical Province of Bamenda', Bamenda: Copy Printing Technology.

Obiora, F. and Ugonna, I., 2001, 'Report on the Seventh Catholic Convention: Ecclesiastical Province of Bamenda', Bamenda: Copy Printing Technology.

Shu, D., 2001, 'Our Medical Services', in W. Knorr, ed., *Full Gospel Mission on its 40th anniversary*, Bamenda: Gospel Press.

Takougang, J. and Krieger, M., 1998, *African State and Society in the 1990s: Cameroon's Political Crossroads*, Boulder: Westview Press.

Tamba, I., 2001, 'Cameroon Stakes and Challenges of the HIPC Initiative', Yaoundé: Frederich Ebert Foundation.

Tanga, P. and Mbuagbo, T., 2002, 'Redressing the Balance Sheet of Women's Empowerment through Associations Networking in Cameroon', *Journal of Applied Social Sciences*, Vol. 2, No. 1 and 2.

Titi Nwel, P., 1995, 'The Churches and the Democratic Upheaval in Cameroon 1982-1993', in P. Gifford, ed., *The Christian Churches and the Democratisation of Africa*, Leiden: E. J. Brill.

Weber, C. W., 1993, *International Influences and Baptist Missions in West Cameroon: German-American Missionary Endeavour under International Mandates and British Colonialism*, Leiden: E. J. Brill.

World Bank, 2000, *Can Africa Claim the 21st Century? An Overview*, Washington DC: World Bank.

III

Associational Life between Traditional and
Modern Society on the Path to Autonomy
and Self-Reliant Development

5

On the Viability of Associational Life in Traditional Society and Home-Based Associations

Emmanuel Yenshu Vubo

Introduction

The notion of civil society, which is at the basis of association life, has gained a new lease of life since the end of the Cold War. In Cameroon the emergence of association life was concurrent with the liberalisation process. Although it has been given a new impetus – to the extent that it pervades all facets of national life (Yenshu Vubo 1997) – the concern with association life has been lived as an exclusively modern one. This joins up with a certain Lockean notion of voluntary association life as the 'product of modernity' (Tester 1992:176). In this regard the notion of civil society is inscribed in the 'modern', 'advanced', and 'civilised', versus the 'traditional', 'primitive', 'backward' antimony and the current evangelists of civil society present it as the appropriate instrument in constructing a new society outside of a largely discredited state.

This view abstracts the question of civil society from its real concern. As Tester (op cit. 5) has put it, the question of the civil society 'can best be understood as a confrontation with the very possibility of society itself – this society, our society'. In this regard we come to view civil society as being at the basis of all societies, the necessary framework for a movement from a state of nature to a state of culture. There is an increasing tendency for traditional association life to erupt into the domain of the modern (Ritzenthaler 1960, Ardener 1975, Nkwi 1985, Diduk 1987, 1989, 1998, 2004). Mamdani (1995:612) has also pointed to the restlessness of traditional society in the modern context. In fact, the indigenous organisation of associations has often risen to the surface during critical movements of transition in the modern era, whether we are talking of opposition to colonial rule, the decolonisation process (cf. Ritzenthaler 1960, Nkwi 1985, Diduk 1989, Breytenbach 1998:39) or the post-Cold War attempts at democratisation (Jua 1993, Diduk 2004, see Forchingong et al. in this volume). Association life is also becoming the central feature of economic, social and political life in the rural areas that have remained largely traditional. This can also be observed in the proliferation of ethnic-based associations in the urban areas (Tostensen, Tvedten and Vaa 2001). Although this is proof of the vitality of traditional association life few studies have paid attention to it, and even where there have been attempts, they have been peripheral to the central issues.

Associations with an ethnic base but laying claims to a development role or function have been a very important feature of association life in Cameroon since colonial times. They have been an important, if not the dominant feature, of popular urban life, creating as it were a bridge between urban and rural spheres, on the one hand, and the traditional and the modern, on the other. In the colonial era they articulated so-called tribal interests, initiating what Ebune has styled the improvement unions (Ebune 2004:62-69),[1] and intervened in a decolonisation process controlled entirely by the colonial powers and directed to the protection of the interests of certain groups perceived to be more favourable to eventual neo-colonial interests. These associations survived into the post-colonial period, constituting in some cases the only safety valve for free expression where associa-tion life in general was outlawed as in the aftermath of the 1967 law on associa-tions (Yenshu Vubo 1998:134, Zambo Belinga 1997:116). These are what have been referred to elsewhere as home-based associations.

The regional drift in political life since the return to multiparty life in politics is also reflected in the nature of certain regional associations that have emerged in the modern period and whose claim is to foster the interests of the people at the regional level (Mbuagbo 2003, Menthong 1996, Miles 2001, Monga 2000, Sindjoun 1996, Tata Mentan 1996, Yenshu Vubo 1998b). While some of these associations are formal structures with a certain history and activism (SWELA), some are informal although their action is overtly public (NOWEDA/NOWEDEP, Bassa-Mpoo-Bati, chiefs associations, unions, or conferences, Ngondo), others are still plainly speaking, clandestine, although they are the object of public knowledge (Laakam, Essingang). All of these associations build on a traditional social base as they try to grapple with the reality of the coercive modern state structure. Advocates of the sanctity of the nation-state as it supersedes local realities and tends towards their obliteration in name of a nation-building process are quick to point to the disruptive and dislocating effects of what others inaptly call irredentist tendencies. Whatever the efforts, more than a century of Christian missionary activity, colo-nial repression and attempts at obliteration by the post-colonial state have not succeeded in putting out the flame of association life at either the local or the regional level. Indigenous peoples have not only maintained traditional associa-tion life, they have succeeded in inventing various forms of associations in response to the developments in the modern era.

Although the mobilisation of some of these movements took on a direction that tended to undermine the goals of collective life and the democratic ideal within the confines of the nation-state (witness the ethnic or ethno-regional drift in most African countries, and especially the Rwandan genocide), we argue here that it is still worthwhile examining the value of local forces in building viable social projects if we still have to live within the pluralistic world that the imperatives of the current nation-state system and the current globalisation process place on the diversity of peoples (see also Yenshu Vubo 2001, 2003). This will fall in line with Sachs's (1995) proposal that one viable strategy in meeting the development challenge is to forge new forms of partnerships among social agents that draw attention away from the 'present imbalance in favour of the central level', and 'to encourage initiatives from the bottom' (Sachs op cit.:34).

The argument in this paper is that these forms of association life are a pointer to forms of autonomy that are essential to development. By refusing to play the game of the state or to acquiesce in a dependency position vis-à-vis the latter, these associations offer a road to self-determination which is essential to development practice. This argument derives its thrust from Aragon's (1995) argument that development of exogenous origin is synonymous with dictatorship or authoritarianism. This conception puts autonomy and self-reliance at the centre of the development effort by arguing that development should grow from within, helping and aiding groups to find their ways within their own cultural patterns; in short, adding a cultural dimension to development.

The study combines ethnographic methods and a survey. Data for this paper are drawn from an ethnographic study of twenty-three traditional associations (rotating savings clubs, solidarity unions, status societies) in six ethnic groups (Moghamo, Bayang, Bafaw, Balong, Barombi, Bakundu) and a survey of twenty-nine home-based associations (cultural and development associations) representing three distinct ethno-linguistic and geo-cultural zones (Momo sub-group of Grassfields Bantu, Cross River Bantu and Coastal Bantu) in Cameroon and from the majority of provinces of the country (South West, Centre, Littoral, North West, South, East, Northern Provinces). We will start with an examination of the development implications of associations in traditional society and then move on to examine the role of home-based associations, which serve as the other end in the continuum.

Development Implications of Associational Life in Traditional Society

Outline for an Understanding

Association life occupies a dominant and even overbearing place in traditional society. In two of the cultural zones that we visited we could identify a large spectrum of associations of an economic, political, cultural and social nature. Although largely expressive of social solidarity that is so vibrant in a mainly traditional rural society, these associations functioned as the basis of survival in the direction of sustainability. They helped generate a forward-looking vision for the society as well as the space for the exercise of democracy and autonomy which a largely truncated citizenship and the rituals of a warped neo-liberal vision of democracy cannot provide. They simply underscore the vitality of the social bonds that are constantly being entered into by local peoples outside the scope of the modern state and which provide the space for the elaboration of an alternative. In general, associations will vary according to the sector of main preoccupation (economy and finance, culture and tradition, the social or solidarity based), according to intensity of social bonds, and the degree of resilience of structure and duration. These associations may also vary according to whether they are more concerned with or derive from individual initiative or whether they result from the pressure of community interest or age-old custom. We will exa- mine the associations under two broad categories depending on the domain of activity. One can affirm that although association life is generally built around solidarity, the rallying point will vary according to whether we are talking of the economy, culture, the exercise of authority, or the enforcement of social bonds. For purposes of this study we will refer to two main categories: the economy, on the one hand, and culture, social solidarity and tradition on the other.

Economy

Economic survival seems to be the motive around which most voluntary asso- ciations operate in the rural areas. At all the sites we visited we could notice farming groups, credit and thrift societies, small savings societies and solidarity savings unions. In fact, in the Moghamo area all associations have a financial side captured in the term 'ashow'. An understanding of these organisational forms is instructive with regard to the background of the so-called informal financial sector that has blossomed in both rural and urban areas in a period when it was expected that financial sector reforms would usher in a period of relatively better conditions in the financial sector (see Awung in this volume).

Rotating Savings Clubs

These clubs are universal all over Cameroon and constitute a key element in the local savings culture. Although a lot has already been written about these societies (Essombe-Edimu 1994), we come back here only to explore the principles in their functioning. Whether it is called 'ashow' with the Moghamo people, 'njangi' with the coastal Bantu-speaking people, the 'nchua/choh' of speakers of Mbam- Nkam and Ring group of Grassfields Bantu, or known by the French term 'tontine', the phenomenon constitutes the core of the savings culture of local peoples with roots buried far in the past (cf. Warnier 1994). Its basic principle of rotating contributions has of recent so pervaded association life in local communities that it constitutes the very soul of this form of social activity. In fact almost every association attempts to establish its own savings society where members take turns in contributing and donating to members. An examination of the 'ashow' of the Moghamo and the 'njangi' of the coastal Bantu peoples will be instructive in this regard.

The 'ashow' begins with a small but reasonable number of people and then grows progressively as more people develop interest in it. Contributions range from insignificant sums – say a few hundred or thousand francs CFA – to more than ten thousand and even as much as twenty-five thousand, which is considerable by the standards of the rural areas. The question arises as to the security of the contribution. In the case of the 'ashow' domiciled in the residence of Elias Teke of Itoh, Batibo, each time a member receives a contribution he or she must present a surety who must not have received his or her contribution as yet. However, the principle here is that of trust and sincerity. Membership will range from less than ten to around fifty while resilience will depend on the age of some of these associations. Although some of them are of relatively recent creation some are more than forty years old. These savings clubs are not restricted to financial transactions as they stretch their activities into the social and cultural domains. Generally there is always entertainment during meetings and contributions to show solidarity with members in situations of either joy or sorrow. Another type of savings association among the Moghamo people is the 'ikeuh'.

The 'njangi' of the coastal peoples operates much on the same principle with regular contributions, which are donated to members in turn. The importance of these structures is that they assist in solving major problems within a family setting such as paying for children's education, building a house, buying farm implements and investing in small businesses.

Small Savings Societies or Solidarity Unions

In both cultural zones studied these kinds of associations go under the much pidginised terminology of 'meetings' (meaning 'association') or 'efferti'. The general principle is for a few people to come together and save regularly, and the savings are either shared at the end of the year or used for a common purpose. Unlike the 'ashow' or 'njangi', which involve considerable amounts of money, the 'meetings' attract relatively small savings.

Among the Barombi, Bafaw and Bakundu, groups that are known as 'meetings', abound. In Barombi Kang for example, there are a variety of meetings, some involving women, some the youth, some farmers. They promote savings and solidarity activities, for example, condoling with bereaved members. Some of these 'meetings' contribute exclusively in the preparation for the end of year festivities in the manner of what Masuko calls 'cooperatives for entertainment' (Masuko 1995:298). In this case members contribute a specific sum of money at regular intervals and the accumulated money is used at the end of the year to purchase consumable items towards the festivities at this period. A prominent type of such solidarity groups is the so-called 'kitchen njangi' or savings union or club whose sole aim is to assist members to procure kitchen utensils. Membership is restricted to women with total enrolment ranging from thirty (as in Kake I) to more than a hundred. There are generally no restrictions on membership except for the fact that members should be viable enough to meet the required sums, which are generally low (for example, 2000 CFA in Kake II). In the case of the 'kitchen njangi' of Kake II there is also a regular savings aspect with no fixed rate. According to our informants there are about fifty such petty financial houses or associations in Kake II.

While the rotating savings clubs are the backbone of local investment in both economic and cultural (education) capital, thus forming the basis for a certain form of transformation, the existence and proliferation of small savings clubs and solidarity unions are indicative of a will to collective survival and proof of the vitality of a largely ignored aspect of civil society at its most rudimentary level. In this way they are both 'social consumption funds' and 'self-help insurance strategies' that have been described elsewhere for southern Africa (Masuko op cit.:279-308). Working largely outside the scope of the capitalist mode of production (with a low level of technology, the absence of an overbearing urban industrial or commercial bourgeoisie), this component of civil society provides a vent for the eventual conceptualisation of alternatives and thus constitutes the space for autonomous action unregulated by the state. Proof of this is the importation of this model into the urban setting where the rotating savings clubs and small savings clubs or solidarity unions constitute the backbone of the financial sector in Cameroon and elsewhere in Africa (Warnier 1994, Essombe-Edimu 1993, Wengue 2004, Niang 2000:136). In their functioning they provide the space for democratic practice that is absent in the neo-liberal model characterised by disenfranchisement, election rigging, exclusion and under-representation. It is also the space of rational, consensual and autonomous management of affairs where global management in the national public sphere has been largely wanting (given the mismanagement of public funds, embezzlement, and corruption). With its stress on the ethos of hard work, the virtues of honesty, sincerity and mutual respect, and the value of reciprocity and continuity, they are veritable schools of ethics indispensable for the development of a society. Niang (ibid.:134-135) has also observed this ethical and moral side and solidarity function of rotating savings clubs and solidarity unions in a Senegalese study.

Culture, Social Organisation and Mobilisation

The rest of the associations, which seemingly do not have a direct development role, can be lumped under the broad category of cultural associations and by extension considered associations with a direct bearing on social organisation, the structure of traditional authority, and mobilisation at both the local and regional level. It is this last aspect that is of capital importance to our discussion, since it connects to development and the search for alternatives. By lumping all else into the category of the 'cultural', we are adopting both a Tylorian sense of culture, and the Marxist conception of the cultural at the level of superstructure (what Gramsci simply designates as structure). Here, culture is equated with identity or to that which defines the group. Within this category one finds local entertainment groups, fraternities or status societies, age-sets, solidarity groups, community-wide fraternities, and cultural and development associations. In some cases these structures transcend the immediate confines of the village in which an association is situated and take on a universal character at regional level. In the section on the legal framework of civil society and social movements, Temngah argues that the state excludes these forms from its definition of civil society. In practice the state is also dismissive of such associational life, which it assimilates to an anti-modern stance, not conforming to so-called natural law, and thus uncivil (see Fonchingong et al. in the present volume). Although virtually outside the scope of modernity, they nonetheless constitute their own domains of civility which merit exploration in their own right, as well as in relation to modernising trends such as democracy, citizenship, development and nation-building.

There have been a variety of calls for the traditional aspects of civil society to be integrated in the study of civil society as one would find it in the modern context (QUEST 1998:9, 12, 13, 15, Mbuagbo and Fru 2003, Breytenbach 1998:39-40). In fact, Breytenbach argues that these forms qualify to be styled 'proto-civil society' because 'the roots of civil society go far back into history, and is not alien to Africa. Once it confronted the colonial state; and now in post-authoritarian Africa, it is resurfacing as the communalisation of politics. The point is that ethnic associations 'should not be excluded simply because they are ethnic...' (Breytenbach ibid.:40). Others before us, such as Fodé Moussa Balla Sidibé, have indeed integrated traditional associations in the study of civil society. In his study of the brotherhood of hunters that covers a wide civilisation area for the Malinké and Bamanan of West Africa (Mali, Côte d'Ivoire, Burkina Faso, Guinea, Senegal, Niger, Gambia, Sierra Leone, Mauritania), Sidibé (1998:91-104) demonstrates that such organisations are the depositories of values which merit to be recognised in their own right and adapted to current realties of the continent. Our decision to include these forms into the study of civil society is for two essential reasons:

- They fall within the domain of associational life like every other form of association. Their adaptation to modern realities makes an important element in understanding the behaviour of non-state actors in the articulation of collective interests.
- They form the background against which we can understand the articulation of certain collective interests as they tend to redefine their role as social change is underway.

Their eruption into modern life transforms them from a mere 'proto-civil society' or the manifestation of communalistic politics (Breytenbach op cit.) or communalistic life (Wiredu 1998) into a vital component of civil society in its own right.

Significance of Traditional Association Life for Development

The characteristic of these associations that is of importance to us is the mobilisation for survival and sustenance, for social, cultural and economic production and reproduction, and growth, however limited that may be. One would be forced to ponder whether this is just a reproduction of poverty or simply stagnation. In other words, is there vitality or are we just dealing with the reproduction of low levels of survival? This is the crux of the matter. One is rather optimistic in observing that in a world largely characterised by ambient poverty, these associations offer a fall-back position. In the case of savings clubs and the savings component of associations they provide a much-needed culture of saving, investment and capital that is lacking in a new culture of consumerism largely bereft of a culture of production. The funds generated also provide the much needed capital for petty household production (farm input, investment in education). One can go further to say that these strategies cannot be considered simply coping mechanisms because the existence of savings implies a surplus or the will to generate surplus.

The proliferation of such associations is proof of the vitality of a certain rudimentary civil society that seems largely overlooked. It would be instructive to interpret them as strategies of existence, continuity and livelihood in their own right, in the way Habermas considers civil society as a way of life (cf. Vilas 1998:71). It is the arena for generating an alternative vision of society both rooted in the past and anchored in the modern world, the space for the exercise of democratic values by way of a self regulating ethic and an autonomy, which a truncated citizenship within the modern state is incapable of providing. It is this autonomy and cultural sustainability that Aragon is referring to when he states that development or development models imposed from outside are synonymous with dictatorship. One should not ask whether they can serve as a model because they are already the model in both the modern urban setting and are the only hope for the common man in the rural areas (cf. Warnier 1994). In fact, they offer greater levels of sustainability and have a far greater impact than institutions deriving from the post-1990 economic and social reforms. Umbrella associations taking the appellation of 'cultural and development associations', which we are going to examine in detail in the next session, are the arena and strategy for reviving the fortunes of communities on the edge of decline owing to a largely alienating modernity which Africans in general have to negotiate.

Coming back to the mode of existence of these associations, which simply escapes the control of the modern state structures, we ask whether they can even be controlled or whether the state could control everything. It is in this regard that we consider them as lying at the very soul of the local society, generating as it were an ancient mystique of vitality and continuity. This falls in line with Julio de Santa Ana's (1998:65) affirmation that 'la société civile est véritablement la conscience d'une nation' (civil society is truly the conscience of a nation). One can then postulate that they are situated at a deeper, more essential substratum than the modern structures of the so-called new civil society that are situated at a more superficial and superstructural level. We can also affirm that this explains the success of the one and the inability of the other to take root (see Enoh Tanjong's study in this volume).

This brings into focus the definition of civil society as a *process*, that is, an emerging and thus real society anchored in history and entrenched in local practices. This process can be opposed to modernity as exemplified in the state ideology of nation-building that is hardly taking root but operates as a superimposed society – or in the words of Goran Hyden 'suspended above society' (in Mamdani op cit.:606), or 'a balloon in the sky' (Osaghae 1998:277) in the wake of the failure of the post-colonial state. One definition considers existing civil society as constitutive of structure in the Gramscian sense (in Santa Ana op cit.). Any other structures posing as civil society which do not take root can only be treated as an intention towards civil society or a dream of civil society that must not be confused with actual existing civil society.

Principal Characteristics of Home-Based Associations or Cultural and Development Associations

In examining the principal characteristics of these associations we will be looking at their objectives, the nature of the association (whether these are local, or regional or sectional), the demographic composition (age, gender), structure and composition (membership, organisation), relations with other organisations and mode of functioning (decision making processes, execution of projects, fund raising, management of projects, selection of leadership structure).

Objectives

Three themes dominate the objectives reported by our respondents: the promotion of solidarity among members, the contribution to the development of communities of origin, and the promotion of cultural heritage. The theme of solidarity pervades the objectives of all associations but becomes heightened when this objective is associated with the promotion of cultural identity. Besides promoting elements of material and non-material culture such as language, religion, dress, food, and authority structure, some of the associations go beyond the solidarity element to the enhancement of a sense of belonging that assimilates the ethnic group to a family.[2] In fact, although some associations' membership is derived from a wide community base, they take the designation of 'Family Meeting' (Famille Musgum de Yaoundé, Famille Lombi du Nkam, Njarenka Family Meeting) while others simply manifest a spirit of family. While the MBOG

LIA ADNA MATEN has the declared objective of bringing together all the Bassa, Mpoo and Bati (treated as families) into a single structure towards common development ('rassembler les familles Bassa, Mpoo et Bati en vue d'un développement commun'), the Association Culturelle et Traditionnelle Elog Mpoo (ACTEM), which is specific to the Mpoo group, wishes to distinguish itself from the former by claiming that it is not an association but 'une association familiale' whose prime objective is 'l'enracinement identitaire et la revalorisation et promotion culturelles'. Such global objectives go to the extent of making claims for the carving of administrative units to correspond to the limits of geo-cultural zones. This is the case of MBOG LIA ADNA MATEN, which is calling for the creation of a Greater Sanaga Province comprising the present Sanaga, Maritime, Nyong and Kelle, and Ocean Divisions that correspond to the Bassa-Mpoo-Bati homeland.

Although some associations mentioned only one of the above three as their objectives, the majority of associations had more than one aim. In fact, the associations with a single objective were in the minority. Only four associations, namely CREDEM, ASSEEC, AJDS, and BANBA – MAMBANDA, mentioned development as their sole objective, while only one association, FAMY, mentioned solidarity as its sole objective. The rest of the associations combined at least two of these objectives with the majority combining all three objectives.

Scope of Associations

Eighteen of the twenty-nine associations we studied were of a regional character. In other words, these are associations whose activities transcend the limits of an ethnic group to encompass peoples with origins from the same cultural zone or administrative district. The rest are community-based organisations limited to particular villages or communities of origin. Although some associations with a regional base are gender neutral, implying that they are open to both men and women, some are clearly women's associations (Lumière du Nkam, AFMAD, and Golden Ladies). Our sample is also representative of youth groups (the students' associations, youth development organisations) whether this is at the level of region or community of origin. At the level of the latter we did not target women's groups given the extensive attention paid to them at the level of traditional association life.

In terms of regional representation we have tried to touch on all cultural zones and geo-administrative areas (North West Province, Bamileke area, Sawa cultural zone, Grand North, the Beti region), although the coastal region (South West and Littoral) has had more attention than all other regions. The coastal region is the principal focus of our study because of the attention it has received as a result of the autonomist claims that ensued from the post-1996 elections period. We are then using the other areas for largely comparative purposes to measure the viability of these tendencies towards autonomy and their utility in a context of decentralisation and regional reorientation of political and administrative life. Our typology contrasts considerably with the four-level typology advanced by Niang (op cit.:112) that breaks down associations in Dakar into associations with a uni-local, pluri-local, regional and supra-regional or national basis. Only our regional associations correspond to Niang's associations with a regional base.

Structure and Organisation

In terms of structure and composition, all associations have formalised hierarchical structures. Typically, an association's constitution makes provision for an executive committee and a general assembly which brings together all members. Apart from an executive committee some of these associations have an advisory council or council of elders. Invariably, the association will have branches nationwide or even in foreign countries, depending on the residence of persons of that community of origin in a locality. This trend is also observed by Zambo Belinga (op cit.:116) among elite associations in general. The adoption of modern modes of organisation with a formalised structure in the style described by Everett Rogers (1960) has also been observed in other contexts such as Dakar (Niang op cit.:104) or the largely traditional rural societies of Cameroon. One can affirm that organisation according to formal modern criteria is thus becoming an almost universal feature of association life in the African context. The general criterion for eligibility for membership is belonging to the community of origin, although there is an allowance for honorary membership.

Age of Associations

Concerning longevity one can classify the associations into three categories: the relatively old associations whose birth is situated in the colonial era (MECA) or in the colonial period but deriving from the very deep distant past – Braudel's *longue durée*[3] – for example, ACTEM, MBOG LIA, Assemblée Communautaire et Traditionnelle de Souza; associations deriving from the pre-1990 post-colonial period (14); and relatively young associations created in the post-1990 period (13). ACTEM and MBOG LIA are associations with origins in a very distant past. Ebune reports that there was a proliferation of home-based associations in colonial British Southern Cameroons generally, going under the appellation of improvement unions (Ebune 2004:62-69).

The year 1990 is taken as an important threshold in the development of associations because of the 1990 law on associations. This is judged against the period following the 1967 law that practically outlawed associational life in Cameroon (Yenshu Vubo 1997). For this period, eleven out of the fourteen associations were targeted. Although selectively targeted, these associations were chosen anonymously (not to say randomly), that is, without prior knowledge of the date of formation. However, it was not the 1990 law on associations or the current phase of liberalisation that facilitated the growth of certain types of associations. The repressive nature of the 1967 law outlawing association life was equally responsible for paradoxically promoting the proliferation of associations with an ethnic base (Yenshu Vubo 1997, Zambo Belinga 1997). The very depth of associations points to the fact that they are not a novel phenomenon but that they owe their existence to a colonial past, which was largely disruptive, and recent modernisation resulting in 'mounting poverty, failing infrastructure and services, and more generally, weak or abdicating governments' (Tostensen, Tvedten and Vaa 2001:5). It is also indicative of the fact that they are linked in historical terms to the 'improvement unions' of the colonial period (see Ebune op cit.).

Inter-Associational Relations

These associations entertain a variety of links with other organisations and structures at local, regional, national (inter-regional) and international levels. At local level, associations of the cultural and development association type are linked to the structures of traditional authority as well as many facets of traditional life in the communities (dance groups, age groups, and local voluntary associations). Some of the associations we studied were either branches of a bigger structure or were emanations of larger movements, for example, Sawa students, Youth of the North, Students of the East. For instance, CEBA is affiliated to the Jeunesse Mpoo, itself an appendage of ACTEM. It also has links with the MBOG LIA that brings together the Bassa-Mpoo-Bati as related peoples sharing a common supra-regional cultural identity.

In the case of the community-based associations and the regional associations or movements, one can say that they are both connected to traditional authority structures, by virtue of the cultural component of their designation, and act as umbrella structures to other bodies situated at a lower level. These associations are also linked to more global structures operating at regional level. ACTEM, which is specific to the Mpoo, has links with MBOG LIA (Bassa-Mpoo-Bati) and Ngondo of the Sawa (coastal peoples of the Ocean, Sanaga Maritime, Nkam, Wouri, Moungo, Nyong and Kelle divisions), structures that are premised on a regional supra-cultural identity.[4] Likewise, BACDU is part of the much wider Oroko Tribal Association, CREDEM part of the Comité de Développement du Groupement Nguen (CODEGRON), that covers the administrative district in which Mgbaga is situated, while FAMY is part of the Associations des Massa, the Musgum being a sub-group of the Massa. One also finds relations operating at a horizontal level in a cross-cultural direction: Sawa students of the CESD having relations with KATE (Sawa), Kul Beti (Beti), students of the Greater North and associations of Bassa-Mpoo-Bati students; NOWEDEP (North West Province) co-operating with SWELA (South West Province); and MBOG LIA linking with Magissa of the East Province. We also find attempts to federate association structures as in the case of the Mutuelle des Associations Culturelles du Cameroun, and the Réseaux National des Habitants du Cameroun. In this way we can say that these associations operate at various levels each linked to the other. It is in this way that the modern is linked to the traditional, the younger generation to the older, rural reality to urban reality. Other links are entertained with state structures and the so-called non-governmental organisations (NGOs) but such links are dictated by the search for external financing. While the links within the local and regional sphere (which the majority are anyway) are established within a spirit of independence and autonomy, links established in the quest for funding are often tainted by a dependency attitude. It is also important to highlight the tendency of certain associations to transcend the parochialism of association life by creating trans-ethnic links and thus fostering cross-cultural relations where others will see only conflict and contradiction. One has to explore the value of this trend in the nation-building project.

Besides the four persons who did not indicate whether they belonged to any association other than the one they were representing, the rest indicated that they belonged to other associations or association structures of a similar nature whether they were home-based organisations, professional organisations, religious orga-nisations, social clubs or federative structures. As such, one can find lawyers in the Bar Association, engineers in the Society of Engineers and teachers in the Teachers Associations. Leaders of community-based associations within specific communities could also be observed to belong to associational structures within the same community or associations of a regional or federative nature. The members of the student associations were also members of associations of a more global and general nature operating within the same region. The president of CEBA is also Secretary General of the University of Douala student branch of MBOG LIA and Secretary General of the Wouri Regional antenna of the Jeunesse Elog-Mpoo (JEM), i.e., the Elog Mpoo Youth Association. The President of AEDELE is also a member of the Amicale des Ressortissants de la Lekié à L'INJS (AMILIS) (Fraternity of Lekié Elements in the Higher School of Youth and Sports). The National President of the AJDS is also a member of the Asso-ciations des Ressortissants Nordistes á Yaoundé and the Association des Ressor-tissants de Petté Résident à Yaoundé, while the Secretary General of the Famille Musgum de Yaoundé is also Secretary General of the Cercle des Etudiants Musgum de Yaoundé (Musgum Student Club in Yaoundé).

Some respondents are involved in more than one home-based association either within the same community or in a regional or federative structure. One can also find respondents in church-based groups (choirs, men and women's fellowships) and social clubs (Alma Mater or Alumni associations, philanthropic societies, and entertainment clubs). A curious case are those belonging to political parties referred to by the CESD respondent, or to structures with strong political connotations (President Biya's Youths, PRESBY) made by the respondent for MBOG LIA ADNA MATEN. Such mentions are indicative of the confusion that can be observed in some circles concerning the difference between political parties and civil society organisations.

In general, it can be observed that respondents were involved and played multiple roles in a variety of associations operating at different hierarchical levels and in varied domains (social, political, cultural, and religious). This shows the very interconnectedness of association life with the elites acting as necessary connection points or the nexus between different levels and domains. Elites are also active in the transmission of skills across a variety of domains in an almost imperceptible manner. In this regard, knowledge obtained in running a professional society is also deployed in home-based associations. One can say that the very interconnectedness of association life as we will see later is at the heart of buil-ding the social fabric and the conviviality that holds promise for Cameroon in a context where the slogans for national unity and integration have yielded little fruit or resulted in just a contrary of the desired results. This also puts the elite leadership at the junctions and connection points between traditional life from which the home-based association are derived, and modern life in which they have been deeply immersed by reason of training, professional involvement and life-style. It is thus instrumental in the management and negotiation of the transi-tion between the largely traditional life of the rural areas and the modernity to which the local peoples are constantly subjected.

The various levels of participation at both local and regional level tend in the direction of our concept of levels of historical awareness and the management of multiple identities (Yenshu Vubo 2003:618). We thus find people participating in associations specific to their communities and also active in pan-regional struc-tures. I have indicated that in the post-1996 period following the Sawa Protests (Yenshu Vubo 1998b, 2003, 2005) some people claiming a pan-Sawa identity retreated to their micro-identity formations to 'provoke a certain cultural revivalism' (Yenshu Vubo 2003:611) that we find in the Elog Mpoo (Bakoko) and Bankon (Abo) associations (ACTEM, MBOG LIA, Assemblée Communautaire et Tra-ditionnelle de Souza), which strive to protect their specific identities. That they are still active in the pan-Sawa movement through structures such as the Ngondo is expressive of participation in two levels of 'historical awareness and action: the level of primordial historic community and... regional trans-ethnic movements' (ibid.). This goes to underline the level of trans-ethnic universality that carries with it 'values of tolerance, accommodation and cooperation that characterise regional level groups [in opposition] to competition, conflicts and animosity' (ibid.:620). In this regard, association life thus presents itself as the school for a trans-ethnic universality via its capacity to provide a framework for conviviality.

Governance Issues: Decision-making, Leadership Choice, Management

Decision-making in these associations is situated at the level of general assemblies and is either by consensus or by open ballot on a universal suffrage basis. Proposals for decisions on important issues arrived at in executive committee meetings are tabled before the assemblies for debate and adoption. It is rather rare to find executive committees taking decisions that are binding on all members. As with the associations emanating from traditional cultural life we can say that, in this way, the associations provide a space for democratic practice and the exercise of autonomy that is lacking within the national space with liberal-democratic pretensions. One has to note that warped legislation and the propensity of the regime to subvert democratic change by conducting a ritual of elections tilted in its favour are at the very basis of the widely reported voter apathy in Cameroon.

The contribution of association life to autonomy and democratic practice is also reflected in the process of the choice of leadership. In general, associations spell out the qualities required of persons who are going to hold positions of responsibility within their ranks. Besides moral qualities, financial viability, social standing, degree of active participation in association life and degree of schooling in home values, knowledge of home language and cultural practices are also generally required. In this regard and to this extent, association life provides an alternative space where people can take autonomous decisions and provide leadership for themselves in a spirit of fairness and tolerance. As we have indicated before, its ideal is to provide a school of ethics to its members, which is largely lacking in the present dispensation. In this regard, the associations correspond to the type of organisation with a non-regulatory and decentralised power structure which promotes participation, solidarity, unity and members' interests found in Niang's typology (Niang op cit.:119).

This spirit of autonomy can also be observed in the execution and management of projects as well as fund raising. Respondents in seven of the associations we interviewed indicated that projects are executed by members in eight associations projects were reported to be executed by an ad hoc committee set up for the purpose. Ten associations reported that they create specific project committees while four associations indicated that their projects were executed under the supervision of the executive committee in the name of the community. Funds are derived principally from the following sources: financial contributions of members; registration fees; income from levies, fines and interest on loans; special fund raising campaigns and donations from elite figures. Such funds are estimated by most respondents at about 80 per cent of the income of the association while the rest is obtained from the state and donor agencies (NGOs, diplomatic missions of foreign countries).

In terms of time management, members (whether ordinary or executive) adjust timetables to suit their professional and family life. However, the watchword was that of sacrifice of time and effort on behalf of community interests, most of the activities requiring a spirit of abnegation. Moreover, the schedule of activities of the association is always organised in a way to accommodate the diverse preoccupations of members, and especially the executive.

One can only evaluate the importance of these characteristics when we evaluate conceptions of development and development practices.

Development Thinking and Practice

Definitions of Development

The majority of respondents advanced definitions of development that alluded to progress or change in terms of process, and social betterment when it concerned content. The idea of progress was captured in terms such as: betterment, improvement, change, advancement, better results, quality of life and struggle, all of them taken in a positive spirit. This is captured by NKONI Cameroon as 'change, movement from one stage of life (society) into another for a positive outcome, improvement in the standards of living'.

In terms of content, although the economic dimension (poverty reduction, improved income/finances, self sufficiency) was taken as basic, other dimensions relating to the environment, social services (education, health, roads, recreation services, electrification, provision of potable water), nutrition, culture (change of mentality, communication, access to improved technologies and social knowledge, improvement in literacy and educational levels, democratisation) were also cited as aspects of development, thus underlining the multidimensional nature of the concept. The respondent for CREDEM interpreted development as a plural matter, since it was 'polysémique' (polysemous) and taken as a 'croissance des biens matériels et l'éducation progressive [vers un changement] des mentalités á partir de l'enseignement des valeurs axiologiques' (growth in material goods and progressive education towards a change in mentalities through an inculcation of values). This was also the view of the respondents of the Famille Musgum de Yaoundé (FAMY), ASEEC, AEDELE, and RAJEB. One can understand these multidimensional conceptualisations of development given the generally high level of education of the respondents. The conclusion to be drawn from this trend is that, compared to ordinary local people whose conceptions of development are limited to social side issues (Yenshu Vubo 1991, Yenshu Vubo and Fonchingong 2002), the largely educated leadership of these associations is very knowledgeable about the most current comprehensive definitions of development (Sachs 1995:22-26).

In terms of actors or beneficiaries, respondents referred to individuals, groups, kin groups, and communities (Famille Lombi du Nkam, Assemblée Communautaire et Traditionnelle de Souza, Njarenka Family Meeting, Nkang Cultural and Development Association) and the global society, stressing in this regard the need to conceive development as involving the individual and the collective as two indispensable and complementary poles. The respondents for BANBA-MAMBANDA and Lumière du Nkam added an inter-generational dimension when they referred to children and the education of the youth (Sachs 1995, Aragon 1995). The necessary interconnectedness between social categories, whether conceived as elites and masses, as indigenes and settlers, or developed and underdeveloped growth poles within the same country, was emphasised by ACTEM and NKONI Cameroon.

Development Priorities of Associations

The prioritisation of development needs took much the same form as the definitions of development: improvement in individual and collective welfare, with the economic as basic but laying stress on improvements in social infrastructure and education. Although the majority of respondents mentioned the provision of roads, health infrastructure (hospitals, health centres), better water supply, electricity, school buildings and the construction of community halls, there was a tendency by others to conceptualise development more as a process of change than the provision of material goods. As such, one could find respondents referring to improvements in health conditions and standards (NOWEDEP) or health education and disease prevention strategies such as HIV/AIDS prevention campaigns (CESD, CEBA, and Golden Ladies). In the same way, there was a stress on education as a global change of mentality, the promotion of schooling (orientation, financial support to students and pupils), promotion of cultural learning ('l'enseignement de la langue et de la généalogie... réhabilitation de l'initiation à la tradition des jeunes Mpoo' - respondent for ACTEM), and the modernisation of farming and livestock breeding methods as opposed to the mere provision of infrastructure. Although there was mention of assistance to farmers in terms of subsidies and the provision of market places, specific mention was also made of the need for a 'good economic and business atmosphere', for food self sufficiency, collective farming, the creation of associations of an economic and financial nature, investment in financially profitable ventures, and several other specific economic activities that could improve the economic situation of individuals. One also finds that while some respondents mention the creation of community halls and recreation centres ('foyers culturels'), there is a parallel stress on reviving and promoting their cultural heritage.

There is also a shift in some responses from the content orientation of the priorities to the spirit and form of development action. The respondent for CREDEM thus spoke of promoting the spirit of collegiality through common initiative groups (CIGs), while a member of NDCO talked of getting people active in 'cooperative or community action groups'. The aforementioned implies that development is seen as not only the improvement in facilities but also the institution of practices and forms of organisation, which alone can ensure that the process is lasting. At the conceptual level therefore the associations' definitions integrate the much-proclaimed aspect of sustainability that came to be at the centre of development thought in the 1990s, albeit in a novel sense. The latter consists in seeing development as a process and a form of action and not only a provision of services and facilities, these processes and organisational forms taking root in people, transforming them, and sustaining the basis of motivations. These definitions of priorities are much in line with proposals for enhancing development activities in the communities as we will see later.

These definitions of priorities contrast considerably with those of the central government that defines development as the provision of infrastructure for social amenities (school buildings, health centres, roads etc.), all in a spirit of paternalism and electoral trade-offs. Such official approaches often end up as the provision of infrastructure with inadequate equipment and staffing. As we have shown before (Yenshu Vubo and Fonchingong 2002:32) the current state of affairs characterised by the pressure from international agencies for the state to limit spending on social services does not permit the erstwhile paternalistic and patrimonial state to live up to its promises regarding the provision of utilities. Faced with this situation, the state often resorts to selective provisioning with an undertone of partisan political discrimination which is at the basis of a 'politics of reciprocity'[5] or electoral trade-offs. The definitions offered by association leaders thus consider the transformation of social structures as the real centre of the process rather than the mere provision of amenities. In this way, people inevitably become not only the beneficiaries but also conscious actors, as they and their social structures are transformed. This also contrasts with the welfare and social infrastructure approach of rural peoples, themselves derived from dominant statist visions of the development decades (Yenshu Vubo 1991, Yenshu Vubo and Fonchingong 2002:14), and points to an evolution in world view as we are dealing here with a much more educated, and therefore, enlightened, leadership.

The Role of Other Actors in Development

The foregoing explains why the roles of associations in development are identified as being not only the identification of projects and the mobilisation of funds, but also education, taken as both the raising of popular awareness and the improvement in social and cultural learning. In this regard, respondents were in the main concerned with the human component of organisation, mobilisation and cultural change.

In the main, most respondents pointed to local peoples and communities as those best placed to undertake development projects. However, some respondents were specific about the quality of people to execute the projects. While the Famille Lombi du Nkam (Yabassi) pointed to experts such as engineers and technicians, the AJDS and LECUDO mentioned businessmen, although under the supervision of the community or associations as commissioning bodies. Only the AJDS and FAMY mentioned the government and the leadership class. This confirms our previous studies, which point to a multiplicity of actors, and not just the 'community', as indispensable actors in the development process (Yenshu Vubo 1991, Yenshu Vubo and Fonchingong op cit.:15).

Respondents who thought that the community or local people were best placed to undertake development action indicated that funds could easily be mobilised at that level (NOWEDEP), that people are conscious of their needs and priorities, and that in the process of execution they are likely to show dedication and the desire for the best. RAJEB'S respondent argued that since the local peoples are beneficiaries there is a greater likelihood that these projects will be protected and put to valuable use by them. The respondents who argued for businessmen, the state and NGOs, advanced financial viability as an asset that was lacking with the communities and associations, although that was not a majority opinion.

These opinions can only be evaluated in relation to the achievements of the associations under study.

Achievements and Gains

One can evaluate the achievements of the associations according to two main criteria: financial value and the nature of projects. We will start our analysis with an evaluation of the financial value of the projects before examining the nature of the projects.

Financial Value of Projects

Table 1 presents a comparative analysis of the financial value of projects according to type of association. The techniques used here are principally descriptive statistics (totals, range, mean, median).

Table 1: Comparative Analysis of Financial Value of Projects (in CFA)

	Type of Association	Number	Value of Projects	Range	Mean	Median
1	Students Unions	3	2324716	781666	774905.3	5,23,333
2	Youth Associations	7	6167546	37,20,000	881078	19,10,000
3	Women's Associations	3	31,650,000	15,450,000	10,550,000	12,275,000
4	Community Development Associations (CDA)	10	2383537000	80,358,000	23853700	40,821,000
5	Regional Development Associations (RDA)	9	185705000	32,500,000	20633888.9	17,750,000
	TOTAL	32	464384262	80, 980, 000	14512008.2	40, 600, 000

What the mean figures tell us is that community development associations (the so-called cultural and development associations or CDAs), and the regional development associations are the most viable structures in terms of financial investment. It is significant to note that the mean for CDAs is greater than that of the RDAs, although the latter cover a greater surface area than the CDAs. This shows that the more localised groups tend to have a greater mobilising capacity than the regional structures that are for the most part either of relatively recent origin, or are only loose structures involving for the most part urban-based elite. The three women's groups have an impressive record with a mean of 10,550,000 CFA, pointing to the increasingly positive role women are playing in development. This point becomes all the more evident when one notices that they are also active at the level of the CDAs and RDAs. Low figures for the students and youth associations are understandable given that these categories of people are characterised by low incomes and a low mobilising capacity.

Figures for ranges and medians point to the wide disparities in the mobilising capacity and financial viability across associations. For instance, one finds one youth group that has only been able to put together 20,000 CFA, while another at the other pole has managed to collect 3,800,000 CFA. Similarly, a women's group at one end collected 4,550,000 CFA, only 22.75 per cent of the capacity of women's groups with the highest financial investment so far (20,00,000) at the other extreme. In the same way, the CDA with the lowest achievement in financial terms could only raise 642,000 CFA as against 81,000,000 CFA for the most successful CDA. Although the difference between the lowest figures and highest sums are quite large, CDAs are not so dramatically wide apart. All in all this points to significant differences in mobilising capacity in the associations, which will determine their achievement levels. These disparities can be explained by the viability of the membership and mobilising capacity of the associations. In that regard, the viability of associations can be said to depend largely on the nature of projects.

The projects are diverse in nature but we can classify them under five different categories: projects of social infrastructure and utilities, institutional development, economic investments or support to economic activities, culture, and a show of solidarity and assistance to the underprivileged. However, projects of social infrastructure provisioning, institutional development and culture (taken as identity affirmation) are predominant. Within the projects classified as social infrastructure and utilities one would place the construction of schools, health centres, roads, bridges and community halls, the rehabilitation of structures (schools, community halls), the provision of water supply and electricity, and assistance in equipping schools (desks, laboratory equipment) and hospitals.

We decided to consider projects as institutional development when they relate to reorientation in organisation or structure. Under this category of projects one would also find the elaboration of existing structures of associations, cooperation with other associations, creation of collective and corporate structures (credit unions, cooperatives), creation of community radio, elaboration of plans and documentation, and contributions to national institutions and structures (grandstand, inter-ministerial block). This adds a much forgotten dimension to the development question: institution building and reorientation of structures.

Developments related to culture, which celebrate identity and the group, tend to stress education and mobilisation as important components of development. This can be seen in the volume of spending on projects of such a nature. In this category one can place the motivation of pupils and students (prizes, internships, scholarships); the organisation of cultural festivities,[6] popular or functional education (health education, training of farmers, seminars); participation in national activities, study visits, exhibitions, provision of didactic materials, information technology (radio station, web site); promotion of discussion forums and enthronements of chiefs. These associations thus carry development beyond the rather simplistic vision which confines it to infrastructure provisioning (see Yenshu Vubo 1991, Yenshu Vubo and Fonchingong op cit.), or improvements in the economy alone. Such projects go to underline the cultural dimension of the associations as an indispensable component of their raison d'être.

With regard to the economy, development efforts are somewhat limited, for example the donation of farming equipment and inputs, the organisation of community farms, and diverse investments as in the cases of AFMAD and ADELE. The relative lack of concern with improvements in the economy has also been observed in previous studies (Yenshu Vubo 1991, Yenshu Vubo and Fonchingong 2002:22). Shows of solidarity are manifested in assistance to the sick, assistance to disadvantaged pupils and students, assistance in funerals and the provision of a training centre for underprivileged children. By and large the view of development projected here as we observed elsewhere is almost exclusively one of social development even when the cultural element is added. As we have indicated before such a view misses out as both the economy and environment are absent (see Yenshu Vubo and Fonchingong 2002, ibid.).

Benefits and Evaluation of Activities

Benefits identified by respondents were primarily of a social nature: social prestige and moral satisfaction (NOWEDEP), pride of belonging to the group, solidarity and mutual self help and social support, social recognition, a sense of public service ('homme public', 'fierté de sacrifice') and social learning. In fact, many respondents indicated that they did not derive any personal benefits from belonging to an association but that the over-riding gains were the spirit of solidarity and the social learning that they acquired as members and as leaders. While the respondents for CESD referred to knowledge of social relations, the AEDELE informant broke up this learning into horizontal or fraternal learning within members, on the one hand, and vertical learning between the younger and the older generations or elites as well as apprenticeship in managerial skills, on the other. This is understandable given that student organisations are composed of young people who are essentially at the learning stage in their lives. The CREDEM respondent was more elaborate when he stated that 'there are no material gains'.

As we have indicated elsewhere, the associations are in this regard schools of ethics that foster the values of sacrifice, abnegation and service to the community so much lacking in the social fabric of the country. The association thus constitutes an important entry point in moral education, which should not be overlooked. It is situated at the very core of the moral fibre of the society itself. What also seemed to matter were the respondents' sense of self-fulfilment in seeing that projects were realised rather than the material benefits that could be derived from the associations' activities. This is precisely the type of ideal action Niang prescribes for the ideal association as being the source of real satisfaction for the group and members of an association ('source de satisfaction pour le groupe et ou les membres de l'association', Niang op cit.:157).

The sense of abnegation, sacrifice and contribution to public service is expressed in members' sense of satisfaction when they succeed in achieving objectives. Only five associations judged the balance sheet of their activities as not being satisfactory. The general tendency was to consider the association's activities as on a good footing despite obstacles and setbacks. In quantitative terms, some organisations rated their success at 50 per cent (MECA, Kumba chapter), 60 per cent (Nkang Development and Cultural Organisation) and between 50 and 60 per cent (Nchang Development and Cultural Organisation, NDCO). However, the impression respondents gave was that development activities were an on-going process which could not simply be evaluated in quantitative and situational terms, that is, at any fixed point in time. What has to be taken note of here is the sense of modesty in evaluating one's own achievement. Although this points to the evident limits of association life – as we remark with financing and expertise – which are the root cause, it is encouraging to discover that people understand that not all is well. It is thus a warning to proponents of the utopian view or of a moralising vision (civil society as the carrier of limitless potential) who are quick to project all sorts of optimism onto associations or civil society. It is encouraging to know that despite setbacks, optimism and belief in the life of associations remains a constant feature of associations.

The Association as an Imperfect but Perfectible Human Project: Problems and the Search for Solutions

Problems

Executive members of associations must accept that some sacrifice (of their time and resources) is required if they are to act effectively. They may face logistical and transport problems. More generally, associational leaders may face destructive criticism that might lead to conflict and cleavages. Tensions may arise from divisions and differences among the executive committees, between the executive members and ordinary members, and between ordinary members. Member participation may be a source of worry as problems of absenteeism, indiscipline, and political interference cause leadership headaches and even associational cleavages of a partisan nature. All these can make the work of coordination tedious and place a serious burden on leaders.

The problems faced by executive committee members are identical with the problems faced by the association as a whole. Some associations underscored the increasing politicisation of associations, especially interference from the dominant political parties, creating serious divisions within the elite to the point of generating deep antipathies. Associating with one set of elites is synonymous with creating enmity with others. A respondent reported that politicians tend to confuse the activities of associations with political activities. People tend to subordinate associations to certain political elites. For Chief Pierre Celestin Pengno of Mbengue, speaking on behalf of ACTEM and the Association of Bakoko (Elog Mpoo) Chiefs, the most crucial problem is that of managing political problems such as the clamour for a province for the Sanaga-Maritime region, which risks eclipsing other problems advanced by Elog Mpoo associations. The risk of political factions manipulating civil society associations reported by other researchers is real in this case. The observation here also shows the difficult situation in which associations find themselves vis-à-vis political parties. Certain associations have at their helm high state officials, representing in a way their regions of origin (Zambo Belinga 1997:116).

However, the ability of the association's leadership to identify this state of affairs as a problem points to a search for autonomy by the associations that should not be overlooked. Associations must be on their guard against the tendency for politicians to interfere in association life and to attempt to exploit the associations' achievements for political ends. It has been argued elsewhere that, contrary to generalisations about the partisan motivations of certain regional autonomy movements, for example, the Sawa movement of the 1990s (Konings and Nyamnjoh 2000, 2003), politicians and especially those of the dominant hegemonic, ruling party have tended to make use of some of these movements when they least expect it (Yenshu Vubo 2005). Although Niang (op cit.:133) argues that the rejection of subordination to political interests reduces the chances of institutional support, the tendency in Cameroon is for such structures to be used in inter-ethnic rivalry for positions in government or the administration. When this occurs, sane and healthy competition between associations, as they strive to develop their respective communities of origin, is replaced with inter-ethnic conflict engineered by politicians competing for advantaged positions.

Financial difficulties are reported by the majority of associations as being both a problem for associations as such, and an issue when it comes to executing projects. However laudable an association's aims may be, for it to be efficient and efficacious, it needs to have adequate finance. Given that funds have to be raised almost exclusively from membership dues, the task may prove difficult in an economic context where the incomes of the majority of local people are low. The generally weak financial situation of associations exposes them to interference from political elites whose donations may only come at the cost of manipulation for partisan ends. Both this political hazard and the resort to international NGOs and other donors, for the most part of Northern origin, seriously corrode the autonomy of associations when agendas have to be modified to suit the funding agencies. The conclusion to be drawn from the foregoing is that the viability of association life depends in part on the general economic conjuncture, although association life may also contribute to the vitality of the economy (see Awung's study in this volume).

The following social constraints are identified as undermining the functioning of associations and their role in project execution: leadership tussles, absenteeism and irregularity in participation in association life, divisions and cleavages, a low sense of sacrifice, the lack of expertise in project execution and management, mismanagement, embezzlement of funds and corruption, and a lack of interest and participation from target communities. These are problems that can be identified in the Cameroonian society in general and which point to the fact that association life is a reflection of the society in which it is situated. In other words, solutions to such problems within associations will also contribute to their solution within the society at large, especially as we have argued that associations constitute schools of ethics. Conversely, the solutions at global level will also be reflected in the life of associations.

Problems in themselves are a pointer to the fact that we are far from the utopian vision that some organisations, especially donor agencies and pro-democracy movements, are wont to project of association life or civil society (Houtart 1998:14, cf. also Tostensen, Tvedten and Vaa's typology 2001:7-26). It also underlines the fact that association life is far from perfect and is only, indeed, a perfectible project. That means that despite the multiple difficulties plaguing associations, there is a commitment to continue in the same spirit. This is sustained by the fact that the evaluation of benefits and activities so far is globally positive. Niang (op cit.:127-130) prescribes a typology of associations according to their capacity to overcome constraints, classifying them according to whether this capacity is holistic, conditioned or marginal. The capacity to master constraints is perhaps the greatest asset for association life, especially in its development function.

Solutions

Various solutions were proposed by a majority of associations. In fact, only three respondents did not propose solutions to the problems identified. Many respondents present the key solution to politicisation of associational life as the affirmation of the apolitical status or the neutrality of associations. While the respondent for CEBA considered that, as a student union, it has to avoid patronage of any sort and refuse alignment with specific elites, he also felt that it is necessary to identify with all currents of opinion and to work more with the local traditional structures. The Secretary General of CREDEM indicated that the association has even already defined its non-political status. The respondent for MBOG LIA, for his part, argued for the accommodation of all shades of political opinion, while Chief Pegngo of ACTEM stated that the association has stuck to its function of cultural revival and to the pursuit of the creation of two adminis-trative districts instead of the call for a Maritime Province that is at the centre of MBOG LIA claims. Scanty or lame as these proposals may be, they point to a necessary step in looking for solutions to a crucial problem which risks compromising an important component of civil society. However, the effectiveness of this approach depends on how lasting they are and whether they take root in the collective conscience of the people.

The solutions advanced to the problem of financing show little originality, although they point to a sense of self-reliance. Associations engage in fund raising campaigns (distribution of letters, the organisation of fund raising galas), and resort to partnerships in development. In this respect, there is a tendency to stay within the limits of financial viability and to jealously guard the association's autonomy. In other words, either the associations stick to the small-scale finances they can raise, or they only associate with partners. This contrasts sharply with associations, non-governmental organisations and common initiative groups created within the context of the liberalisation process whose funding is almost exclusively of external origin, and at times even seems to constitute their only raison d'être (see Enoh Tanjong's study in this volume). This explains the sustainability of the associations in a context where a certain civil society of modern origins has thrived only as a financial colony of big business, principally through NGOs of northern origins acting in many cases just as an outlet for finance from the latter (Yenshu Vubo 1998a:46-47). In this regard, we can say that the home-based associations do not only cope without lavish funding, they have also learnt to cope outside this current of assisted and dependent civil society life.

Concerning managerial problems, respondents mentioned stricter measures to cope with financial mismanagement, to exercise greater supervision, technical evaluation, monitoring and self-evaluation, all of which are measures which seek remedies from within the associations themselves rather than from beyond. This tendency strengthens the drive for autonomy through self-regulatory mechanisms. In no case did respondents mention recourse to legal or judicial procedures or external auditing, which are public and objective mechanisms for coping with problems of this nature. It is likely that recourse to such procedures will compro-mise the spirit of trust, fraternity, solidarity and sacrifice that is at the basis of this type of association.

The same type of remedial measures are proposed as a way out of the problems of indiscipline and lack of motivation or enthusiasm within associa-tions and the target communities where development projects are implemented. To such problems respondents proposed more education, sensitisation and an encouragement to hard work, thus seeking to preserve the voluntary nature of the associations. The watchword in this regard is making the people aware of the need to participate rather than be forced to act; in other words encouraging voluntary participation based on a reasoned awareness rather than on blind participation based on coercion. One would conclude that although the associations have an ascriptive basis (home of origin), they do not operate along the ascriptive lines that are characteristic of traditional life. Ascription is only a basic criterion for membership, while participation is expected to be voluntary and based on rational understanding.

To problems of a technical nature respondents reported the increasing resort to feasibility studies or technical assistance prior to project execution. Others proposed the resort to technical expertise where this was necessary but lacking. This is where the community is aware of its obvious limitations and considers itself as primarily a mobilising force. This is equally our observation with rural peoples who indicated the lack of technical expertise as a major limitation (Yenshu Vubo and Fonchingong op cit.:30). As we have noted before there are major areas in which local peoples and associations are lacking and in which they definitely need external support, especially from national governments within whose framework they operate (ibid.). Financing and the provision of expertise are two of these key domains. However, where local people are assisted in these areas, the assistance should not compromise the autonomy of the people in problem identification, organisation and mobilisation. This point helps to explain the following proposals by respondents:

- Development projects should be people-centred, implying that they should not be exclusively technocratic or the affair of experts alone;
- Development projects should be supervised by the community involved, implying the autonomy of the community in its development as opposed to technocratic authority, political influence and the financial weight of external agencies;
- Development projects should be those that cultivate a spirit of communalism, implying that projects that destroy the unity of the community in the name of technical and economic efficiency lose their raison d'être;
- Development projects should be orientated towards self employment and self-sufficiency, thus fostering autonomy and discouraging dependency;
- Development projects should also involve private enterprises, financial institutions and common initiative groups (CIGS), thus filling the gaps that lead to economic and financial dependency. In other words, development projects should not be limited to piece-meal collectivist projects whose financing depends on donations and small-scale levies or dependence on external sources;
- Development should be mental, that is, it should comprise an educational process as opposed to the view that development comes down to infras-

tructure provisioning, which seems to have dominated development activity until recently;

- Development activity should target all categories of people and should be undertaken by people who have the interest of the community at heart and whom the community members trust. In other words, development should be a collective activity whose beneficiaries are not only the greater community but whose leadership is derived from a social contract built on trust. People should not only constantly support development activities both morally and financially. They should have a leadership that is responsible towards them and responsive to their needs and aspirations.

Notes

1. Ebune has identified four such 'improvement unions' created along ethno-regional lines and the geopolitical divide of the British colonial period in Cameroon. These are the Bamenda Improvement Union, the Bakweri Improvement Union, the Mamfe Improvement Union and the Oroko Improvement Union. Empirical evidence also shows that such structures existed at micro-community level.
2. The reference to family has also been observed as being at the basis of association life in Dakar, Senegal (Niang 2000).
3. Braudel (1969:50-51) has stated that certain structures become stable elements over an infinity of generations and even end up as determinants of historical processes by their very long-term duration. This is the fate of structural forms which survive over relatively long periods of time and which are therefore situated at the level of the *longue durée*.
4. For more on this see Yenshu Vubo (1997, 2003) and Austen and Derrick (1999).
5. This is captured in the pidgin English expressions 'Politik na njangi' (politics is reciprocity), or 'you scratch my back I scratch your own' (One good turn deserves another) used by former Prime Minister Simon Achidi Achu. This actually meant that social services were allocated based exclusively on support for the regime.
6. Alone they constitute 23 per cent (85,500,000 out of 363,554,263 CFA) of all expenditures cited.

References

Ake, Claude, 2000, *The Feasibility of Democracy in Africa*, Dakar: CODESRIA.

Amin, Samir, 1989, *Africa and the Challenge of Development. Essays*, ed., Chris Uroh, Ibadan: Hope Publications.

Aragon, L. E., 1995, 'Building Regional Capacity for Sustainable Development in the Amazon', UFRJ/EICOS, ed., *Social Development: Challenges and Strategies*, Rio de Janeiro: UFRJ/EICOS.

Ardener, S., 1975, 'Sexual Insult and Female militancy', in S. Ardener, ed., *Perceiving Women*, London: Malaby Press.

Banock, Michel, 1982, *Le processus de démocratisation en Afrique. Le cas du Cameroun*, Paris: L'Harmattan.

Braudel, F., 1969, *Ecrits sur l'Histoire*, Paris: Flammarion.

Breytenbach, Willie, 1998, 'The Erosion of Civil Society and the Corporatisation of Democracy in Africa', QUEST Vol. XII, No. 1, Special Issue: Proceedings of the Interdisciplinary Colloquium on State and Civil Society in Africa, Abidjan, 13-18 July.

Diduk, S., 1989, 'Women's Agricultural Production and Political Action in the Cameroon Grassfields', *Africa*, 59 (3).

Diduk, S., 1987, 'The Paradox of Secrets: Power and Ideology in Kedjom Society', Ph.D. Thesis, Indiana University.

Diduk, S., 1997, 'Civil Society and Institutionalized Resistance in the Cameroon Grassfields', Working Paper Prepared for the Centre for Cross-Cultural Research on Women, University of Oxford, 29 November 29.

Diduk, S., 2004, 'The Civility of Incivility: Political Activism, Female Farmers and the Cameroon State', *African Studies Review*, Vol. 47, No. 2, September.

Ebune, Joseph B., 2004, 'Contributions of Self-Help Associations to the Growth and Development of British Southern Cameroons, 1922-1962: A Historical Perspective', *Epasa Moto. A Bilingual Journal of Arts, Letters and the Humanities*, Vol. 2. No. 1.

Essombe-Edimu, J. R., 1993, 'Contribution à l'analyse essentielle de la tontine africaine', *Africa Development*, Vol. XVIII, No 2.

Houtart, F., 1998, 'Editorial', *Les Cahiers Alternatives Sud*, Vol. V, No. 1.

Hyden, G., 1983, *No Shortcuts to Progress: Africa's Development Management in Perspective*, London: Heinemann.

Jua, R., 1993, 'Women's Role in Democratic Change in Cameroon', in Nalova Lyonga et al., eds., *Anglophone Cameroon Writing*, Bayreuth University: Bayreuth African Studies 30/Weka No.1.

Konings, P. and F. B. Nyamnjoh, 2000, 'Construction and Deconstruction: Anglophones or Autochtones', *The African Anthropologist*, Vol. 7, No. 1.

Konings, P. and F. B. Nyamnjoh, 2003, 'Negotiating an Anglophone Identity. A study of the politics of recognition in Cameroon', Leiden and London: Brill, Afrika-Studiecentrum series.

Mamdani, Mahmood, 1995, 'A Critique of the State and Civil Society in Africanist Studies', in Mahmood Mamdani and Ernest Wamba-dia-Wamba, eds., *African Studies in Social Movements and Democracy*, Dakar: CODESRIA.

Masuko, Louis, 1995, 'The Zimbabwean Burial Societies', in Mahmood Mamdani and Ernest Wamba-dia-Wamba, eds., *African Studies in Social Movements and Democracy*, Dakar: CODESRIA.

Mbuagbo, Oben Timothy and C. Fru, 2003, 'Civil Society and Democratisation: The Cameroonian experience', *Journal of Social Development in Africa*, Vol. 19, No. 2, July.

Menthong, H.-L., 1996, 'La construction des enjeux locaux dans le débat constitutionnel', in Melone, S., A. Minkoa She and L. Sindjoun, eds., *Le Reforme Constitutionnelle du 18 Janvier*

1996. Aspects Juridiques et Politiques, Yaoundé: Fondation Friedrich Ebert and Association Africaine de Science Politique (Section Camerounaise)/GRAP.

Miles, M., 2001, 'Women's Groups and Urban Poverty: The Swaziland Example', in Tostensen, A., Inge Tvedten and Mariken Vaa, eds., *Associational Life in African Cities. Popular Responses to the Urban Crisis*, Uppsala: Nordic Africa Institute.

Monga, Y., 2000, 'Au Village. Space, Culture and Politics in Cameroon', *Cahiers d'Etudes Africaines*, 160, http://etudesafricaines.revues.org/document46.html

Niang, Abdoulaye, 2000, 'Les associations en milieu urbain dakarois. Classification et capacités développantes', *Africa Development*, Vol. XXV, Nos. 1 & 2.

Nkwi, P.N. 1985, 'Traditional Female Militancy in a Modern Context', in Barbier, J. C., ed., *Femmes du Cameroun. Mères Pacifiques/Femmes Rebelles*, Bondy: ORSTOM/Paris: Karthala.

Osaghae, E, E., 1998, 'Rescuing the Postcolonial State in Africa: A Reconceptualization of the Role of the Civil Society', QUEST Vol. XII, No. 1, Special Issue: Proceedings of the Interdisciplinary Colloquium on State and Civil Society in Africa, Abidjan, 13-18 July.

QUEST, 1998, 'Synthèse des travaux et des débats/Synthesis Statement of the Colloquium', *QUEST* Vol. XII , No. 1, Special Issue: Proceedings of the Interdisciplinary Colloquium on State and Civil Society in Africa, Abidjan, 13-18 July.

Ritzenthaler, R., 1960, 'Anlu: A Women's Uprising in the British Cameroons', *African Studies*, 19 (3).

Rogers, E. M., 1960, *Social Change in Rural Society. A Textbook in Rural Sociology*, New York: Appleton-Crofts Inc.

Sachs, Ignacy, 1995, 'Searching for New Development Strategies. The Challenges of the Social Summit', World Summit on Social Development, Copenhagen, 6-12 March: MOST Policy Paper 1.

Santa Ana de, Julio, 1998, 'Eléments Théoriques pour comprendre la société civile', *Les Cahiers Alternatives Sud*, Vol. V, No. 1.

Sidibé, Fodé Moussa Balla, 1998, 'La confrérie des chasseurs traditionnels et les valeurs authentiques de l'enracinement de la societé civile africaine', *QUEST*, Vol. XII , No. 1, Special Issue: Proceedings of the Interdisciplinary Colloquium on State and Civil Society in Africa. Abidjan, 13-18 July.

Sindjoun, L., 1996, 'L'Imagination constitutionnelle de la Nation', in Melone, S., A. Minkoa She and L. Sindjoun (ed.), 1996, *La Reforme Constitutionnelle du 18 Janvier 1996. Aspects Juridiques et Politiques*. Yaoundé: Fondation Fredrich Ebert and Association Africaine de Science Politique (Section Camerounaise)/GRAP.

Tatah Mentan, E., 1996, 'Constitutionalism, Press and Factional Politics. Coverage of Sawa Minority Agitations in Cameroon', in Melone, S., A. Minkoa She and L. Sindjoun, (ed.),1996, *La Reforme Constitutionnelle du 18 Janvier 1996. Aspects Juridiques et Politiques*. Yaoundé: Fondation Fredrich Ebert and Association Africaine de Science Politique (Section Camerounaise)/GRAP.

Tester, Keith, 1992, *Civil Society*, London: Routledge.

Tostensen, A., Inge Tvedten and Mariken Vaa, 2001, 'Preface', to Tostensen, A., Inge Tvedten and Mariken Vaa, eds., *Associational Life in African Cities. Popular Responses to the Urban Crisis*, Uppsala: Nordic Africa Institute.

Tostensen, A., Inge Tvedten and Mariken Vaa, 2001, 'The Urban Crisis, Governance and Associational Life', in Tostensen, A., Inge Tvedten and Mariken Vaa, eds., *Associational Life in African Cities. Popular Responses to the Urban Crisis*, Uppsala: Nordic Africa Institute.

Vilas, Carlos V., 1998, 'L'heure de la societe civile', *Les Cahiers Alternatives Sud*, Vol. V, No. 1.

Warnier, J. P., 1994, *L'Esprit d'Enterprise au Cameroon*, Paris: Karthala.

Wengue, Marie Yvonne, 2004, 'Analyse sociologique des organisations financières informelles: cas des tontines, Douala': Unpublished Maitrise thesis in Sociology, University of Douala.

Yenshu Vubo, E., 1991, The Rural Community and its Development in Cameroon. A case study of the Community Development experience in Bafut, Unpublished Doctorat de 3e Cycle thesis in Sociology, University of Yaoundé.

Yenshu Vubo, E., 1997, 'Balanced Rural Development in Cameroon within a Democratic Context', in Nkwi, P. N. and Nyamnjoh, F. B., eds., *Regional Balance and National Integration in Cameroon: Lessons Learnt and the Uncertain Future*, Leiden: African Studies Centre/ Yaoundé: International Centre for Applied Social Science and Training (ICASSRT), ICASSRT Monograph No. 1.

Yenshu Vubo, E., 1998a, 'The Evolution of Official Attitudes to Grassroots Initiatives in Cameroon', *Community Development Journal*, Vol. 33, No. 1.

Yenshu Vubo, E., 1998b, 'The Discourse and Politics of Indigenous/Minority Peoples' Rights in Some Metropolitan Areas of Cameroon', *Journal of Applied Social Sciences. A Multidisciplinary Journal of the Faculty of Social and Management Sciences*, University of Buea, Vol. 1, No. 1, October.

Yenshu Vubo, E., 2001, 'Changing Inter-community Relations and the Politics of Identity in the Northern Mezam Area', *Cahiers d'Etudes Africaines*, XLI-1, 161.

Yenshu Vubo, E., 2003, 'Levels of Historical Awareness. The Development of Identity and Ethnicity in Cameroon' *Cahiers d'Etudes Africaines*, XLIII (3), 171, 2003.

Yenshu Vubo, E., 2005, 'Levels of Historical Awareness. The Development of Identity and Ethnicity in Cameroon', *Cahiers d'Etudes Africaines*, XLIII, 3, 171.

Yenshu Vubo, E., 2005, 'The Management of Ethnic Diversity in Cameroon: The Coastal Areas', in Fomin, E. S .D. and Forje, J. W., eds., *Central Africa: Crises and Reform*, Dakar: CODESRIA Books.

Yenshu Vubo, E. and Che C. Fonchingong, 2002, 'The Rural Communities of Cameroon and its Development in the Era of Post-Developmentalism', Paper Presented at the 10th General Assembly Conference of CODESRIA, December.

Zambo Belinga, Joseph Marie, 1997, 'Equilibre Régional, Replis identitaire et Fragilisation Croissante de l'Intérêt National: Vers un Effet "boomerang" de la Politique des Quotas au Cameroun', in Nkwi, P. N. and Nyamnjoh, F. B., eds., *Regional Balance and National Integration in Cameroon: Lessons Learnt and the Uncertain Future*, Leiden: African Studies Centre/Yaoundé: International Centre for Applied Social Science and Training (ICASSRT), ICASSRT Monograph No. 1.

6

Traditions of Women's Social Protest Movements and Collective Mobilisation: Lessons from Aghem and Kedjom Women[1]

Charles C. Fonchingong,
Emmanuel Yenshu Vubo and Maurice Ufon Beseng

Introduction

For the past two decades there has been a sharpened interest in a previously neglected aspect in anthropology, namely, women's collective mobilisations. The available literature is replete with material that links the oppression of women with the introduction of private property and capitalism (Boserup 1970, Hafkin and Bay 1976, O'Barr 1982). The expansion of capitalist interests has been at the basis of the marginalisation and disempowerment of women in the periphery of the world capitalist system. The reactions to this situation have been the manifestation of various forms of resistance. Thus, in accounts of resistance movements in Africa, women's roles and their experiences remain largely on the margins (Ranger 1994, O'Barr and Firmin Sellers 1995). The present paper attempts to examine some recent resistance movements that derive from colonial and post-colonial developments in the North West Province of Cameroon.

The Kedjom and Aghem women's movements which constitute the focus of the paper represent female indigenous institutions fighting against actions that impinged on women's farming activities and access to land for other productive activities. This has called for innovative ideas and new dynamism even in traditional forms of resistance. Women using these traditional strategies of resistance are directing them to aspects of human survival since they contribute to the livelihood of the community. This is an extension of their productive and reproductive roles, which they consider sacrosanct, inalienable and non-negotiable. As Guyer (1995) notes, in almost every region women have access to some kind of productive resource or a particular market which provides them with an income of their own. When such interests are threatened, it calls for action(s) to redress the situation. It is clear that most of these movements occur in a rural setting, in which all women, the vast majority of whom are illiterate, participate. They defend women's access to and rights over land and vehemently resist all practices that threaten to or compromise their hold on other productive resources.

The Kedjom (Fombuen), Kom (Anlu) and Aghem (Ndofoumbgui) women's movements are rural phenomena with underpinnings in urban life (see Diduk 2004). For instance, the Takumbeng,[2] women's movement of the Bamenda metropolitan area came into the limelight in the context of Cameroon's democratic transition. There is overwhelming evidence that the Takumbeng is composed of urbanites from ethnic groups around Bamenda with variations in cultural attributes and manifestations as they bring together women from adjourning villages like Kedjom, Bambili, Bambui, Wum, Mankon, Nkwen and Mendankwe that do not share similar linguistic and cultural traits. The present involvement of women's movements in politics is an urban-based phenomenon with a strong regional colour (Jua 1993). Each group mobilised its own members and their meeting point was the protest ground. They had key members in the wards who mobilised others during street protests. It should be noted that the group transcended the barriers of ethnicity, though not of class and educational level. Elsewhere, research has shown manipulation through extraneous forces by virtue of the fact that most of the women participating are illiterate and ignorant, and sometimes did not understand the implications of their actions and the battle they were engaged in (Jua 1993, Yenshu Vubo 1995, Diduk 2004). The visible barriers of class and educational attainment did not affect the cohesion of the group, though the very literate women rarely participated. By virtue of their numerical strength and collective mobilisation for a common cause, the women were able to overcome many impediments. It is argued elsewhere (Staudt 1986, 1987) that elite women have become active participants in the creation of ideologies that preserve their elite status but undermine and subordinate them as women. Resistance movements become mostly the weapon of weak peasants (see Scott 1985).

Seen within this perspective, the Aghem women's movement became famous as early as 1968 when the first major dispute pitting farmers and grazers broke out. The then Wum Division that comprised the present Menchum and Boyo Divisions has gone down in history as the birth place of the female protests of the immediate pre-independence period (Awasom 2002:4) and since then has occupied a prominent place in women's protests in the Cameroon Grassfields, providing a stimulus to the other women's mass mobilisation movements. Under the umbrella organisation, 'ndofoumbgui', the Aghem women's activities have evolved from local demonstrations in the Aghem community such as the recent sit-in at the chief's palace to protest marches that transcend local community borders. For instance, in 1973 they were involved in a march that covered a distance of 80 kilometres from Wum to Bamenda to protest against abuses arising from farmer-grazer problems. Preceding this movement is the much quoted Anlu of the Kom which was very vocal in the immediate pre-independence period. Diduk (1989) has demonstrated how this movement, born of resistance to a certain interpretation of colonial policies and inscribed within the politics of decolonisation (see Nkwi 1985), spilled over into the Kedjom communities wherein we find the Fombuen making their appearance in public for the first time. This appearance has however become a permanent feature that does not limit itself to the concerns of gender alone but also dictates patterns of participation in modern political life. A fuller account of recent events will situate us in this respect.

This chapter takes a historical, anthropological and comparative approach in situating the trajectory and parallels of two women's protest movements in Cameroon. With the benefit of hindsight, we examine the discourse of social protest and women's resistance in countering male hegemony, transgressions on women's agricultural activities in the agrarian economy and practices that denigrate womanhood and motherhood. The antecedents of women's collective action pioneered by the Anlu and Fombuen are replicated, albeit indifferently by the Takumbeng in the difficult route to Cameroon's democratic transition from the 1990s.

The main thesis of the paper is that women's collective action cannot only be situated within the context of traditional roles exercised in traditional society during the pre-colonial and colonial era. The mutations and extension of those roles have underpinnings in contemporary society. In this light, Takougang and Krieger (1998) and Diduk (2004) observe that the roots of the modern protests in the Cameroon Grassfields captured in the term 'Takumbeng' involved female elders in the past. Kolawole (1997) posits that African women's collective mobilisation and the question of self-assertion and empowerment are glossed over or effaced from mainstream women's theorising. She argues that it is necessary to probe the unexplored areas of the African woman's audibility and visibility to assess the limits of her position as a muted category. Research conducted by Diduk (2004) in the Cameroon Grassfields situates the highly disruptive but mystically charged nature of women's mobilisations and their effectiveness in opening spaces for popular dissent on the national stage.

This ethnographic study attempts a response to the inadequacies in the presentation of female resistance by examining the parallels in the frequent women's movements in Cameroon with specific emphasis on three forms of ethnic associations: the Fombuen society of Kedjom Keku and the Ndofoumbgui (Aghem).

Women's Traditional Associations and the Discourse of Social Protest: The *Ndofoumbgui* of the Aghem

Political action by women in the North West Province of Cameroon is a cultural given that has become an integral part of the collective conscience of the people at a group level and what Bourdieu calls 'habitus' (2004) at the individual level.

Transgressors of the moral order whatever their status – cattle herders, bar brawlers, or representatives of the state – defy such women at their peril, risking a supposed mystical power of reprisal belied by their apparently humble rural status (Diduk 2004). Against this backdrop, women's movements like the Fombuen, Ndufoumbgui and Takumbeng have taken a prominent place in the discourses and practices of social protest in the North West Province of Cameroon.

Due to their protracted demonstrations and riots, the Aghem women have occupied a leading place in the politics of Cameroon in general and Menchum division in particular. Wum is on record to have witnessed the worst demonstrations in the history of farmer-grazer conflicts in the North West Province The nature of their demonstrations permits one to draw parallels with the Anlu of Kom. This is clearly evident in the narrative of the Aghem women leader. She notes that in 1937, three chiefs, Kelly Kwala, Fung-u-Tsang, and Keba Mbong, under the leadership of Fon Bambi I, negotiated with Major Walters – the then colonial administrator of Wum Division – for the coming of Fulanis (grazers) locally called the 'Akus'. In 1943, the Fon and these chiefs allocated three grazing areas situated in the outskirt of Kesu, Zonghofuh and Waindo villages. Unfortunately, when the first cattle arrived at Wum in 1957, they were not taken to the designated areas, thus precipitating the first major dispute of farmer-grazer conflict in 1968. As cattle trespass on farmlands became rampant, coupled with the lukewarm attitude of local traditional authorities to rectify the situation, Aghem women marched naked in Wum in 1972.

As the situation degenerated in 1973, more than one thousand women marched from Wum to Bamenda,[3] a distance of about 80 kilometres, to complain to the Governor about the matter. This led to the creation of the 'Nseke Commission', named after the then Governor of the North West Province, whose role was to delimit farmland from grazing land. Unfortunately, the commission failed to relocate grazers to the three areas that had been designated by chiefs but instead allocated the areas that were currently occupied by both farmers and grazers.

Consequently, pressure on land had increased with the increase in both the human and cattle population. Incidents of destruction of farmlands by cattle quadrupled. This and other causes triggered the next Wum affray in 1981. 'Though not solely reported as a female protest, women were very instrumental in the Wum affray between Fulani grazers and Aghem farmers which saw the intervention of government soldiers leading to nine fatalities and a number of women wounded' (Chilver 1989:402). The consequences of the 1981 affray were shocking. The Aghem women lost nine of their husbands while several women sustained severe injuries. There was a general outburst of rage at the chiefs, local administrators and the Fulani who were perceived as enemies. This resulted in increased solidarity among the women and a reinvigoration and fortification of the female traditional institution called 'ndofoumbgui'.

Ndofoumbgui spokeswomen reported that after the 1981 affray they requested the men to refrain from active participation in farmer-grazer conflict as it was solely their responsibility. There was an absolute need for every Aghem woman to belong to *ndofoumbgui* to enable them to successfully tackle their opponents. This shows the level of determination of the women. A plethora of female traditional institutions now exist in Wum, all geared at mobilising women for greater activism and involvement in the *ndofoumbgui*. The women's resolve was motivated by the inability of the local administration to effectively resolve farmer-grazer disputes. They argued that using 'commissions of inquiry' to probe issues often proved futile. They cite the 2003 Aghem women's sit-in action during which the Governor of the North West Province created a seventeen-man commission to look at the problems. Although the commission had only fifteen days to present a report with proposals on how to resolve the conflict, by 23 December 2003 when we interviewed a women's movement leader there was 'no sign of the commission anywhere'. Even at the time we are writing this paper there are no indications that the administration has got anywhere with solutions to the problems. This only goes to underline either the dubiousness of the administration in handling conflict situations of explosive dimensions or their reluctance to intervene in domains that are complicated.

The 2003 *ndofoumbgui* uprising of the Aghem women was provoked by attempts to limit women's access to communal land, an act which was interpreted as a disenfranchisement with far-reaching effects on Aghem social and cultural life. The background was the order from the local administrator, head of the farmer-grazer commission, that farmers quit farmland occupied by close to 600 women in favour of two grazers in respect of Prefectoral Order No. 60 of 28 March 2003. This order is said to have annulled order No. 144 of 12 December 2003 that was in consonance with earlier recommendations that called for the demarcation of farmlands from grazing land. Given the uncertainty that characterised the period when these orders were to be implemented, cattle invaded farms and destroyed crops. The women thought they had been tricked to quit the area in favour of the grazers. According to a *ndofoumbgui* leader, this provoked about 8000 Aghem women to take seven traditional rulers including the *kedeng*[4] of Aghem, Bambi III, hostage through a sit-in strike. For forty-eight days (14 September 2003 to 2 December 2003), the *ndofoumbgui* women occupied the courtyard of the Deng Keghem. During the protest period the women stood their ground, braving both torrential rains and scorching sun. They accused the traditional rulers (custodians of the land) of selling their farmlands to the more influential cattle owners. As was the case with the Pare women's uprising (O'Barr 1976) they suspended all marital and other domestic responsibilities. It may be observed that poor sanitation conditions caused many of the women to develop illnesses and injuries. One of the protesting women was reported to have had her leg amputated due to a tetanus infection she contracted during the sit-in action. Women from neighbouring villages, as was the case with women during the demonstrations by the neo-traditional Takumbeng, extended support in the form of food and drinks to their protesting *ndofoumbgui* colleagues.

The 2003-2004 Fombuen Uprising and Socio-political Reforms in Kedjom-Keku

On 17 May 2004 a mammoth crowd of resident Kedjom Keku people gathered at the border between their settlement and the neighbouring village of Bambui, both to prevent a Fon[5] who had ruled them for twenty-five years from returning to the community, and to banish him from the same community. At the forefront of this history-making event were heads of the corporate political units, *vetiveloh*, (literally 'fathers of the community'), senior king makers (*vechevefon*), *ntsningsegeng* (retainers of the governing society, Kwifon) and the avant-garde members of the women's movement, Fombuen. While the first three categories of actors in this drama represented the cream of traditional political power, the fourth was an age-old institution that sanctioned women's opposition to social abuse, political oppression or economic alienation (Diduk 1987, 1989). For once, both the local dominant status group made up of men and the moral guardians of the society made up of the women, were at one to restore order and redress the de-structuring process that a quarter of a century of what community members diagnosed as misrule had set in.

This very significant act was the culmination of a protracted period of unheeded control and sanctions by Kwifon but also unending protests and appeals for better rule by the women through the Fombuen. This was one of the rare moments that the Kwifon dictum that they were always together with the women in ruling the community became literally true. In a sense, this was a perfect marriage of male and female power. This action led to the banishment of the incumbent Fon and the choice of a new one for the community. Several attempts by the local administration to reinstate the banished Fon were futile and although the modern administration originally hesitated to endorse the changes within the hierarchy of the community, it finally had no choice but to agree with the local community. A detailed study of this political event with far-reaching implications for the political anthropology of the region in particular and Cameroon in general will be the subject of a separate study, but it will be instructive to evaluate the role of women in these developments.

The background to the event comprised grievances related to misrule and social injustice, large scale alienation of land to big cattle farmers, insensitivity to the plight of farmers – the majority of whom are women – a false representation of natives (subjects) to the administration and a plethora of other minor complaints. Some of these grievances had been the subject of tussles between the Fon and leading traditional authorities (here represented by Kwifon), several petitions by these authorities to the local administration and protests by women. The most recent of these conflicts had crystallised around a farmer-grazer conflict that pitted food cultivators against cattle farmers in the fertile high land in another settlement (Kefem). Although this area had been declared exclusively farmland by the technical authorities in charge of farming and grazing in a previous ruling, the Fon and some of his acolytes had still surreptitiously succeeded in settling cattle herdsmen on the area. A combination of shifting cultivation and bush fallowing on the one hand, and extensive grazing on the other soon brought the local people and the grazers into a long drawn-out conflict. Peaceful attempts by villages to obtain redress from the Fon and local administration were fruitless as the Fon persistently labelled farmers as criminals who were 'stealing cattle'. Such a misrepresentation actually led to the arrest and jailing of some local farmers; others who were merely resisting encroachment on their farms were charged before judicial authorities with theft of cattle. In such an atmosphere, which lasted for more than two decades, the community felt itself to be the victims of aggression by the cattle owners with the connivance of the Fon who was supposed to be an objective judge, a source of community continuity and sustenance, and guarantor of social justice.[6]

Each time there was a crisis between the farmers and the cattle owners and in which the Fon tended to criminalise the farmers to the administration, the women protested before the Fon and the local administration, either at sub-divisional, divisional or provincial level. The protest marches and sit-ins of the Kedjom Keku women either at Tubah or Bamenda have now become legendary. Whether this was during the confrontation between local farmers and the late Jurebure at the Kwinchum part of Kefem in the 1980s, the confrontation between farmers and the famous and much dreaded business magnate and kingpin of the ruling CPDM party, Alhadji Baba Ahamadou Danpullo, in the 1990s in the Mbwangang area, and the more recent conflict between farmers and Alhadji Youssoufou at the Abongfen segment of Kefem, women were an active and vocal element of the protest movement that sought redress for farmers. The action of the 1980s recognised farmers' rights over the Kwinchum segment of the Kefem area while the protest of the 1990s led to the recognition of their rights over Mbwangang and the imposition of a 49 million CFA fine to be paid by the grazer Baba Danpullo. The most visible gains of the riots spanning 2003-2004 were that the grazers at Abongfen were dislodged through the concerted action of youth and women. Moreover, the administration has considered the acquisition of land by Youssofou as illegal and called on him to 'regularise' his situation in Kedjom Keku. The banishment of the Fon from the community and his replacement came to crown local people's action. The timid reaction of the administration in recognising the changes at the helm of the local community have only gone to legitimise the popular nature of social protest, which was initially branded as an 'insurrection' or a 'rebellion'. The modern administration is on the way to endorsing such changes only because they have ushered in a period of social peace and the absence of unrest that was characteristic of the community over the past two and a half decades. What remains to be seen is whether these gains will be consolidated in the future.

The women in their action drew inspiration from historical antecedents which were inscribed in a long-standing tradition of protest and a culture of dissent. We find here a rare case of institutionalised dissent that contrasts with attempts by the Fon to criminalise the actions of the protesters. Most respondents whom we encountered pointed to the first manifestation as having been registered in the reign of Fon Vubangsi in the 1940s-1950s. This pioneer protest was intended to call the attention of the late Fon Vubangsi to the wanton destruction of crops by uncoordinated grazing practices, in which his cattle were involved. Then, the problem was resolved by setting up a ditch as a protective device against the Fon's cattle to protect the crops from livestock. Other marches occurred in the 1980s and early 1990s during the period of political effervescence. The protests of the 1980s were restricted to localised community-based issues such as the destruction of crops by small ruminants as well as cattle (Diduk ibid), while the protest of the 1990s were more in consonance with the wider neo-traditional activities of the women in the Bamenda metropolitan area that were inscribed within the wider political protest that was characteristic of the region (Diduk 2004), although the farmer-grazer problem was still very much in the background.

By tracing their actions to historical antecedent, the women were reaffirming rights to resistance and protest. The capacity to resist, derived from a tradition couched in a distant past, is in itself social capital because it is an accumulation of collective values. It was the re-enactment of a culture of resistance to perverse forms of social domination and alienation. In this way, the women ultimately take on themselves the role of judges of local governance practices. It is in the same way that they are hard in their judgment of local administrative authorities whom they consider complacent in the search for solutions to social crises of this nature.

Besides the role of judges of history that the women take on themselves, the women also join the men as prime movers of history. In joining hands with the men to chase away a ruler considered despotic and insensitive, they assert their rights to self-determination and momentarily recover their autonomy as actors in their own right in the face of a hesitant administration. What is interesting is the fact that the justification for their actions is not the much-trumpeted gospel of human rights. It is simply legitimacy derived from a history of institutionalised dissent and protest. It is also the affirmation of the traditional right to act as custodians of land and as claimants to land in their own right. In other words, they are not only farmhands or persons with user rights as is often wrongly portrayed in modernist circles. One of the leaders of the women's movement, Tabitha, indicated that as mothers they have greater rights to farmland than even the men. When advocating changes they did so in the interest of their children and their husbands whom they also assimilate to children. The woman's job is to protect the rights of her children, she affirmed. In this respect, it is motherhood, much more than wifehood (see Farnyu and Yenshu Vubo 2005), that gives the women a central place in Kedjom political life. In this motherhood role, women have to assert the right of every community member to food, which is the crux of the struggle over land. It has to be noted that when we say women's protest is institutionalised as is dissent in traditional life, we are saying that it forms an integral part of the social life, is acceptable to everyone and sanctioned as a political institution.

The Fombuen that gives form to this element of dissent and protest maintains only a skeletal structure, as is also the case with the Anlu of the Kom (Nkwi 1985, Ardener 1975, Ritzenthaler 1976) and the Mawu of the Bayang. Every adult female can become a member, while the leadership is made up of jesters and clowns (*vugwe*). Its personality is amorphous and its actions spontaneous and on the spur of the moment. Fombuen thus exists but does not have a permanent structure. When it accomplishes its mission it can dissolve back into the community where it hibernates until it is provoked to resurface with the advent of a new crisis. Recent developments that seem to crystallise its activities have not subtracted from this simple logic that owes its operational efficiency to the very nature of its simplicity. The inability of the modern administration to understand the logic of this mode of operation has led many an administrator to read manipulation into its activities as some people consider Fombuen members as lacking in knowledge of the issues of modern politics (see R. Jua op cit.). But on the contrary, frequent incursions into the modern sphere have led the women to develop a heightened awareness of current political issues, even if only in their own way. One may not also exclude the possibility of politicisation as such movements tend to act as powerful instruments of mobilisation. The very resilience of these women in all kinds of weather conditions and their resolve to have their voices heard is daunting. For two and a half decades running these women have not missed a single year to protest (marches, sit-ins). The most recent protest lasted from around mid-2003 to mid-2004 during part of which they organised a boycott of the palace and the Fon and practically governed the community. With the near collapse of the traditional system of government, the Fombuen took over the day-to-day administration. It checked abuses by community members, settled disputes and kept order in the most astonishing manner. Even members of Kwifon (the highest traditional administrative institution) were not spared. The modern administration was also compelled to pay attention to its discourse and include them in all conflict resolution initiatives. In fact, the Fombuen gave power to the community in the end by giving power to the men in the face of a perverse traditional despotism, the rising capitalist interest of the cattle owners, and an ambivalent administration (see also Konde 1991 in the case of Anlu).

Response of Local Traditional and Administrative Authorities

The local traditional and administrative authorities have been very cautious in resolving framer-grazer conflicts that border on women's land rights and undermine agricultural productivity. The Aghem and Fombuen examples show the excesses and pitfalls in the procedures employed by these authorities. Since the Fulani supply most of the protein in the form of beef, and also pay tax on their stock, and the women's food crops are vital (Fonchingong and Ufon, forthcoming), it is becoming a difficult task for administrators to break the deadlock.

As a result of the importance of the cattle economy in Menchum Division, particularly with regard to the economic interests of local administrators, they have been playing divisive tactics when it comes to resolving farmer-grazer problems. There are claims and counter claims as both parties reproach each other for fanning the conflict. The cardinal question is: how come for over half a century now no definite solution has been found to the farmer/grazer confrontation that has plagued the province?

In the Aghem case, the First Assistant S.D.O of Wum affirmed that, 'since the chiefs are poor, they easily fall prey to Fulani influence - allocating them vast areas of land which is usually farming land in exchange of cash and when a problem arises, they will run to the administration pleading for help'. The cattle farmers in question corroborate this view. Alhadji Manto revealed that when he first arrived in Wum, a chief sold him a parcel of land, and he only later discovered that women were farming on the other side. When he complained, the chief told him to continue to graze on the piece of land. For Chief Ben Afue of Naikom village, 'the S.D.O and D.O. in conjunction with the Divisional chief of lands and surveys issue land certificates to grazers, who as persons holding formal title to land, dominate women and even threaten to take them to court'.

From the foregoing, it can be seen that the actions of local authorities have been imprudent. Like their predecessors, these administrative authorities have found themselves caught in a dilemma, because pleasing the farmers means losing out on the much needed cattle money. They have therefore failed to respond effectively to farmers' problems while reaping the necessary funds to sustain themselves and the administration. One *ndofoumbgui* leader indicated that they no longer needed commissions of inquiry and unfulfilled promises.

From interviews conducted with women, men, and the traditional and administrative authorities, it is clear that people subscribe to the gendered ideology of women's contribution to the rural and urban economy in terms of food production and family upkeep. Tih Amban, tihloh (head of a corporate political group in Kedjom Keku), aged 74 and a farmer, argues that 'without the efforts of women, village communities will never develop. Men are warriors and very aggressive. Women have to control them such that they take proper decisions'. Asked if the Fombuen women's protest was legitimate, he said that 'women have confronted the Fon several times on a land dispute at Kefem. Farmland that belongs to the Kedjom Keku people was sold to the Fulanis; the women therefore did not have access to this land. Cattle destroyed crops that have been sown on this land. Kedjom Keku belongs to all not to a single individual in the name of a Fon. He had no right to sell the land, which belongs to the Kedjom Keku people. Our women are supposed to cultivate on this land and nobody has the right to refuse them access to this land. That is why the women's movement was right when they protested'.

Recognising the greater visibility of women in agriculture and community development, most of the interviewees considered that the actions of the women were appropriate. However, some of the traditional and administrative authorities reproached the women for employing strategies that are antisocial, inimical to culture and uncivil in disposition. The Provincial Delegate for Women's Affairs/ Director of Women's Empowerment Centre Bamenda is of the opinion that 'The Delegation of Women's Affairs do not encourage women associations that operate as secret societies such as the Takembeng of Nkwen and the Fombuen as you call it in Babanki. We encourage development associations. The practices of these secret societies, which operate as associations, are disgusting and expose women's privacy (walking naked on the streets)'. She indicated that all traditional laws and customs must be respected as long as they are not repugnant to natural justice. Waylen (1998) contends that women have taken over public space not normally seen as part of their domain for protests, and use their bodies as symbolic and metaphorical devices to subvert the dominant discourse of womanhood.

By describing the women's activities as not conforming to the tenets of mo-dern law wrongly identified with natural justice, the Delegate is simply subscribing to the Eurocentric-American centred view of its justice system as universal and all other systems as deviant. The state official attempts here to place restrictions on the contours of traditional law and its practices by subjecting them to 'natural justice'. Just how natural this justice is, is open to question. It is simply the expres-sion of a selective attitude of the administration towards civil society organisa-tions that has also been highlighted by Temngah (in this volume). What one can say is that the state fails in its attempt to choose its own civil society as these so-called civil society structures fail to take root. On the contrary, the despised uncivil women with their rustic mannerisms succeed in gaining the full status of a vibrant civil society.

Being antithetical to state actions and attitudes, women's movements constitute symbols of resistance to excesses from traditional and administrative authorities. The source of their authority, as Diduk (2004) observes, is not just the fact that they are rooted in a pre-colonial ideology and the social institutions of female moral guardianship. It is that these indigenous roots are essentialist; grassfields women, by their very nature, act in defence of production and reproduction.

Other officials share the view of the Delegate of Women's Affairs concerning the destabilisation that the women's actions can produce. The Senior Divisional Officer of Mezam opines that: 'The women of Kedjom Keku did not request a meeting with me. They came here as individuals. They intended meeting me as a group. I refused because the association is not registered. The administration does not recognise associations that are not registered. Such associations promote social disorder. I receive development associations and professional groups. Thus, four women from Kedjom met me and complained about a land dispute in the village. I realised after having discussions with them, it's a chieftaincy problem. A commission was therefore set up to study the problem and submit its report. I am still expecting the report'.

This insistence on receiving the women only as an association reflects a selective attitude towards civil society bodies. In this way, only modern associations are given administrative approval and considered as falling within the scope of the acceptable. The insistence that organisations fall within the scope of modern law can be interpreted as an attempt to control all facets of public life in a pervasive hegemonic drive. We are led to question whether the state can legislate on everything or subject all aspects of social life within the scope of the law (see Temngah in present volume).

One way of reading attempts to subject civil society to the regime of modern law when people act to assert traditional rights is that this is a juridification of rights which 'contributes to the surveillance and disciplining of the individual' (Foucault in B. Jua 2002). In other words, instead of guaranteeing rights, legislation restricts them. To the administration the women are infringing on the law by enacting practices outside the ambit of the relevant legislation, whereas the women strongly believe they are exercising their rights offered to them by their society. This leads to a confrontation between the two logics which ends up in an impasse for lack of a modus vivendi. This is the ambiguity of the attitudes of the modern society vis-à-vis traditional institutions. Refusing to receive the women as a traditional association because it is not registered but receiving them as individuals exhibits a modernist bias that stresses individuals as citizens but negates the social institutions that shape them as social beings. However, the very resilience of these institutions renders them indispensable in modern space. By inscribing their dissenting voices within the realm of disorder, the administrator relegates the activities of these associations as well as traditional life to the status of the anti-social, hence backward and criminal. With a characteristic western bias the traditional is assimilated to the primitive.

Another reading will consider this attitude as representative of more recent attempts to criminalise dissent by criminalising the instruments of this dissent. Such attitudes arose with the rise to prominence of the neo-liberal programme (Wacquant 2000) but have gained greater weight with the developments of the period after the so-called 9/11 events that have largely defined international attitudes to violent forms of protest. In this regard the administrator falls short of calling the protesting women terrorists. Even then the actions are branded in a communiqué by the same administration as an insurrection.

Even the analysis of the problem is dismissive. By reducing the social problem to a local political issue the administrator admits his inability to come to terms with the social crises that rock the state. Reading all social problems with a political lens therefore re-situates the political actor which the administrator is and enables him to treat the question of dissent as essentially a challenge to the state or constituted order. This also dictates the state's attitude: repression where the threat of breach of peace is sufficiently serious; being dismissive where the threat is at its very least; cosmetic reforms with no far-reaching import where the threats are not too serious but the issues are the source of perennial and protracted complaints. The creation of commissions of inquiry which yield little fruit is one strategy of not only buying time but also warding off social problems without addressing them. We have seen in the case of the Aghem women's movement – and it is common knowledge in Cameroon – that the appointment of commissions of inquiry is one of the surest ways of killing off a burning social crisis. The fact that local peoples finally resort to their own effective strategies of tackling social problems and effecting reforms in the way Kedjom Keku people are doing, points to the fact that the civil society is increasingly capturing its own space where the state fails or acts ambivalently.

Counting the Gains of Women's Protest Actions

Criss-crossing Rural and Urban Spaces

A noticeable activity of the women's movement as presented in this study is the attempt to conquer more spaces in the search for solutions to burning problems. The rural milieu is increasingly transformed as women take their protest actions to urban areas in order to seek redress from administrative authorities.

This analysis presents the role of the Ndofoumbgui, Anlu, Fombuen, and Takumbeng as women turning to more intensive political activism. This trend ties in with Andrew Apter's (1999) call for understanding socio-political processes in Africa from the perspective of 'the base', or the people themselves, in this case female subsistence farmers who engage in and talk about making political history. It is important to capture the reasons behind the actions and motivations of women's protest actions. James Scott (1985, 1990) has stressed that peasants, in general, may be savvy political actors, but their structural position often requires them to challenge the political elite and influence formal institutions only through unorthodox means such as work slowdowns or songs expressing ironic contempt for the powerful. Farmers may become critics, but primarily through indirection; they challenge at a slant to avoid the wrath of the state. By contrast, the case of female farmers in the North West Province of Cameroon suggests that they can be very direct and wilful in raising criticisms and pressing for change, whether in regard to local or national issues (Diduk 2004). In an interview with the Senior Divisional Officer of Mezam (September 2004), he indicated that he thought that women within his jurisdiction are 'enjoying their rights. The women are very conscious of their rights and always protest once their rights are tampered with. That is the reason why the Kedjom women are always protesting'.

If the state is seen as patriarchal and their policies unjust towards women, then women's experience can be seen as one of exclusion from state resources, inequality of access, neglect and outright oppression (Parpart and Staudt 1989). Through public singing, verbal insults, dancing, and demonstrating in public and by generally seizing control of resources and political outcomes (Shanklin 1990), women attempt to force the offending party to change his or her behaviour. Women are ready to respond to the reticence and nonchalance of administrative authorities. This unrelenting attitude could be likened to female resistance in the Niger Delta region of Nigeria. Protesting women from the Itsekiri and Ijaw communities have been pressing for concessions from oil companies. On one occasion, defiant women's leader stated the women's resolve candidly when she said that: 'The Federal government and oil companies like to oppress us. Since we are already suffering, we did not mind if we died on the flow stations...' (Ukeje 2002). As claim makers, women's resistance activities are largely borne by their pains of childbirth and pangs of motherhood that urge them to create order where chaos is imminent (Ngwane 1996). In this regard, we would be correct in affirming that these movements do not only criss-cross rural and urban spaces, but also stand astride the traditional and modern worlds. They derive their legitimacy from the traditional setting but, in order to articulate the problems of the contemporary period, they make incursions into the modern sphere. In this way they are the necessary connection between history and the present and constitute a bridge into the future.

The Gender Question

It can be deduced from women's activism in the area under study that women and men are both conscious of their roles in society. There is a greater recognition of women's roles in subsistence agriculture and their importance in guaranteeing livelihoods. Diduk (2004) argues that the cultural emphasis on women as guardians of crops and community sustenance clearly sets them apart. Their special status is given expression in routinely essentialised conceptions of gender that are articulated by both men and women in rural and urban communities in the region. What we observe here goes beyond the current dominant discourses and practices around the gender question that evokes far-fetched modernistic notions with little connection to the day-to-day realities of the common folk. There is a conscious attempt in the area under study for women to occupy a critical position as prime movers of the history of their societies. Problems of gender relations gain greater credibility when a synergy is achieved between the two streams of the gender question. The current gains of the present protests go only to strengthen the traditions of protest and the cultural capital of dissent and in this way foster the democratic culture of pluralism of discourses and practices. In this way traditional institutions are also definitely carriers of positive values.

Transcending Local Concerns

These movements also transcend the immediate localities within which they emerge. Such transcendence may be derived from a long-distant past, as in the commonality of practices such as those in the institutions of the speakers of Ring Group of Grassfields Bantu (see above), or expresses itself as a spill-over effect from the rural into the urban, a chain effect from recent events. It was observed that the women's protest movement of the 1990s touched a large number of groups and addressed issues of wider national import, although they were localised in space. Consequently, although the Takumbeng of the Bamenda metropolitan area was most vocal at this moment (Diduk 2004), a variety of such movements soon arose all over the country. We can specifically refer to the *mawu* of the Bayang and a plethora of similar movements in the Nso, Bali Nyonga, Bakossi and Ewondo areas. The gains of each group only go to strengthen the culture of resistance of the women as prime movers of history.

Notes

1. The division of labour in this paper is as follows: the general design, hypotheses and analysis on the Takembeng and the Aghem women by Charles Fonchingong, in-depth theoretical insight and the section on Kedjom Keku by Emmanuel Yenshu Vubo, and the field work on Aghem by Maurice U. Beseng.

2. The term in its primordial usage in the area under question and as reflected in political anthropology (Aletum 1977, Warnier 1985) points to a male regulatory society open to princes in contradistinction to *kwifor* (a commoner regulatory society) in the royalty-commoner divide that characterises the binary structure of traditional political organisation in the region. Diduk (2004:52) rightly traces the origins of the usage to this source but affirms that it is 'not clear why this is so'. We can observe that this is much in the direction of what Hobsbawm (1992:1) has styled the invention of tradition and more so of the kind he describes as '... emerging in a traceable manner within a brief period – a period of a few years perhaps – and establishing themselves with great rapidity'. In this case the women adopt known, highly respected and revered social symbols and give them new meanings in the search for a new social order. It is in this regard that the actions both claim to be politically correct within the traditional sphere and lay claims to innovation.

3. Bamenda is the provincial capital of North West Province of Cameroon.

4. The Aghem term for King.

5. Local term used by a variety of groups to refer to a King. In the present form it suffers from an anglicised deformation but has gained currency and is often equated with kingship. Within the central Ring group of Grassfields Bantu it is pronounced as 'foyn' (Kedjom, Kom, Oku, Mmen) or 'Mfon' (Nso). Within the Mbam-Nkam community of Grassfields Bantu it goes under the appellation of 'Mfor' (Ngemba speakers), 'Mfon' (Pati-Nun) or 'Fo' (other so-called Bamileke peoples and affines). Its rudimentary meaning points to the

importance of a person or headship of a group. The Bayang, situated to the immediate south of the Grassfields region of Cameroon, also use the term 'nfor' to refer to a chief.

6. On the powers of the Fon in the region see Fowler (1993:255) who affirms that 'epic notions of qualities' required of Grassfields Fon expect him to 'use occult powers and mystical agencies to increase the population and material wealth of his kingdom. The king is explicitly associated with the fertility of the earth...'

References

Aletum T., 1977, 'Exploration of Traditional Political Institutions towards National Development', Yaoundé: ISH.

Apter, A., 1999, 'IBB = 419: Nigerian Democracy and the Politics of Illusion' in John Comaroff and Jean Comaroff, eds., *Civil Society and the Political Imagination in Africa*. Chicago: Chicago University Press.

Ardener, S., 1975, 'Sexual Insult and Female Militancy', Shirley Ardener, ed., *Perceiving Women*, New York: John Wiley and Sons.

Awasom, S., 2002, 'A Critical Survey of the Resuscitation, Activation, and Adaptation of Traditional African Female Political Institutions to the Exigencies of Modern Politics in the 1990s: The case of the Takumbeng Female society in Cameroon', Paper presented at the 10th General Assembly of CODESRIA, Kampala, Uganda, 8-12 December, 2002.

Bourdieu, P., 1994, *Raisons Pratiques. Sur la théorie de l'Action*, Paris: Editions du Seuil.

Boserup, E., 1970, *Women's Role in Economic Development*, New York: St. Martin's Press.

Cleaver T. and Wallace M., 1990, *Namibian Women in War*, London: Zed Books Ltd.

Chilver, E. M., 1989, 'Women, Cultivators and Cash Crops: Phyllis Kaberry's *Women of the Grassfields* Revisited', in P. Geschiere and P. Konings, eds., Proceedings/Contributions, Conference on the Political Economy of Cameroon: Historical Perspectives, June 1988. Leiden: African Studies Centre Research Reports No. 35: 383 – 422.

Farnyu, W. T. and E. Yenshu Vubo, 2005, 'Gender and Rural Economy in the Wimbum Society, Cameroon: A Study in Perceptions and Practices with particular reference to the Land Question', Paper presented at the Workshop on Women, Popular Culture and Land Use, University of Buea, 10-15 January.

Fowler, I., 1993, 'African Sacred Kings in the Cameroon Grassfields', *Ethnology*, June.

Guyer, J., 1995, 'Women in the Rural Economy: Contemporary Variations', in Hay, Margaret and Stichter, Sharon, eds., *African Women South of the Sahara*, London: Longman.

Hafkin, N. and Bay, G., eds., 1976, *Women in Africa: Studies in Social and Economic Change*, Stanford, CA: Stanford University Press.

Hobsbawm, E., 1994, 'Introduction: Inventing Traditions', E. Hobsbawm and T. Ranger, eds., *The Invention of Tradition*, Cambridge, New York and Melbourne: Cambridge University Press.

Jua, R., 1993, 'Women's Role in Democratic Change in Cameroon', in Nalova Lyonga et al., eds., *Anglophone Cameroon Writing*, Bayreuth University: Bayreuth African Studies 30/Weka No.1.

Jua, N., 2002, 'The State, Traditional Rulers and "Another Democracy" in Post-colonial Cameroon', *Africa Insight*, Vol. 32, No. 4.

Kolawole, M., 1997, *Womanism and African Consciousness*, New Jersey: Africa World Press.

Konde, E., 1991, 'The Use of Women for the Empowerment of Men in African Nationalist Politics: The 1958 "anlu" in Cameroon', Working Papers in African Studies, No. 47, Boston, Massachusetts: African Studies Centre.

Ngwane, G., 1996, *Settling Disputes in Africa. Traditional Bases for Conflict Resolution*, Yaoundé: Buma Kor House Publishers.

Nkwi, P., 1985, 'Traditional Female Militancy in a Modern Context', in Jean-Claude Barbier, ed., *Femmes du Cameroun*, Paris: ORSTOM Karthala.

O'Barr, J., 1982, *Perspectives on Power: Women in Africa, Asia and Latin America*, Durham, NC: Duke University Centre for International Studies.

O'Barr, J., 1976, 'Pare Women: A Case of Political Involvement', *Rural Africana*, 29.

O'Barr, J. and Firmin-Sellers, K., 1995, 'African Women in Politics', in M. Hay and S. Stichter, eds., *African Women South of the Sahara*, London: Longman.

Parpart, J. and K. Staudt, eds., 1989, *Women and the State in Africa*, Boulder, Colorado.

Ranger, T., 1994, 'The Invention of Tradition in Colonial Africa', in E. Hobsbawm and T. Ranger, eds., *The Invention of Tradition*, Cambridge, New York and Melbourne: Cambridge University Press.

Ritzenthaler, R., 1976, 'Anlu: A Women's Uprising in the British Cameroons', *African Studies*, 19, 3.

Shanklin, E., 1990, 'ANLU Remembered: The Kom Women's Rebellion of 1958-1961', *Dialectical Anthropology*, Vol. 15, No. 2-3.

Staudt, K., 1986, 'Class Stratification and its Implication for Women's Policies', in Claire Robertson and Iris Berger, eds, *Women and Class in Africa*, New York: Africana Publishing Company, Holms and Meier.

Staudt, K., 1987, 'Women's Politics, the State, and Capitalist Transformation in Africa', in Leonard Markovitz, ed., *Studies in Power and Class in Africa*, New York: Oxford University Press.

Takoungang, J. and Krieger, M., 1998, *African State and Society in the 1990s: Cameroon's Political Crossroads*, Boulder, Colorado: Westview Press.

Ukeje, C., 2002, 'From Aba to Ugborodo: Gender Identity and Alternative Interpretations of the Discourse of Social Protest among Women in the Oil Delta of Nigeria', Paper presented at the 10th General Assembly of CODESRIA, Kampala, Uganda, 8-12 December.

Wacquant, Loic, 2000, 'Modifications du role de l'Etat et conséquences sociales. L'Impact des politiques néoliberales dans les sociétés occidentales', Conference paper presented at the 2000 World Social Summit, Geneva. CETIM.

Warnier, J. P., 1985, *Echanges, développement et hiérarchies dans le Bamenda précolonial (Cameroun)*, Stuttgart: Franz Sterner Verlag 76.

Waylen, G., 1998, *Analysing Women in Third World Politics*, Buckingham: Open University Press.

Yenshu Vubo, E., 1995, 'Indigenous Society and multiparty Politics in Cameroon in the early 1990s', Paper presented at the Annual Conference of the Pan African Anthropological Association (PAAA), Nairobi, Kenya, 15-19 October.

7

Micro-credit, Financial Sector Reform and Welfare

Wilfred J. Awung

Introduction

In 1989, the Cameroonian government began implementing a Structural Adjustment Programme (SAP) as part of the World Bank and International Monetary Fund's prescription to solve the country's economic crisis. A financial sector reform was instituted as part of the reform programme and this aimed at ridding the economy of insolvent financial institutions and putting the financial sector on a sound footing. The reform programme has been completed and new privately owned commercial banks have appeared in the Cameroonian banking sector.

However, restrictions continue to be in place, which make it difficult for many ordinary Cameroonians to patronise commercial banks. Thus, the informal financial sector continues to be the major source of financial services for Cameroonians. They have served Cameroonians well but their services are limited by many factors such as the small size and short cycles of the loans, which make them unsuitable for long-term investment purposes. Non-governmental organisations (NGOs) and cooperative credit and savings societies have appeared on the Cameroonian financial scene as part of the decentralised financial programme, providing credit services. The main objective has been to meet the financial needs of ordinary Cameroonians, especially the small-scale business, and the poor urban and rural dwellers. These NGOs lend to groups and make use of joint liability, peer selection, and investment in repeated financial transactions to overcome the informational constraints in financial markets (Zellner et al. 2001). They seek to upgrade the services of informal financial groups by providing credit services along banking lines. They attempt to overcome the limitation of informal and formal financial institutions by providing the poor with best practices that will help them overcome their financial problems and improve their welfare. By providing their members with services such as training, book keeping, auditing and supervision, they hope to overcome the weaknesses of both the formal and informal services. Thus with the financial sector reform, there have been adaptations and innovations in the country's financial institutions, especially those serving the poor.

Financial sector reform has gone alongside the increased role of the informal sector in the economy. The informal sector accounts for 60 per cent of employment in the economy and is made up of mostly small and medium-sized enterprises. The entrepreneurs in this sector face numerous constraints, especially finance. The question then is whether the financial sector reform is of assistance to the informal sector.

The objective of this study is to analyse the evolution of informal credit institutions in Cameroon since the commencement of the Structural Adjustment Programme. The study will also explore the impact of financial sector reform on the well-being of the people.

The Structure of the Financial Sector in Cameroon

The simplest form of credit institution in Cameroon is the informal financial credit institution popularly known in pidgin English as 'njangi' in the English section of the country and 'tontines' in the French-speaking section of the country. These rotating savings groups abound in a context of a largely flawed banking system. They are formed when the demand for credit is excessive in the formal market resulting from the quantitative restriction on transactions or from the imposition of a price ceiling (Agenor 1995). Informal financial operators include moneylenders, landlords and rotating savings groups.

Rotating savings groups are the most prevalent forms of informal finance arrangements in Cameroon. Two variants of these rotating savings groups exist. In the first type, a number of people meet at fixed intervals and collect a fixed sum of money which is loaned to different members of the group each month. Sika and Strasser (2001) maintain that there are two variants of this type of informal financial schemes: in the first, the order of the members who receive the money is determined in advance by consensus. The number of members determines the loan period, which defines the length of the loan cycle. An equal amount of money is distributed each month free of interest. In the second type, the money collected is auctioned and all members of the current round who have not yet received a loan may bid for it. The highest bidder gets the money. The profit made in the primary market is then divided into small amounts, which are auctioned in the secondary markets. This money in the secondary market is treated as short-term loans, which must be repaid with interest.

The second type of rotating savings group is more flexible, accommodating people with different incomes. The money collected is similar to a joint fund, which is available to individual members of a loan stock. At every turn, new contributions are shared into packets of money whose amount depends on the number of members taking part and the level of loans they seek. An arbitration body is usually available to satisfy everybody. In this case loans have a short cycle, usually one month, and the interest rate is set at 5-10 per cent per month.

Informal financial organisations have several weaknesses. The cycle depends on the number of members, and where there are few members, the cycle may last for less than a year. Thus their loans are short-term in nature, meaning that loans cannot be put into long-term investment ventures spanning many years. The short-term nature of their loans restricts their investment to speculative activities. In addition to the above the cost of credit in these markets usually between 5 per cent and 10 per cent per month is higher than what obtains in the formal markets. Furthermore, the amount of money transacted in these markets is limited to members' contributions, thus making it impossible for people to obtain large loans from these markets. Members of informal financial groups needing more money have to look elsewhere for financing. In most cases, the loan is granted to the person who wins the ballot. Often this person may not need the money at the time. Someone else may have a profitable business venture but may fail to get the loan when it is most needed. Thus, it is difficult to match needs and the availability of funds.

Given the above limitations, numerous attempts have been made to upgrade the functions of informal financial institutions in Cameroon, especially in rural areas. Cooperative loans and savings societies, NGOs and credit unions, have been created with the aim of providing micro-credit to the poor people. They are considered semi-formal financial institutions because their services are limited to savings and deposit activities only. These include ordinary savings and deposit accounts for members of local mutual funds. According to Amin et al., (1999), Cameroon's cooperative law of 1992 gave leeway to savings and cooperative societies in the rural areas of the country. Since 1995, the registration of these societies has been increasing although most of them are located in the urban areas and are patronised by a relatively wealthy clientele. Today, there are approximately 300,000 customers of these cooperative loans and savings societies in Cameroon. Various micro-credit institutions have different structures, mostly patterned after successful rural credit programmes for the poor in South East Asian countries such as the Grameen Bank in Bangladesh. They have a network of various actors starting from the villages to commercial banks and NGOs. A good example is the MC2 or the 'Mutuelle communautaire de croissance', sponsored by the Afriland Bank (formerly CCEI Bank) and ADAF.

Also, NGOs now operate in the rural areas of Cameroon, supplying credit to the poor. The donor community and multilateral finance institutions particularly support these NGOs by providing the funds which are lent to people at reduced rates of interest. This is because it is believed that NGOs can lead in the drive for institutional innovation in financial services available to poor people by training poor people and helping them finance self-help groups. By supporting self-help groups implement sound micro-financial practices and networking, NGOs help informal financial groups better serve the poor.

In 1989, there were nine commercial banks with 274 branches, four development banks, a social security fund, and a series of cooperative credit unions spread throughout Cameroon. These banks were concentrated in urban centres and were patronised mostly by traders and civil service employees. They had mobilised significant savings from the private sector and public sector enterprises. A 1973 law made it mandatory for the state to acquire 25 per cent of the share equity in commercial banks. This piece of legislation was abused as politically insolvent loans were granted to people without collateral. By 1989 when the Cameroonian economy went into a crisis, the commercial banking sector was characterised by bad debts and consequent insolvency.

The Structural Adjustment Programme, the Poor and the Credit Needs of Cameroonians

The implementation of the structural adjustment programme in Cameroon was intended to restore the economy on a path of growth. The adoption of market-oriented policies meant a reduction of the role of the state in economic activities. This programme had significant ramifications on the common people, especially the rural dwellers whose standard of living has deteriorated significantly. The producer prices paid for agricultural export commodities such as cocoa and coffee were slashed and brought in line with world market prices.

There was a freeze in employment in the civil service, the withdrawal of subsidy to public sector enterprises, an elimination of subsidised agricultural inputs, and the liberalisation of the country's external trade. Many people lost their jobs, especially vulnerable groups such as women and children. The employment rate fell by 10 per cent from 1984 to 1991 and reached 17 per cent by 1995.

Studies on poverty in Cameroon since the implementation of the SAP programme reveal that poverty has increased in both absolute and relative terms. The 1996 household consumption study revealed that 51 per cent of the population were unable to meet a minimum consumption basket (poverty line) and 23 per cent were unable to meet even the food component of this basket (extreme poverty line). The poverty line used was 148,000 CFA francs with adjustment for regional prices. Poverty, which varied according to region, was predominantly a rural phenomenon with 86 per cent of the poor living in rural areas and women being poorer than men.

The second household consumption study in 2001 pointed to the fact that most Cameroonians were living with an annual income below the poverty line of 232,547 CFA francs which represents the estimated annual income necessary for an individual in Yaoundé to buy a 'minimal basket' of essential food and non-food items, including health, education, and housing expenditures. Amin (2001) analysed rural poverty and agricultural development in Cameroon and came out with the same results as the previous two studies. He found that poverty is prevalent in Cameroon; it is more of a rural than an urban phenomenon and affects women more than men. It projected that the structural adjustment will seriously compromise the middle class in the country. What these studies have in common is that since the implementation of the adjustment programme, conditions of living have worsened for most Cameroonians. Access to social services such as schooling has declined and health care services have deteriorated considerably, becoming death traps for many. In short, Cameroonians cannot meet their basic needs for survival. The material and financial resources to satisfy their basic needs are lacking and this thus renders them vulnerable to all forms of deprivation.

As unemployment rose and joblessness became the norm, the informal sector became the last resort. This sector is attractive because its activities are unregulated and its capital requirements are humble compared to other sectors of the economy. Fonjong and Endeley (2004) have pointed out that in the informal sector of Cameroon, women act as farmers, food crop retailers, food vendors, exploiters of NTFP, hairdressers, restaurant operators, second-hand clothes vendors, telephone call box operators, basic provision store operators, seamstresses, local beer parlour operators, locally distilled wine and palm wine vendors, interior decorators, and fish smokers. Many men also do business in the informal sector and face similar problems as women, chief of which is lack of finance. In order adequately to tackle poverty-related issues, it is important to design a study which carries out a comparative analysis of both men and women.

Statement of Problem

The informal sector has become the main avenue for fighting the economic crisis. It provides at least six out of ten households with an income. As such it is the most rapidly growing sector in the Cameroonian economy and is considered a social safety net due to its ability to absorb workers shed by the public sector and the shrinking private sector. Given the ease of its establishment, most of the informal sector endeavours are concentrated in commercial activities. However, because most of the businesses are often considered small and medium-sized enterprises, finance is their major problem. They are considered 'unbankable' because they lack the necessary collateral for loans, often require small amounts of money as opposed to large-scale manufacturing, and loan application procedures are complex and time-consuming.

Several institutions have developed outside of the formal financial system with the objective of addressing the finance needs of these businesses. The Cameroonian government took steps to promote semi-formal financial institutions by creating the National Micro Finances Programme Support Project in November 2000. Also known as decentralised financial groups, they aim at providing financial services to the poor not served by commercial banks. Decentralised financial groups are expected to alleviate poverty by helping the poor to participate in financial services. The project aims at overcoming the financial problems of rural dwellers. Its objectives are: (i) to increase the access to micro-credit in rural areas from

100,000 people to 500,000 people and then to 1,250,000 people at the end of the first phase of the project in 2006. (ii) From an institutional angle, its aim is to improve the standing of micro-financial organisations with respect to the traditional financial sector, thus enhancing their capacity in relation to donor-assisted micro finance. (iii) From an environmental point of view, it aims to increase production and consumption of food in order to modernise agriculture and preserve the ecosystem.

Despite the financial innovations provided by micro finance institutions since the commencement of SAP, few empirical studies have been carried out to analyse the impact of micro finance on poverty alleviation. The problem then is to discover what these innovative institutions managed to do to meet the finance needs of the informal sector.

Some studies have analysed the financial problems of the enterprises especially those patronised by women. Amin et al., (1999) analysed the financial sector reform and women's survival strategies. They found that despite the financial sector reform women were not well served by formal financial institutions. As such women patronise informal and semi-formal financial sources for their finance needs. This is because they are easily accessible, have faster services and low transaction costs. Fonjong and Endeley (2004) analysed the importance of micro-entrepreneurial activities in poverty reduction and the constraints they faced in Cameroon. They found that the role of the informal sector in poverty alleviation has increased with the implementation of the structural adjustment programme. Women are significant actors in this sector but they face numerous constraints, such as a lack of time, lack of capital, lack of skills, limited market, and an unfavourable policy environment such as high taxes and harassment from the forces of law and order. Although the thrust of this paper is on general poverty alleviation, it is limited to women. It fails to address the problems of the informal sector finance problems on institutions and by gender. Male and female entrepreneurs may face different constraints and different resource allocation preferences.

Since finance is the major problem which these entrepreneurs face, this study attempts to address this problem by focussing on the various financial sectors of their activities. It analyses the finance problems of the poor and the continued prominence of the informal financial sector in meeting the finance needs of the poor since the implementation of the SAP.

Methodology

(a) Data Sources and analysis: For this study we needed as large a sample as possible, containing participants in the various financial sectors of Cameroon. The data used here were generated from primary data collected from respondents between August to December 2004 in four of Cameroon's ten provinces where informal, semi-formal and formal financial sectors exist. Despite the proliferation of financial institutions, many Cameroonians still do not patronise all of these institutions. Thus, it was difficult finding the right respondents to produce the desired information.

b) Sampling: The respondents were selected from the following provinces: Littoral with 106 respondents, Northwest with 67 respondents, West with 66 respondents and Southwest with 43 respondents. The uneven nature of the breakdown of the provincial respondents is due to the population distribution of these provinces, the economic opportunities in the area, and the culture of the people. The Littoral has the highest number of respondents because it is the centre of commercial activity in Cameroon. The North West Province has the second highest respondents because of the dynamic nature of the people and the fact that the enumerators were familiar with the terrain. The West province had only 66 respondents because of the difficulties of communication with the indigenous people there. The Southwest province has the least number of respondents because it has the lowest population amongst the four provinces from which respondents were drawn. Only 250 of the questionnaires from the 284 respondents were properly answered and it is these questionnaires that are used for our analysis.

The respondents were selected through a multi-stage sampling procedure. First, through simple random sampling, the communities to be sampled were identified. Second, for the sake of convenience, we used a purposive sampling technique to identify the individual respondents. Data were solicited on household demographic characteristics such as size of household, asset composition and ownership, credit and savings transactions, age of household head, uses of credit, and welfare of respondents. Simple descriptive statistics such as the arithmetic mean and percentages are used to analyse the data.

Findings

In Table 1, some demographic characteristics of the sample households are presented. The results reveal that women headed-households make up 31.1 per cent of the population. Male-headed households make up 68.9 per cent of the total of respondents. In terms of education attainment, 48 per cent of all respondents have some form of primary education. A breakdown by sex shows that 30.4 per cent of male respondents had primary education and 17.2 per cent of all female respondents had primary education. In terms of secondary education, 30 per cent of all respondents had some form of secondary education. While 20 per cent of all male respondents had some form of secondary education, only 10 per cent of all female respondents had. In terms of university education, 22.4 per cent of all respondents have some form of it, with 4 per cent of the women having attained university education and 18 per cent of the men. This finding reveals that the higher the level of education, the lower the number of respondents who attained it.

In terms of occupational distribution, one surprising finding is that only one male respondent was a farmer. It is surprising because more than 50 per cent of the population is engaged in agriculture, the major activity for most Cameroonians.

This anomaly might be due to sampling error. However, more women respondents take part in farming than men with 7.6 per cent of the female respondents being farmers. Teaching seems to be a major activity for most urban-based Cameroonians, with 26 per cent of all respondents being teachers: 18.4 per cent of the male respondents and eight per cent of the female respondents followed this occupation. Two-fifths (22 per cent) of all respondents are civil servants, with 16.8 per cent of all male respondents and four per cent of all female respondents working in the public sector. This is because Cameroon has a large civil service sector. Two per cent of the male respondents are in the military. Trade and self-employment is an attractive endeavour for all Cameroonians. About 29 per cent of all respondents are in the trades or self-employed sector. Of this number males are 21 per cent and females seven per cent. This high number shows the efforts Cameroonians are making in fighting the crisis by engaging in their own small-scale businesses. In our data, only men are in business and they form only four per cent of the population. Women's absence in business may be due to constraints such as lack of capital.

Table 1: Demographic Characteristics of Households in the Sample

	Male %		Female %		All %	
A) Sample Size	171		79		250	
B) Household Size	855 (68%)		338 (31%)		1293	
C) Mean Age of Household Head	49.4		27.5		29.1	
D) Educational Attainment of Household Head						
Primary school	76	30	43	17.1	119	48
Secondary school	50	20	25	10	75	30
University	45	18	11	4	56	22
E) Occupation of Household Head						
Farming	1	-	18	7	19	7.6
Teaching	46	18.4	20	8	66	26
Civil servant	42	16.8	10	4	52	22
Trades and self employment	52	20.8	18	7	70	29
Military	6	2	0	-	6	2.4
Business	14	5.6	13	5.2	27	10
Others	10	4	0	-	10	4
Total	171	68.4	79	31.2	250	101

The mean age of all the respondents is 29.1 years meaning that most of the respondents were relatively young; however, the mean age for female respondents is 29.1 years while that for male respondents is 49.4 years, meaning that female respondents were almost half as young as the male household heads.

Table 2 presents results for financial institution participation, which is a breakdown of the manner in which the respondents are members of financial institutions by sector and by sex. It reveals that most of the respondents belong to one form of financial institution or other. Informal financial institutions or rotating savings group are the most popular: 30.4 per cent of the male respondents and 14 per cent of female respondents are members of informal financial institution. A closer look at the female data will reveal that close to half of the female respondents are members of informal financial groups. Only 4.1 per cent of women patronise commercial banks. This may be due to the fact that banks are still inaccessible for most women who find it hard to meet their requirements such as collateral and the huge amount needed to open an account. About 20 per cent of the male respondents belong to a formal financial group.

Table 2: Participation of Household Heads in various Financial Institutions by sector and by sex

Types of Institutions	Male %		Female %		All
Banks	50	20.2	10	4.0	24.2
Semi-formal	20	8.1	23	9.3	17.4
Informal	76	30.7	35	14.1	44.8
Formal/informal	10	4.0	4	1.6	5.6
Informal/semi formal	8	3.2	3	1.2	4.4
Formal/semi formal	7	2.8	2	0.8	3.6
Total	171	69	77	31	100

Source: Field Data.

Men tended to patronise commercial banks more because most of them are in businesses which involved heavy transactions unlike the small-scale activities that women are involved in. A significant number of respondents, 17 per cent - patronise semi-formal institutions. In gender terms, 9.4 per cent of the women respondents patronise semi-formal institutions while 8 per cent of the men respondents also patronise commercial banks. These semi-formal institutions are becoming popular because they address the credit needs of the informal sector and use self-help groups as surety in making their decision. Since many women belong to these groups this explains their preference for them. Also, some male and female respondents patronise more than one institution: they use formal/informal, formal/semi-formal and informal/formal sectors as a means of diversifying risk.

Table 3 brings out the point that although most of the respondents patronised informal financial groups, commercial banks granted the highest amount of loans to its customers, both male and female. This is because commercial banks have more money at their disposal than the rotating saving groups and semi-formal groups. Also the duration of their loans is much longer, which means that their loans can be put to long-term investment purposes. Informal rotating savings groups give out the least amount of loans. The small size of their loans reflects their low volume of transactions and the short-term nature of their activities. Semi-formal savings and loans cooperatives give out more loans than rotating savings groups, which means that self help groups who need long-term loans should start thinking of patronising this group.

Table 3: Loan Transactions and Their Characteristics

	Male	Female	All
Informal credit			
Loan size	8,600,000	4,870,000	13,470,000
Loan maturity	3 months	3 months	3 months
Annual interest rate	8-10 per cent	8-10 per cent	8-10 per cent
Default rate	3 per cent	none	3 per cent
Semi-formal			
Loan size	16,510,000	6,179,000	22,689,000
Loan maturity	one year	one year	one year
Annual interest rate	4 per cent	4 per cent	4 per cent
Default rate	none	none	none
Formal			
Loan size	24,500,000	8,650,000	33,150,000
Loan maturity	3 years	3 years	3 years
Annual interest rate	3 per cent	3 per cent	3 per cent
Default rate	none	none	none
*Sample size	171	79	250

Source: Field Data.

From Table 4 it can be seen that a large percentage of loans from the informal sector are used for non-productive activities such as consumption durables, food, health and social events. Loans from formal sector and semi-formal sectors are mostly used for investment purposes. Because semi-formal financial institutions grant most of their loans to groups who have investment ventures, they have become the main source of loans for investment purposes. There are no loans from the semi-formal and formal institutions for consumption because they emphasise investment. This makes it possible for creditors to repay the loan when it is due. Also a higher proportion of loans from the semi-formal and formal sector are used to repay other loans because the amount of money involved is large and getting more loans is contingent on repaying past loans.

Table 4: Uses and Sources of Loans in CFA Francs

USES	Informal		Semi-Formal		Formal	
	Male	Female	Male	Female	Male	Female
Food	200,000	400,000	-------	359,000	------	-------
Health	250,000	300,000	310,000	360,000	------	-------
Social events	1000,000	320,000	-------	460,000	------	-------
Consumption durable	2000,000	750,000	450,000	1000,000	1000,000	750,000
Farm implements	1,500,000	500,000	300,000	500,000	500,000	1000,000
Farm inputs	3000,000	650,000	4250,000	800,000	4,000,000	1,200,000
Non-Farm Input	2000,000	1250,000	3000,000	950,000	3,500,00	1,700,000
Business investment	350,000	200,000	4000,000	1,250,000	7000,000	3000,000
Reimbursement of other loans	1,000,000	500,000	1,500,000	500,000	4000,000	1000,000
Total	8,600,000	4,870,000	16,510,000	6,179,000	24,500,000	8,650,000

Source: Field Data.

The loans are repaid in order to avoid a situation where one's collateral can be seized by the banks. Loans from informal sources are used for social consumption purposes and investment in cultural capital (education); one can say that in the short term they help clients meet their welfare needs.

Summary and Conclusion

This study has attempted an analysis of financial sector reforms and its impact on meeting the financial needs of Cameroonians. It described the impact of the structural adjustment programme on poverty in Cameroon. It shows that poverty in Cameroon worsened with the implementation of the structural adjustment programme. As a result, social services such as education and health deteriorated. Cameroonians could not meet their basic needs and the informal sector became the hope for the common man, providing them with employment. However, the informal sector activities faced many constraints, chief of which was lack of finance.

An attempt was made to analyse the structure of the financial sector since the commencement of the structural adjustment programme. It reveals that with the financial sector reform, insolvent commercial banks have been liquidated, while commercial banks that had some prospects of growth were merged. New regulations regarding the opening of bank accounts were introduced and the requirements for opening new banks defined. New commercial banks have appeared in the Cameroonian financial sector and the total amount of deposits in the banking system has increased, suggesting some success in the reform programme.

The decentralised financial sector, which includes cooperative savings and loans societies, and credit unions, are now functional as semi-formal financial institutions. These institutions have been brought under the regulatory authority of

COBAC. Despite the proliferation of semi-formal financial institutions and the appearance of new banks in the country, the informal sector remains the main source of loans for most Cameroonians. This is because their services are most suitable to the needs of Cameroonians. However, an equal number of respondents sampled patronise both the semi-formal and formal sector. This indicates an acceptance of the semi-formal financial sector as an important part of the financial sector despite its relatively young age.

The continuous dominance of the informal financial sector as the main source of credit calls into question the success of the financial sector reform. This can be explained by the fact that the financial sector reform failed to improve on their services. Small-scale savers operating in the informal sector were denied their services because of restrictions which made it difficult for them to patronise the commercial banks - such as the large amount of money needed to open savings accounts and the fact that only large-scale entrepreneurs with collateral can patronise commercial banks. Therefore it is suggested here that the semi-informal financial sector be upgraded by implementing best practices, which can make them overcome their current weaknesses such as extending their loan cycles and attracting more clients. This will enable them to play a role as a complementary sector in the search for alternative financial sources within the economy.

References

Agenor, Pierre Richard, 1995, 'Macroeconomics Management with Informal Financial Markets', *International Journal of Finance Economics*, Vol. 1, 87-101.

Amin, Aloysius, 2001, 'Rural Poverty and Agricultural Development', Paper presented at the Colloquium Pauvreté et Développement durable held at the Université Monstequieu, Bordeau 1V, Paris: UNESCO.

Amin Ntongho Rebecca, Regina Nsang Tawah, and Aloysius Amin, 1999, *Financial Sector Reform and Women's Survival Strategies*, Washington: The World Bank, Rural Development Group.

Fonjong, Lotsmart and Joyce Endeley, 2004, 'The Potentials of Female Micro Entrepreneurial Activities within the Informal sector in Poverty Reduction in Cameroon: Opportunities, Constraints and the Way Forward', Unpublished paper, Department of Women and Gender Studies, University of Buea, Cameroon.

Littlefield, Elizabeth and Richard Rosenberg, 2004, 'Micro Finance and the Poor: Breaking down Walls between Micro Finance and Formal Finance', *Finance and Development*, June.

Republic of Cameroon, 1996, 'Cameroon: Poverty Reduction Strategy Paper', Yaoundé: The Government of Cameroon.

Republic of Cameroon, 2000, 'Interim Poverty reduction Strategy Paper', Yaoundé: The Government of Cameroon.

Sika, Jean-Marc and Balz Strasser, 2001, 'Tontines in Cameroon: Linking Traditional and Semi-formal Financial Institutions Systems', *Development and Cooperation*, No. 1, January/February.

Zellner, M., Manohar Sharma, Akhtern U. Ahmed, and Shahidur Rashid, 2001, 'Group-Based Financial Institutions for the Rural Poor in Bangladesh: An Institutional and Household-level Analysis', International Food Policy Research Institute Research Report No. 120.

Zellner, Manfred, 2001, 'Promoting Institutions in Microfinance: Replicating Best Practices is not Enough', *Development and Cooperation*, No. 1, January/February.

IV

Non-Governmental Organisations

8

Focus and Quality of NGOs as Partners in Development

Enoh Tanjong

Introduction

With the present levels of poverty, most developing countries have turned to non-governmental organisations (NGOs) for much-needed sustenance and development. Africa's political upheavals, natural disasters and the general rate of poverty awakened the need for an alternative solution to these problems. With a few dozen NGOs at the beginning of the century, 1987 showed a marked increase with several thousands the world over (Berg 1987).

Globally, there has been a marked improvement in the field of NGOs as seen from the creation of a 'consultative status' put in place by Article 71 of the United Nations Charter adopted in similar forms all over the world. This charter calls for a liberal policy towards NGOs. It remains to be seen whether the granting of an international status would truly help lighten the constraints against freedom of movement to which NGOs aspire.

In Cameroon, the history of NGOs is fairly recent. More than ten years after the emergence of NGOs in the country, the question of how far NGOs have come to provide alternatives to the shortcomings of the highly centralised and authoritarian governments from 1960-1989 has become a recurrent one.

The end of the monolithic political system in favour of multiparty democracy in Cameroon ushered in the democratisation process in 1990. This process led to the liberalisation of laws governing the formation of associations and organisations. The government passed into law a series of bills meant to liberalise public space (freedom of association, freedom of the press and multipartyism) through a document entitled 'Cameroon: Rights and Freedoms' (1990) (Law No 90/052 and Law No 90/056 of 19 December, 1990).[1]

So far, the general feeling is that the fear and intimidation that characterised the monolithic era have been gradually replaced with a spirit of freedom and liberty. Associations and organisations are no longer considered forums for political agitation and threats to the leadership of the one-party oligarchy. Consequently, the rapid growth of NGOs in Cameroon between 1990 and 1995 has been attributed to the new spirit of liberalisation (Tanjong & Ndeso-Atanga 1995).

With the passing of the 1990 law on freedom of association, the tendency has fluctuated from exaggerated optimism in the early 1990s to cynicism in the early 2000s. Emerging NGOs in Cameroon are increasingly not fulfilling the aspirations of the people. Cameroon is today among the bottom 19 per cent in the low human development category (*Human Development Report* 2003). The fundamental question is why the exaggerated optimism regarding the promise of NGOs in Cameroon has now turned into cynicism.

As Fonjong (2001) explains, the early optimism might have been partly a result of the catastrophic effects of the economic crisis in the late 1980s and the harsh adjustment measures that later followed in the 1990s. Many saw NGOs as a possible organisational avenue to counter the effects of the crisis. According to Fonjong (2001:227), 'government influence has waned'. It has been unable to meet the basic needs of the people, leaving the population to take charge of their destiny through self-reliant development. Community groups and NGOs have been closing ranks to reduce the development gap thus created. The change in national economies and the effects of international trade have magnified the need for NGOs in world affairs. Governments as well as international organisations like the United Nations and the Bretton Woods Institutions consult these NGOs regarding development issues.

Early Optimism

The advent of NGOs raised the hopes and aspirations of many in Cameroon. NGOs came at a time when the country was going through the devastating effects of the economic crisis, which had a trickle-down effect on all sectors of national life. Government was unable to provide the much-needed development to counteract the crisis. NGOs came as a breath of fresh air that would check the excesses of government and serve as agencies of development. Public expectations regarding the activities of NGOs at the time were high. It was envisaged that NGOs would provide health services, reduce unemployment, carry out rural development, care for the environment, educate the rural masses, help the private sector, ensure increased productivity, construct roads, provide loans and offer scholarships - an unrealistic scenario that experience would show to be so.

During the period of the Cameroon economic depression, unemployment was at its peak with over 35 per cent of the active labour force without jobs. Living in an agricultural economy, many people resorted to subsistence agriculture while most civil servants took up petty trading and other income-generating businesses (Fonjong 2001). The health system was collapsing with a ratio of a thousand patients to one doctor. It was amidst this general malaise that the public saw NGOs as offering a new solution to the difficult equation the Cameroon economy was posing at the time.

Moving from a highly centralised one-party system to a semblance of multiparty democracy gave a flicker of hope and up to a point exaggerated optimism. Bitter differences over the high- handedness of government during a quarter century of repression made NGOs appear as God-sent. NGO activities were seen as a veritable source of income, particularly for retired and retrenched civil servants. Coming at a time when Cameroon was witnessing the devaluation of the CFA franc in 1994 and the privatisation of state-owned corporations, many civil servants were retrenched. The coming of NGOs was seen as preparing the way for these jobless and retired civil servants to plough back profits into their private bank accounts.[2]

Another explanation for the early optimism surrounding NGOs in Cameroon was the perception of boundless funds that northern NGOs could disburse. These hopes were further compounded by the euphoria created by these northern NGOs through the organisation of field-level activities, workshops and training seminars for capacity building for potential actors in the domain of local NGO activity.

International NGOs such as PLAN International, HELVETAS, SNV, and the German Technical Cooperation (GTZ) had already been given credit for enormous rural development projects and the high quality of goods and services offered to grassroots communities. Their human and material resources like qualified manpower, four-wheel drive cars, well-furnished offices and good pay packages were such as to stimulate the people to foresee the creation of projects which would transform the lives of local communities. National NGOs saw these services as worth emulating and this generated a high degree of optimism among NGO leaders.

Conceptual Framework

The World Bank Operational Directive (1991) defines NGOs as 'private organisations' that pursue activities to relieve suffering, promote the interests of the poor, protect the environment, provide basic social services, or undertake community development. In wider usage, the term NGO is applied to non-profit organisations, which are independent from government and have development-oriented goals (Farrington 1999). With such a variety of goals, it is quickly noticeable that there must be an array of different types of NGOs.

Korten (1989) noted that the term NGO embraces a wide variety of organisations including Voluntary Organisations (VOs), People's Organisations (POs) and Governmental Non-governmental Organisations (GONGOs). Community-Based Organisations (CBOs), Citywide Organisations, Village Development Organisations (VDOs), and national and international organisations also exist (Cousins 1991). However, since the proliferation of non-state institutions in the late 1990s in Cameroon, the term NGO has been used in a blanket fashion to imply all organisations that are not directly linked to government services and operations (Tanjong & Ndeso-Atanga 1995).

Various reasons have been proposed for the creation of NGOs in Third World countries. Some researchers claim that they were created to provide much-needed development in the economic, political and social domains. Others assert that NGOs were intended to be stop\gap measures against the excesses and failures of the public sector in the development process.

However, the euphoria that followed the creation of NGOs has today died out, as most developing countries are not experiencing the positive fruits of their projects. NGOs have not assisted in the building of roads, major schools and hospitals, or the provision of welfare services to citizens.

This paper addresses the nature of emerging NGOs in Cameroon in terms of their focus, their activities and the public assessment of them as alternatives to governmental institutions.

Theoretical Framework

There is now a significant body of literature on the focus and quality of NGOs in development (for example, Micou 1995, FAO 1994, Farrington, Bebbington et al., 1993, Wellard and Copestake 1993, Caroll 1992, Fowler, Campbell, and Pratt 1992, Clark 1991, Cernea 1988, Tanjong and Ndeso Atanga 1995).

According to Brown (1996), the state is no longer seen as the sole planner and service provider. The role of NGOs has come increasingly to the fore over the last ten years. The end of the Cold War, coupled with expanding international trade and the burgeoning information age, has led to a broad recognition of the role that the civil society has to play in international development. In many countries that are still dependent on foreign assistance to initiate and sustain development initiatives, the trend is now to encourage decentralisation of government activities, and the greater provision of what were once exclusively public services by alternative private entities. Clark (1996) explains that the World Bank is placing increased emphasis on helping NGOs play a more effective role in development activities. It does so by encouraging dialogue with NGOs and using its influence to promote policies and legal environments favourable to them.

One concern with the role of NGOs is that they may become dependent on their Northern counterparts in Europe and America, and on governments. This dependence has in some cases reached such a level that donors are able to call the tune whenever they like. The result is that African NGOs (Cameroon inclusive) have adopted a Northern agenda, to the detriment of local interests. Such NGOs change their development profiles to suit the whims and caprices of the donors (Kengo News 1993). This trend has also been observed in other African case studies cited in the general introduction (cf. in this regard Mohan 2002, Hearn 2001).

In search of development alternatives in Africa, what paradigm can NGOs use to combine internal socio-political and economic change with the capacity to master external relations with northern NGOs? One logical answer is what Amin (1994:334) has called 'delinking'. By 'delinking', Amin does not propose a complete separation of NGOs from external agencies, but a system that offers new opportunities for African NGOs to develop their own approach, with a large margin of relative autonomy, to achieve internal changes at some distance from the global trends.

Well aware of the present levels of NGO activities, major theoretical perspectives have been developed to analyse NGOs as alternative agents in the development process. Among the major paradigms, modernisation theory, dependency theory, and at present theories of alternative development and the free flow of information have been put forward. But the role, methods and objectives of NGOs in development have varied as theoretical frameworks have come and gone. At present, development is seen as critically dependent on the active participation of the communities with NGOs. The key phrase is 'Development from Below'. This approach to development is described as participatory, endogenous and self-reliant.

Systems theory has also been important in forming new ideas for the design and delivery of NGO initiatives. Private sector analysis has been a core tool in new approaches to development. These approaches help to identify the constraints, particularly with regard to economic development and the measures required to come up with solutions to these constraints.

A central claim of the innovation theory widely corroborated in practice is that making users active partners in innovation leads to an increase in development. This insight has grown in reaction to early innovation models, which adopted a linear perspective on the diffusion of innovation processes. Innovation diffusion models have widely noted that the initial uptake of development tends to be driven by a few highly motivated adopters - in this case NGOs. Theories of diffusion of innovation might be appropriate in providing insight on issues concerning public versus private stewardship of development.

The subsidy theory asserts that this institutional form is a response to the many implicit and explicit subsidies made available to NGOs by the state (Weisbrod 1988). Activities such as education, health, poverty alleviation and welfare are encouraged through a variety of subsidies to both charitable organisations and their financial contributors.

A different view of the rationale of NGOs is provided by the public goods theory, which states that NGOs exist to satisfy the residual unsatisfied demand for public goods in society. It argues that the state tends to provide public goods only at the level that satisfies the media and voters; where demand exceeds this level or where heterogeneous demands exist, NGOs step in to fill the gap.

The contract failure theory suggests that NGOs arise where ordinary contractual mechanisms do not provide the public with adequate means to police producers (Hansmann 1987). The argument here is that when contracts are difficult to define, people are likely to trust NGOs more than commercial firms. When the public is unable to monitor or evaluate certain outputs and services (for example, disaster, relief and care of the elderly) they are likely to turn to organisations with no profit motive for producing and delivering the outputs and services.

The consumer control theory explains the existence of a category of NGOs in terms of the superiority of direct consumer or patron control when the market and government are unable to ensure the desired performance (Kabanda 1996). It is argued that consumer control may help eliminate information asymmetry and the adverse consequences of monopoly for members.

These theoretical perspectives provide alternative explanations of why NGOs emerge and survive in society and point to the conditions under which this institutional form is likely to perform better than the market and the state.

Literature Review

The Role of NGOs in Development

NGO involvement in development activities in Africa has grown rapidly since independence. According to Bratton (1989), Africa's first modern NGOs emerged in the latter days of colonial rule as ethnic welfare associations (see Ebune 2004). Paul and Israel (1991) argue that how one looks at NGOs and their development roles often depends on deeper questions of how one looks at development and the role of the state.

The concept of non-governmental organisations has met with increasing interest during the last two decades. It is a facet of social development to which the public has adapted at a relatively fast rate. The World Bank states that NGOs are neither protected by power nor are they legitimated by elections. Mostly, they appear as actors in the field of international politics without having control over territory and population. As a result of the significant variance in the nature and role of NGOs, definitions should be narrowed so as to limit a spectrum that stretches from the churches to the Mafia. The Bank in this vein highlights the decisive characteristics of NGOs as being their non-profit status and their abstention from participation in state power.

The concept of development in itself is a complex one. Neher (2003) associates the concept with a cluster of terms such as modernisation. He cites early development paradigms that viewed development as the abandonment of traditional ways and the adoption of 'modern' practices as exemplified by the West.

Similarly, Rostow (1963) portrays development in the form of traditional Asian and African societies struggling to mimic western culture. Amin (1994) thinks that the essential part of this definition is left out, namely that the underdeveloped countries form part of a world system; that their integration into this system forged their special structure which henceforth has nothing in common with what prevailed before their integration into the modern world.

Dissanayake (1981) looks at development as a process of social change that has as its goal the improvement of the quality of life of the majority of people without doing violence to their natural and cultural environment. It also seeks to involve the generality of people as closely as possible in this enterprise, making them masters of their own destiny.

He further states that his definition is different from those presented by the scholars who defined development in the 1960s. For instance, Rogers and Shoemaker (1971) in Dissanayake (1981) defined development as a type of social change in which new ideas are introduced into the social system in order to produce higher per capita income and standards of living through modern production methods and improved social organisation.

According to Ngwa (2002), development for most people in rural Africa has meant disempowerment of all kinds. It has meant marginalisation and subordination for the rural masses, in favour of a city-based power elite. For the excluded, development has come to be associated with less and less control over their lives and resources. It has meant increasing centralisation of power in the hands of a powerful coterie of corrupt indigenous elites.

Hence, many developmental blueprints resulted in the virtual loss of traditional paradigms, customary communication channels, local ideas and indigenous contributions. According to Ngwa, since the government-owned media have been part of the power structure, they could only have supported development that kept people in an imaginary society, which constantly looked outside itself for improvement.

It is clear that the basic framework of a viable development process requires rethinking. Wignaraja (1976) posits that this very act of rethinking would seem to require new kinds of information and retraining of actors in the process as well as a new methodology. Once there is a broad agreement on a feasible alternative, even in the form of an idealised construct, then we will be in a position to see what kind of information is required and of course what kind of processes should be envisaged.

Seers (1969) pointed out quite rightly in the following comment:

> The questions to ask about a country's development are therefore: what has been happening to poverty? What has been happening to inequality? And what has been happening to the economy? If all three of these have declined from high levels, then beyond a doubt, there has not been a period of development for the country concerned. If one or two of these central problems have grown worse especially if all three have, it would be strange to call the result development even if the per capita income doubled.

Dissanayake (1981) comments that this statement clearly reflects the newer attitude to development. It is in this sense that development is applicable and not as a synonym for economic growth, but as a term, which also includes distributive justice and human fulfilment. Older approaches to development during the 1950s and 1960s propounded the argument that what was needed was rapid economic growth by means of industrialisation. Heavy emphasis was laid on capital-intensive technology and centralised planning. The guiding principle seems to have been that the only way in which the less developed countries could make progress was by emulating the industrially advanced countries and taking the same historical path that they traversed. Rostow's influential work, *Stages of Economic Growth: A Non-Communist Manifesto* (1963) had a profound impact on this type of thinking. In his book, he identified five stages of development for a country: the Traditional Society, the Precondition for Take-off, the Take-off, the Claim to Maturity, and the Age of High Mass-Consumption.

As Adelman (1975) points out, not only is there no automatic trickle-down of the benefits of development; but the development process leads typically to a trickle-up in favour of the middle classes and the rich.

Schiller and Nordenstreng (1975) observed that the notion of a relatively isolated nation developing in accordance with the conditions determined mainly within the society remains almost untouched. In the opinion of these two authors, this is a fundamental consideration that cannot be overlooked. They make the point that while advocates of the approach to development and communication like Everett Rogers (1976) talk of external causes of underdevelopment and dependence theory, such notions do not significantly influence their conception.

The Agenda-Setting Function of NGOs

Agenda-setting according to Kabanda (1996) is the bringing of welfare issues to the attention of relevant decision makers. NGOs sometimes exert pressure from outside, intent on both the formation and implementation of policies, programmes and plans. They use campaigning - a visible activity directed at a certain constituency - and lobbying - a direct and often private approach to individuals or small groups of people. NGOs are supposed to act as a counterweight to state power, protecting human rights, opening channels of communication and participation, providing training grounds for activists, and promoting pluralism.

Annis (1986) describes NGOs from the Latin American perspective as a thickening web of grassroots organisations. This is because the strength of the voluntary sector as a development agent is not found in the size of its individual organisation as much as in their number and variety, their ability to evolve and their ever-shifting networks and coalitions. To focus on the performance and scale of individual NGOs is to risk losing sight of the aggregate phenomenon that they represent: a movement attempting to return the control of development to the people.

The literature on NGOs is multifaceted, covering the economic, political and managerial dimensions of the non-profit sector. There is a sizable literature on the economics of the non-profit sector that consists of theories of the role of NGOs and their behaviour (Hansmann 1987, Rose-Ackerman 1980). The dominant approach is to explain the phenomenon of NGOs in terms of the failures of the market and the state.

Douglas (1987) argues that studies of the politics of the non-profit sector have focussed on the reasons that NGOs perform public functions that normally fall within the purview of the government. Voluntary action is viewed here as an adaptive response to the constraints of majority rule and equitable distribution criteria. Ramanathan (1982) adds that a modest body of knowledge exists also on the dynamics of managing NGOs concerned with the planning, financing, budgeting, controlling and evaluating NGO activities. The focus here is on the internal management problems of NGOs, an applied area of direct relevance to the training and development of NGO staff.

Brown (1989) and Korten (1984) analyse the rationale of NGOs from a number of perspectives. They argue that the comparative advantage of NGOs lies in their ability to innovate, to adapt to local conditions, and to reach and work with the poor. These positive features are a function of their basic values, special skills, small size, limited resources, flexibility, and freedom from political constraints. Their weaknesses stem from some of the same characteristics - particularly their value commitments, small size, independence and administrative flexibility.

Brodhead et al., (1988) point out that many NGOs grew out of true volunteer tradition. A group of people decided to commit their uncompensated time to righting a social wrong. Eventually they become strong enough to raise funds to hire a small paid staff to support their volunteer efforts. As an organisation gained credibility it was able to attract further funding and hire more paid staff. Eventually the paid staff displaced the volunteers, with the argument that volunteers could not be expected to meet the necessary performance standards.

According to Ginsburg (1991), NGOs have become increasingly visible and active in various sectors of social life including education. NGOs have received greater attention in government, international organisation reports and policy documents as well as in scholarly literature. NGOs are characterised and evaluated in quite different ways.

Some reasons for the contradictory representation of NGOs are that they constitute a heterogeneous set of institutions, and not just because of the different sectors in which they work or the gender, racial, ethnic and social class characteristics of participants (see in this regard Tostensen, Tvedten and Vaa 2001:11). These institutions include grassroots operations intricately interwoven into social movements as well as non-profit businesses run by professionals. Some NGOs are locally based institutions that operate on shoe-string budgets derived from the resources of those involved, while others are international entities with sizeable budgets built from grants and contracts from international organisations.

NGOs are characterised differently in the literature because authors bring different perspectives to the analytical task. The difference in perspectives is to some extent captured by typologies or mapping of social theory paradigms. For example, analysts employing equilibrium perspectives tend to paint a different portrait of NGOs than those using the lens of conflict theory.

However, analysts and those who are grounded in similar paradigms may differ in their depiction and evaluation of NGOs because of differences in their conceptions of the space available for democratic participation within the state versus civil society. In democratic political systems, one would applaud the increasing role of NGOs only to the extent that one viewed the state or the public sector as unresponsive or inefficient. Cameroon seems to fit squarely into this categorisation.

Robbins (2002) suggests a few reasons why NGOs have become increasingly important in the past decade. For instance, communication advances, especially the Internet, have helped create new global communities and bonds between like-minded people across state boundaries. There are now increased resources, growing professionalism and more opportunities in NGOs. He also stresses the media's ability to increase awareness when the public demand that their governments take action of some kind.

Perhaps most important, Robbins (op cit.) suggests that some people believe NGOs have developed as part of a larger neo-liberal economic and political agenda. Shifts in economic and political ideology have led to increasing support of NGOs from governments and official aid agencies in response. Neo-liberal economic and political agendas have proposed a greater role for NGOs.

Neo-liberalism is a dominant ideology being promoted around the world today by the US and various other nations, and is known as the Washington Consensus. One of the many aspects of this ideology is to minimise the role of the state in the social sector (health, social welfare, provision of social goods and services, and education).

Robbins (2002) argues that NGOs are growing because of increased amounts of public funding. However, NGOs that are not dependent on state aid are the exception rather than the rule.

Another reason for the existence of NGOs is that people come together in independent groups to promote some type of activity that is not being undertaken by the government. Alternatively, governments may already be involved in an activity but groups are formed in order to challenge the way government is handling the matter (Kabanda 1996).

Mainstreaming Women in NGOs

NGOs might have done much to mainstream women in development in Cameroon but their efforts fall short of meeting the strategic needs for a long-term solution to the relative lack of empowerment (Fonjong 2001). The focus of NGOs on women during the economic crisis was crucial since women were more severely affected than men. More women than men became unemployed, household incomes fell, subsidies to agriculture became selective, and the informal sector was flooded by newcomers (including men and wives of the elite). Women needed assistance to find new survival strategies to maintain their crucial roles in society (Fonjong op cit).

Fonjong (2001:227) asserts that inadequate skills limit women's effective participation in development. Many NGOs in Cameroon have focussed on making women more productive and competitive in the job market. Training is organised in workshops, seminars, demonstrations and training centres, emphasising the acquisition of knowledge, skills and information as basics for self-reliant development, which better equips the women. The intent is to increase organisational and technical capacities of these NGOs.

NGOs as Civil Society Organisations

In their quest to improve the quality of life of citizens, NGOs have become active partners and relevant actors in the civil society. NGOs have been acting as a means of bringing about sustained improvements in the well-being of individuals. However, civil society in most of sub-Saharan Africa (Cameroon inclusive) has been very docile in the articulation of public policy. Nyamnjoh (1999) identifies civil society as those independent and politically active bodies, religious, professional, cultural and special interest groups, that fall outside the structure of government. Civil society in this case refers to the vital space and network of potentially independent organisations that prove instrumental for the authentic articulation of public interests.

Monga (1995) adds that the civil society thus comprises all organisations whose actions have helped or are helping to amplify the affirmation of social identity and the rights of citizenship, often in opposition to those in power whose natural tendency is to repress such identities and rights.

Methodology

A multiple approach of qualitative and quantitative research methodologies was used in carrying out this study. Three methods were used: content analysis, semi-structured interviews and a survey.

Content Analysis: A content analysis of 268 NGOs in Cameroon was conducted using the Directory of NGOs in Cameroon (1997) and the African Civil Society Contact Directory (www.nivblodon.kabissa.org), which lists all NGOs in Cameroon (1999-2003). The objective of the content analysis was to identify the areas of focus of NGOs in the country.

Semi-Structured Interviews (SSI): A series of semi-structured interviews was conducted with the leaders and management of eleven NGOs in Fako Division of the Southwest Province. This was based on a random sample of the NGO leaders and management. The semi-structured interviews were based on the following thematic issues: the mission of the NGO, operation and management systems, quality and capacity, sources of funding and external relations.

Survey of Cameroonians: In January 2004, a cross-sectional probability sample of 600 heads of households in the Buea municipality was surveyed. Face-to-face and self-administered interviews were conducted with the sampled respondents from the following neighbourhoods: Bolifamba, Bomaka, Bonaberi, Bonalyonga, Bokwoango, Small Soppo, Great Soppo, Molyko, Buea Town, Longstreet, the Government Residential Area (GRA) and Bonduma.

A Systematic Random Sampling (SRS) technique was used to draw respondents from the twelve neighbourhoods. In each neighbourhood, an alternate sampling of houses was made and within each household, heads of households were interviewed. The response rate of the survey was 90.3 per cent.

The study focussed on the Cameroon public's perceptions of NGOs as alternatives to development. It thus examined public assessments of the development-oriented activities of NGOs and their capacity to act as alternative agents in the process of social change.

Results

Focus of NGOs

An examination of the focus of NGOs in Cameroon from the content analysis revealed that 5.2 per cent of the 268 NGOs studied direct their interventions at rural communities, while 4.9 per cent targeted urban communities. Surprisingly enough, an overwhelming majority (89.9 per cent) of the NGOs did not indicate their area of intervention.

This poses a practical problem in terms of the level of operation of these NGOs and how far they are carrying out their activities in the field. One may tend to believe the assertion that these NGOs are 'briefcase' bodies, since they did not spell out their areas of operation.

NGOs (particularly international NGOs) started operations in Cameroon way back in the early 1940s. But it was not until 1990 with the passing of the freedom laws that national NGOs witnessed an upsurge. Today, there are over 300 NGOs in Cameroon ranging from Village Development Organisations to Service Providing NGOs (SPNGOs).

From the content analysis, the major focus of NGOs in Cameroon can be placed under the portmanteau concepts of urban and rural development (31 per cent). These are quite elusive concepts because they do not specify the exact nature of NGO activities.

Other reported areas of focus were education (28 per cent), environment sustainability and agro-forestry (24 per cent), health and HIV/AIDS (16.3 per cent), and sport (0.4 per cent). Curiously, none of these NGOs reported being active in politics despite the fact that we are experiencing democratic pluralism in Cameroon. Evidence from the survey data also suggests a similar trend in the various categories of NGO focus: Health, education, agriculture, and environmental sustainability. A lack of focus is indicative of the elusive nature of

Cameroon's NGOs. This has implications for effectiveness and the ability of these NGOs to impact on grassroots communities.

NGO Governance

From the semi-structured interviews in Limbe and Buea sub-divisions, NGO leaders revealed that most of the organisations had been founded by a few charismatic individuals with a strong commitment to a cause or purpose and a definite set of ideas about how to serve that cause.

Overall, membership of most national NGOs is still relatively small and tied to family or tribal lineage. Few NGOs can claim a national scope because of their lack of resources, capacity, infrastructure and focus. Consequently, most NGOs are limited in geography and focus.

NGO leaders maintain the direction of the NGOs in line with their stated objectives. Leadership is more effective if it is open to as wide a variety of opinions and talents as possible in order to be effective and utilise all the talents and enthusiasm of its staff and members, as well as to avoid insularity and stagnation. The role of effective leadership is to manage the attention of employees by articulating a set of intentions or a clear vision of the outcome, goal or direction of the NGO, and by making these ideas tangible and meaningful to employees. NGO leaders in Cameroon can be more effective if they are focussed, constant and consistent, so that they will be trusted and followed.

Above all, leadership fosters the involvement and participation of the NGO membership and the community which the NGO serves. The best method is the participation of NGO leaders, members and the community in realising the objectives of the NGO. Developmentally, this participation is the best method of ensuring the success and sustainability of an NGO and its programmes.

The Quality and Capacity of NGOs

The quality and capacity of NGOs depends on the effective combination of its human and material resources. These human resources must possess the skills, the motivation and the opportunity to make the best contribution of which they are capable to the NGO. They also need to be organised and relate to each other in ways that are conducive to productive outcomes. It is worth noting that the level of education (academic qualification) of NGO staff is a vital aspect for the efficiency of the NGOs. This is because working with an unqualified staff may not yield the required output. Also, recruited workers might have acquired little or nothing as far as the objectives of the NGO are concerned. NGO staff must have the capacity and technical know-how to be able to access the new technologies of information and communication. NGOs with poorly qualified staff fall short of meeting the needs and aspirations of the communities which they serve. This confirms studies in other African contexts (see Mohan op cit., Hearn op cit., Cameron 2001, Mercer 1999). Conversely, NGOs with a qualified staff have registered some degree of success. This accounts for their capacity to provide quality goods and services to the local population.

From observation, most of the NGOs do not have offices. This explains why they use private sitting rooms and one-room apartments as offices. An office is supposed to be a very vital place for consulting and has to be well equipped. Talking about equipment, most of these NGOs, as one of their objectives, pursue computer literacy training programmes for their members and the local community but do not have the required equipment.

In most of the offices, there is no basic equipment such as stationery, computers and files. Most of the NGO leaders claim to have equipment that is not readily available. Although the leaders were hesitant about answering questions with regard to finance, their subordinates testified that most of their leaders embezzled the funds. This is one of the factors that have undermined the effectiveness and credibility of NGOs in Cameroon. NGO members have resorted to strike action when the leaders could not give a proper account of the money in their coffers. Evidence suggests that there is a significant wave of corruption among NGOs although most people are of the opinion that corruption is only prevalent in governmental organisations. This is eloquent testimony to the fact that many people working in NGOs are there for personal profit.

In order to be effective and efficient an NGO needs to ensure that it uses all the skills and experience of its staff appropriately. It can do this by providing them with every opportunity to use their skills, experience and to be creative and take upon themselves the responsibility for improving the ways in which work is done. In addition to having adequate resources and the necessary cash flow, the NGO needs to have a sufficiently diverse resource base and long-term plans for meeting its resource needs.

More than half (58 per cent) of the respondents strongly agreed with the statement that NGOs are sources of private funding and wealth. Similarly, 43.7 per cent reported that most NGOs do not actually exist (they are 'briefcase' NGOs), while 56.4 per cent of the respondents also agreed that Cameroonian NGOs rely heavily on their Northern counterparts for funding. On a positive note, 37.3 per cent of the respondents agreed that NGOs are alternatives to development as opposed to 28.7 per cent who disagreed.

From the data, more than half of the respondents (58 per cent) accuse NGOs of corruption. This is an ethical indictment of Cameroonian NGOs by the respondents. In the current democratic dispensation, most people look to NGOs for honest developmental efforts, and NGO leaders need to win the support of the masses by directing funds to the right development projects instead of amassing wealth for themselves.

When the respondents were asked to advise NGO leaders in the dispatch of their duties, 18.7 per cent called on the NGOs to be honest, 9.3 per cent requested that they should embark on rural development while others referred to assisting and educating the poor (7.7 per cent), proper management of funds (7 per cent) and the need to stick to the non-profit making motive (3.7 per cent).

While some NGOs employ staff in the usual way, others have turned these organisations into family businesses. Some NGOs have all members of their families as the main workers or policy makers of the institutions. Very often, this happens because the leaders do not want to spend money; leading to poor and unproductive outcomes.

This notwithstanding, it is generally true that NGOs with a qualified management and staff stand a greater chance of succeeding in achieving their objectives. Though many leaders claim that their NGOs have a number of staff working for them, it was observed that this was not always the case. The leaders were acting as public relation officers for their NGOs.

Cameroon NGOs and the Dependency Syndrome

The increasing level of poverty in Cameroon has led to a high dependence on international NGOs for both financial and material aid. Most NGOs receive a great deal of assistance from international NGOs, but the problem is not that they are receiving such funds, but what it is that they do with the money. As already noted, most of the offices do not have the basic equipment that an office is supposed to have. As a result, there is gross mismanagement of funds. Some NGOs do claim that they have not received any assistance from international organisations.

Long-term reliance on one or few donors or fund sources can result in the NGO becoming complacent about its financial future and failing to take steps to generate its own funding. It can result in serious problems of continuity and service delivery if the funding ceases for any reason. An NGO is more secure in this area if it has a one-to-three-year fund availability projection. NGOs need a variety of fund sources that can pick up any shortfalls and avoid excessive dependency on specific donors, and must be able to demonstrate at any one time alternative ways of meeting programme commitments and cash needs.

Presently, international NGOs have curtailed donor funds to national NGOs. International aid is now being directed to the ailing economies of Eastern Europe and the former Soviet Union. The question is, how can these national NGOs overcome the dependency syndrome? There are two possible ways: to collect funds locally from the private sector and from governments, and to move into income-generating activities. However, this may be easier said than done. There are several reasons for this problem.

The government and NGOs usually look for funding from the same source - the North. This can lead to government undermining NGOs as it sees them as competitors for the same funding. In addition, the government thinks that NGOs do not have adequate resources.

The private sector in Cameroon is very weak. They need all the profit they can keep whether legally or otherwise. At the same time, donations are not tax-deductible; hence there is no incentive for the private sector to donate funds to NGOs. But what is more important, the private sector does not understand the concept of NGOs and even the idea of foundations. Many of them see the NGO 'watchdog role' as being anti-industry and anti-private sector.

Not all NGOs work in areas where income generation is a feasible alternative. Examples are NGOs working for the provision of water to poor communities, adult literacy, and primary health care in slum areas. Furthermore, many beneficiaries of NGO services do not expect to pay for them. So the question may be posed: How long will national NGOs continue to depend on Northern NGOs for survival? The answer is 'for ever', if action is not taken by both the government and the NGOs themselves. The government therefore must look at NGOs as useful partners in development and provide adequate resources to these NGOs.

The only realistic alternative would be if the government agrees to give at least one per cent of tax revenue to NGOs. This would make NGOs depend less on Northern NGOs and, as a result, form a solid base for effective service delivery in local communities.

Public Assessment of NGOs

Although studies of public perceptions of NGOs are few, the last decade has witnessed increasing interest in the activities of NGOs in Cameroon. Evidence from the data suggests that a majority of the respondents first obtained information about NGOs from the mass media (74 per cent) while 26 per cent of the respondents first had information about NGOs from inter-personal sources. The following mass media sources were singled out: radio (57.7 per cent), television (7.3 per cent), newspapers (five per cent), magazines (2.3 per cent), and the Internet (1.7 per cent). The respondents also reported that they obtained information about NGOs from inter-personal sources: friends (11 per cent), NGO leaders (7 per cent) and family relatives (6 per cent).

The findings reveal that the mass media still plays a major role in informing people about the work of NGOs. However, there exists evidence to suggest that inter-personal channels are more persuasive than mass media appeals. In other words, the diffusion concept is far more fruitful in explaining how the mass media can exploit the powers of inter-personal channels to get the message across.

Also, greater credibility and understanding are two of the obvious reasons for the persuasiveness of inter-personal sources of communication. From these observations, it is therefore obvious that NGO leaders must be able to exploit both the news media and inter-personal channels in their development-oriented activities.

With the passing of the law on freedom of association, public expectations around the activities of NGOs were high. These expectations were re-echoed in the survey data: 17 per cent of the respondents expected NGOs to concentrate on increasing economic activity and reducing employment. Others hoped for advances in the development of rural areas (12.3 per cent), the improvement of the agricultural, educational and health sectors (9.7 per cent), assistance to government in the dispatch of duties (6.7 per cent), the provision of humanitarian services (5.3 per cent), and the reduction of corruption (4.7 per cent).

From the plethora of expectations regarding NGOs in Cameroon, it is clear that the public still anticipate that NGOs will prove to be effective partners in development. But the activities of NGOs are not meeting the needs and aspirations of the people who are looking up to them with optimism. The public expects the NGOs to focus more on providing much-needed employment. This expectation comes against a backdrop of high unemployment levels of around 30 per cent of the active labour force. When the respondents were asked to make an assessment of the focus of NGOs in Cameroon, 41.7 per cent reported that the NGOs focus on health activities, 37.7 per cent on agriculture, environmental sustainability and forestry (29 perc ent), education (24 per cent), social activities (21.7 per cent), economic activities (19 per cent), cultural activities (16.3 per cent), sport (8.3 per cent), religion (6.7 per cent) and politics (6 per cent).

The findings do suggest that NGOs in principle at least deal with real life issues because most focus on health activities, especially the fight against HIV/ AIDS, human rights, child labour and women's emancipation. There are other NGOs, which assist rural women in the agricultural and health sectors by providing farm tools and health care facilities for rural development.

From the survey data, other priority areas of focus are agriculture, which so far is the mainstay of the Cameroon economy with over 70 per cent of the labour force found in this sector. Also, the respondents singled out education as another major area of focus of NGOs. As a developing country, Cameroon still needs to invest much in the educational sector for training and capacity building. The recent trends towards professionalisation, technical education and vocational training will be helpful in moulding an industrial society in the not too distant future.

Current Cynicism

According to the survey data, public expectations of NGOs as reliable alternatives to public sector development have dropped considerably over the last decade. The optimism that welcomed the advent of national NGOs in Cameroon has turned to pessimism, as the average NGO is not meeting the needs and aspirations of the grassroots communities. The following reported reasons were advanced as to why NGOs are no longer considered as alternatives to development. Self interest, lack of funds, their existence as briefcase organisations, mismanagement of resources, corruption, ineffective leadership and government interference were among the reasons advanced for the ineptness of national NGOs in Cameroon.

NGO quality and capacity is generally weak across Cameroon. Most of the NGOs are out for self-aggrandisement. Even those that have clearly specified objectives do not possess the necessary funds for effective operation. Planning and coordination is inadequate at all levels because of the ineffective leadership. Mismanagement of resources becomes a problem among national NGOs because they lack planning capacity. Therefore, donors do not engage in coordinated planning and NGOs operate according to the whims and caprices of the donors. For example, NGOs will rarely identify areas of intervention in grassroots communities which are not in line with the specific needs of the donor agencies. Funds are therefore often misdirected and poorly managed.

Corruption among national NGOs is at its peak. Huge sums of money destined for community-based development projects are siphoned off into private coffers. The population is largely ignorant of NGOs which claim to carry out activities in their area. Some NGO leaders have reported that government is hindering the implementation of most of their projects due to the fact that some of them have not yet obtained the required documents to enable them to carry out their development projects. This explains why most NGOs operate as 'briefcase' institutions and to a certain extent in a clandestine fashion.

As mentioned earlier, the rising hopes and aspirations of the early 1990s were gradually replaced by cynicism as national NGOs sprang up in every nook and cranny causing a cacophony of development-oriented activities. It is against this backdrop that the government promulgated Law No. 99/014 of 21 December, 1999, reorganising and redefining NGOs in Cameroon. According to article 2 (1) of that law, an NGO is any local or foreign association which has been authorised under the law in force, and accepted by the administration to participate in the execution of development activities in the general interest of the local population.

Another noticeable trend is the fact that both government and NGOs are competing for funding from the same sources. Consequently, there is mutual suspicion and tension between government and NGOs. This contributes to the current cynicism around the role of NGOs in development.

The 1999 law exerts excessive control on NGO activities by the Ministry of Territorial Administration and Decentralisation in terms of structure and operation. The administration must be informed about the composition of the NGO hierarchy and any changes within this structure. This new law questions the much-trumpeted talk of NGOs as 'private organisations', as this government interference is viewed as having a negative impact on NGO activities (Owona 2004).

One of the major critiques among Cameroon development watchers on the failure of national NGOs to meet the needs and aspirations of the local population is the absence of an enabling environment in the legal, economic and political aspects of national life. From the legal framework, it was not until 1999 that a law was signed putting an end to the anarchy created by several hundreds of loosely knit associations posing as NGOs (see Temngah in the present volume).

This legal environment came with strings attached, as it introduced a lot of government control over the composition and activities of NGOs.

From the economic standpoint, there is the absence of a resource base (human, material and financial), which national NGOs could use to carry out mainstream rural development projects. Development in Cameroon has been tied to political leanings. Development activity is therefore heavily politicised (see also Yenshu in the present volume). Ndzie (2004) adds his voice to the cynicism that surrounds NGOs today in Cameroon when he notes that anyone who needs money, fame, varied sources of finance, funding and a high standard of living in Cameroon turns around and creates an NGO. This paints a picture of how NGOs have become sources of private wealth and funding.

In spite of the litany of public pronouncements commenting negatively on NGOs, the public seems very concerned about their activities, and still has not lost all hope that they can constitute alternatives to public sector development. However, most NGOs have veered off the path that led to their objectives. Little wonder thus that the public is making a clarion call on NGO leaders to be honest in the management of their funds, create partnerships with the government, and fight corruption etc.

Conclusions

While the above findings may not exactly capture the current state of affairs regarding NGOs as a whole, they nonetheless give some insight into their various areas of focus, the Cameroonian public perceptions, and their operation and management systems. There is evidence of mixed feelings and scepticism on the part of the respondents. In order to adjust and make fruitful contributions to the development process, it is important for NGO leaders, staff, members and stakeholders to be aware of what the Cameroonian public thinks about them.

NGO staff should consist of men and women with a real understanding of the problems faced by grassroots communities and who are committed to the alleviation of the problems they face. NGOs should budget for socio-economic, environmental and resource management activities, so as to be able to generate effective indicators for monitoring and evaluation, and to identify clearer objectives. Local beneficiaries of projects should be given adequate training by the staff of NGOs so that they will be better able to decide on the initiatives to be carried out, and so that the skills necessary for carrying out projects can be transferred to the local community. While social, political and economic changes continue to affect the development process in Cameroon, development remains a crucial issue that must be addressed at all costs. NGOs therefore have a vital role to play in the development process.

Further studies on the environment in which NGOs operate in Cameroon are needed to examine their successes and failures vis-à-vis the current democratic dispensation. Speculations are rife that the state is frustrating the efforts of NGOs in Cameroon. This is against a backdrop of the state not creating an enabling environment for their effective operation. However, it is useful to know that there is the need for a self-righting process in the way NGO activities are currently being carried out. The pace at which they are implementing the present development process is inevitably slow. Cameroonians are aware of the challenges. The solutions may not be found as quickly as the problems are acknowledged.

The question can legitimately be posed as to whether international NGOs can serve a liberating or recolonising purpose in Cameroon as new missionaries of development. For now, there is a delicate, thin, dividing line between international and local NGOs, determined by the basic philosophies of intervention fluctuating between direct and indirect approaches. The first phase of international NGO activity was direct and based on the argument of operational efficacy. The major setback to this approach was the fact that it was not adapted or responsive to the needs of local peoples. This led to a change to an indirect approach, which set out to build capacity for local NGOs who would in the long run take over from them. In this regard, international NGOs provided the training to local NGOs and operated through the latter by funding them on the grounds that the local partners were more conversant with local realities. The capacity-building and proxy approach are no longer tenable. International NGOs are no longer sub-letting their functions to the locals but are using the very argument to justify their continued presence in the country. The fear is being entertained that if local NGOs acquire the requisite capacity they will replace or displace international NGOs. This explains why the capacity-building mission is not serious or has no end in sight. In such a situation, there is surely going to be a long period of cohabitation, as international NGOs continue to maintain a posture of paternalism and retain niches in order to escape replacement by local partners or competitors. The image that presents itself is one of international NGOs striving to remain in business, because, after all, the NGO sector is a lucrative one that mobilises substantial funding and provides a sizeable amount of expatriate employment.

Notes

1. For a detailed analysis of the legal framework of civil society and social movements following these reforms see Temngah (in this volume).
2. This is equally the opinion of Herbert Endeley, Chairman of Cameroon Mountain Conservation Foundation (CAMCOF), a local NGO, who thinks that NGOs failed because retired civil servants who were responsible for failure through red tape became recycled as initiators and managers of the budding NGOs (*Eden* newspaper, September 2004).

References

Adelman, I., 1975, 'Development Economics: A Reassessment of Goals', *The American Review*, LXV.

African Civil Society Contact Directory (see all listings on Cameroon 1999-2003), www.kabissa.org or www.nivblodon.kabissa.org

Amin, Samir, 1994, 'The Issue of Democracy in the Contemporary Third World', in Ulf Himmelstrand et al., *African Perspectives on Development*, New York: St. Martin's Press.

Annis, Sheldon, 1987, 'Can Small Scale Development be a Large Scale Policy? The Case of Latin America', *World Development*, (Supplement, autumn).

Berg, Robert J., 1987, *Non-Governmental Organisations: New Force in Third World Development and Politics*, Michigan: Center for Advanced Study of International Development.

Bratton, Michael, 1988, 'Poverty, Organization and Policy: Towards a Voice of Africa's Rural Poor', (unpublished).

Brodhead, Tim, Brent Herbert-Copley, and Anne-Marie Lambert, 1988, *Bridges of Hope? Canadian Voluntary Agencies in the Third World*, Ottawa: The North-South Institute.

Brown L., David and David C. Korten, 1989, *The Role of Voluntary Organizations in Development*. Boston, MA: Institute for Development.

Brown, Michael, 1996, ed., *Non-Governmental Organizations and Natural Resources Management: Synthesis Assessment of Capacity-Building Issues in Africa*, New York: World Learning Inc., CARE, WWF.

Clark, John, 1991, *Democratizing Development*, London: Earthscan.

Cameron, Greg, 2001, 'Taking Stock of Pastoralist NGOs in Tanzania', *Review of African Political Economy*, No. 87.

Caroll, Thomas F., 1992, *Intermediary NGOs: The Supporting Link in Grassroots Development*. Hartford, Conn: Kumarian Press.

Cernea, Michael, 1988, 'Nongovermental Organizations and Local Development', World Bank Discussion Papers, no. 40. Washington DC: The World Bank.

Cousins, William, 1991, 'Operational Directive 14.7', Washington, DC: The World Bank.

Dissanayake, Wimal, 1981, 'Development and Communication: Four Approaches', (unpublished).

Douglas, James, 1987, 'Political Theories of Non-Profit Organizations', (unpublished).

Ebune, Joseph B, 2004, 'Contributions of Self-Help Associations to the Growth and Development of British Southern Cameroons, 1922-1962: A Historical Perspective', *Epasa Moto. A Bilingual Journal of Arts, Letters and the Humanities*, Vol. 2, No. 1.

FAO (Food and Agriculture Organization), 1994, 'FAO Collaboration with Asian NGOs for Participatory Rural Development: The Case of ANGOC', Rome: FAO.

Farrington, John, 1997, *Improving Agriculture/NGO Extension*, London: FAO.

Fonjong, Lotsmart, 2001, 'Fostering Women's Participation in Development through Non-governmental Efforts in Cameroon', *The Geographic Journal*, Vol. 167, No. 3, September.

Fowler, Alan, Piers Campbell and Brian Pratt, 1992, *Institutional Development and NGOs in Africa: Policy Perspectives for European Development Agencies*, Oxford: The International NGO Training and Research Centre (INTRAC).

Ginsburg, M., 1991, *Understanding Educational Reform in the Global Context*, New York: Garland Publishing.

Hearn, Julie, 2001, 'The "Uses and Abuses" of Civil society in Africa', *Review of African Political Economy*, No. 87.

Hansmann, Henry, 1987, *Economic Theories of Non-Profit Organizations*, Boulder, Col: Lynne Rienner Publishers.

Kabanda, Pherrys, 1996, 'The Role of NGOs in the Third World', Paper presented at the National Development Studies Week on behalf of the National Coordinator, Uganda National NGO Forum.

Kengo News, 1993, 'Kenya Energy and Environment Organizations', Vol. V, No. 3, July.

Mercer, Claire, 1999, 'Reconceptualising State-society Relations in Tanzania: Are NGOs Making a Difference?', *Area*, 31, 3.

Korten, D., 1989, *Getting to the 21st Century: Voluntary Action and the Global Agenda*, Connecticut: Kumarian Press.

Law No 90/052 of December 19th 1990.

Law No 90/056 of December 19th 1990.

Law No 99/014 of December 21st 1999.

Micou, Ann McKinstry, 1995, 'NGO Development Training in Southern Africa: Promoting South-South Linkages Through Information-Sharing, Vol. 1: Botswana, Lesotho, Namibia, Swaziland & Zimbabwe', New York: Institute of International Education: Southern African Information Exchange Working Paper, No. 29.

Mohan, Giles, 2002, 'The Disappointments of Civil Society: The Politics of NGO Intervention in Northern Ghana', *Political Geography*, 21.

Monga, C., 1995, 'Civil Society and Democratisation in Francophone Africa', *The Journal of Modern African Studies*, No. 33 (3).

Ndzie, Guy Pancrace, 2004, 'ONG et Business', *La Nouvelle Presse*, No. 129, Tuesday 6 January.

Neher, William, 2003, *International Communication: Concepts and Cases*, Ontario: Wadsworth.

Ngwa, George, 2002, 'Communication and Empowerment of the People', in Festus Eribo and Enoh Tanjong, eds., *Journalism and Mass Communication in Africa: Cameroon*, Washington DC: Lexington Books.

Nyamnjoh, Francis B., 1999, 'Media pluralism and civil society in emerging African democracies', in Luke Uche, ed., *Mass Communication, Democracy and Civil Society in Africa: International Perspectives*, Lagos: Smagh and Company, Nigeria Ltd.

Owona, Francois, 2004, 'ONGs: Splendeur et Misère', *La Nouvelle Presse*, No 129, Tuesday 6 January.

Paul, S. and A. Israel, 1991, 'Non-Governmental Organizations and the World Bank: Cooperation for Development', Washington: The World Bank.

Ramanathan, K.V., 1982, *Management Control in Non-Profit Organizations*, New York: Wiley.

Republic of Cameroon, 1990, *Cameroon: Rights and Freedoms. Collection of Recent Texts*, Yaoundé: Edition SOPECAM.

Robbins, Richard, 2002, *Global Problems and the Culture of Capitalism* Second Edition, Boston: Allyn and Bacon.

Robinson, J. P., 1971, 'Toward Defining the Functions of Television', in Robinstein, E.A., Cumstock, G.A, and Murray, J. P., eds., *Television and Social Behaviour*, Washington, DC: Government Printing House.

Rose-Ackerman, Susan, ed., 1980, *The Economies of Non-Profit Institutions: Studies in Structure and Policy*, Yale Studies on Non-Profit Organizations, New York: Oxford University Press.

Rostow, Walt, 1960, *Stages of Economic Growth: A Non-Communist Manifesto*, New York: Oxford University Press.

Schiller, Herbert and Kaarle Nordenstreng, 1975, *Globalization and Business Practice*, London: Macmillan Press.

Seers, Dudley, 1969, *Development in Perspective: An Asian Study of Development*. London: Heinemann Press.

Tanjong, Enoh and Ada Ndeso-Atanga, 1995, *Networking in Natural Resource User Organizations in Cameroon: Field Experiences*, Yaoundé: AMA.

Tanjong, Enoh, 1999, 'The Politics of Democratic and Media Pluralism, Press Freedom and Civil Society in West and Central Africa', in Luke Uche, ed., *Mass Communication, Democracy and Civil Society in Africa: International Perspectives*, Lagos: Smagh and Company, Nigeria Ltd.

Tostensen, A., Inge Tvedten and Mariken Vaa, 'The Urban Crisis, Governance and Associational Life', Tostensen, A., Inge Tvedten and Mariken Vaa, eds., 2001, *Associational Life in African Cities. Popular Responses to the Urban Crisis*, Uppsala: Nordic Africa Institute.

United Nations Development Programme (UNDP), 2003, *Human Development Report*, New York: Oxford University Press.

Weiss, W., 1969, 'Effects of Mass Media of Communication', in Lindsley, G. and Azonsan, E., eds., *Handbook of Social Psychology*, Vol. 5, 2nd Edition, Addison: Wesley Publications.

Weisbrod, B. A., 1988, *The Non-Profit Economy*, Cambridge, MA: Harvard University Press.

Wellard, K. and James Copestake, eds., 1993, *Nongovernmental Organizations and the State: Africa*, London: Routledge & Keagan Paul.

Wignaraja, Ponna, 1976, 'A New Strategy for Development' (unpublished), www.webartery.com/prime/ngostudy.htm-101k

www.worldbank.com/premnote/ngo

9

NGO Involvement in Environmental Protection in the North West Province

Ndenecho Emmanuel Neba

Introduction and Objectives of the Study

The past decade has seen a steady growth in non-governmental organisations at the local, national and international level – along with an increasing interest from both donors and the NGOs themselves in seeking ways to make NGOs more effective. The profile of NGOs has grown among policy-makers, activists, and researchers in both the North and the South. NGOs now feature prominently in discussions on service delivery, advocacy and lobbying, social movements, philanthropy and charity giving, building 'civil society', and social entrepreneurship. This rich diversity of NGOs in both the North and the South is widely celebrated, with a growing number of publications devoted to them. Although there are voices challenging the claims which are made for NGOs, these are generally restricted to the context of humanitarian assistance in emergency situations, and NGOs continue to be the 'flavour of the month' in development circles.

There has been a general and rising interest among countries on environmental issues, most especially environmental protection, since the United Nations Conference on Environment and Development (UNCED) or the Earth Summit, held in Rio de Janeiro, Brazil in June 1992. In principle, this conference expected countries to recognise the complementary relationship that exists between development and the environment. The challenge of environmental protection was made formal by the Cameroon government's recognition of NGOs as partners in natural resource management and rural development. The challenge is that NGOs must perform efficiently in realising local, regional, national and global environment plans, which means they must have adequate capacity and resources. This requires an appraisal of the financial means and sustainability of NGOs, of cooperation between NGOs and GOs (Governmental Organisations) in tackling natural resource management, with the focus on the grassroots resource users, the degree of participation (empowerment), and the global dimension of the activities of NGOs. This chapter seeks to identify NGOs involved in development work and to appraise their input in the environmental protection process in order to establish a base for cooperation between local and international NGOs and to elaborate strategies in achieving sustainability through local resource mobilisation, organisational strengthening and the institutional development of civil society.

Methodology

Data for this study were obtained from the SNV-sponsored project reported by Marion Wiendels (1994), and a study by Ndenecho (2003). Information was gathered from interviews with one representative of each relevant organisation. To be of interest in the framework of this research, an NGO had to meet the following five criteria (Wiendels 1994):

- The organisation is active in the region at the moment, which implies that co-workers are either established on a permanent base, or are playing an important role in enabling organisations which are physically present to execute their activities. To be included an organisation has to have at least one office based in Cameroon.
- The organisation is not a base organisation. A base organisation is defined here as an organisation existing due to the initiative of the target population.
- The organisation is either in direct contact with the target population, or works directly with organisations which are in direct contact with them.
- The organisation aims at the development of the area.
- The organisation is apolitical and non-commercial.

These criteria apply to governmental and non-governmental organisations. An inventory of organisations operating in the domain of rural development and environmental protection in the region was made using an established list of NGOs, a telephone directory, and knowledge of organisations which are active in the region acquired through interviews and field surveys. The organisations are analysed on the basis of size of means, ratio of means, continuity, cooperation, level of integration, objectives, degree of participation, process approach, and international dimension.

The study set out to achieve the following research outputs:

- An inventory of organisations operating in environmental protection and rural development in the region.
- The geographical location of NGOs in the region.
- The degree of spatial concentration of NGOs in the region.
- Typology and roles of NGOs.
- Graphic presentations of NGOs based on the parameters studied.
- Weaknesses and limitations of NGOs.

- The scope for achieving greater efficiency in sustainable environmental management and protection.

A special case was made of the involvement of an international NGO (Helvetas) in watershed management in collaboration with local stakeholders and beneficiaries at local level. This refers to the case of the Tubah watershed protection project.

Characteristics of NGOs

Typology of Development Organisations

The field survey established the following typology of development organisations involved in environmental protection issues. This typology will enable us to evaluate the contribution of NGOs.

- Membership Organisations (MO): These are farmers' organisations that are involved in agricultural development and the marketing of produce. The main MOs are the Cameroon Cooperative Credit Union League (CAMCCUL) and North West Cooperative Association (NWCA). MOs mainly serve the interests of their members. The problem with some of these organisations is that for a long time they were organised by government officials rather than by farmers themselves. They were supposed to work for farmers but also implement government policies.

- Donor organisations targeting communities (DOs): These organisations are active in poverty reduction programmes at the grassroots. They started by giving aid to people in distress. Unfortunately, most of these have been more successful in instilling a dependency attitude among local people by leading them to expect free inputs, tools and credit at favourable rates rather than in emphasising the importance of improving managerial capacity. The main DOs include the North West Development Authority (MIDENO) and church organisations. In order to raise finance, they sometimes try to create the image that their target group is in a very difficult situation that will not improve without external support. Unfortunately, their target groups include poor people in complex, diverse and risk-prone environments where the agro-ecological and socio-economic situation is very difficult. They evidently lack the capacity to handle environmental and resource management issues under these circumstances. Most of them are isolated while others may assign projects to other organisations.

- Community based organisations (CBOs): These are very active in the region and include Farmer Groups, Forest User Groups, Bee Keeping Groups, Tree Nursery Groups, Common Initiative Groups, Villages Development Associations, and socio-cultural and development organisations involved in rural road construction projects, rural water supply schemes, community forest management, watershed protection, provision of basic village socio-economic infrastructure, and the rational use of village natural resources. Unfortunately, they face the same limitations experienced by grassroots support organisations because they are championed by local and external elites.

• International NGOs and Public Service Organisations: These are international support organisations. They help membership organisations, CBOs, and local NGOs in developing countries through financial and material support, training and expertise. These are based in the developed countries but are represented in the study area to provide training and expertise. They also act as a channel to transfer donor assistance to local NGOs, CBOs and membership organisations. Those active in the region include AFVP (Association Française de Volontaires du Progrès), Bird Life International, Food and Agricultural Organisation, Swiss Association for Development and Cooperation (Helvetas), German Agency for Technical Cooperation (GTZ), Heifer Project International (HPI), INADES (Institut Africain pour le Développement Economique et Social), Netherlands Development Organisation (SNV), and Plan International. Although operating under different legal statuses these organisations have the common characteristic of possessing high technical capacity and the financial means to implement their policies.

• Local NGOs: These are local organisations receiving direct funding from international and Northern NGOs in order to reinforce local civil society through the development of new partnerships. Several of these bodies proliferate in the study area as there has been an emergence of a new generation of local NGO 'contractors' since the 1990s.

Viability of NGOs

International NGOs have more financial resources than local NGOs, DOs and MOs. They promote a great deal of rhetoric about partnership and enhancing civil society as they channel the majority of their funds to local NGOs through semi-contractual arrangements for service delivery projects. There is an exaggerated emphasis on specific sectors and services to the detriment of a wider strategy of funding long-term goals, which cut across sectors, such as poverty reduction and strengthening civil society. Unfortunately, these funds are channelled to a very small number of local NGOs, thus several local NGOs present misshapen organisational profiles. The lack of financial means threatens continuity, leads to poor cooperation among the NGO community, and to a poor integrative approach, participation, and process approach by several local NGOs. The local NGOs have no international dimension.

Membership organisations such as CAMCCUL, NWCA and Bamenda Vegetable Cooperation (BVC) have considerable means at their disposal and reach many people in their areas of operation. CAMCCUL is limited only to the rural finance sector and isolated in its organisational network. However, its influence in rural savings and credit generation is enormous. NWCA used to have a large impact in the development process for it had the monopoly in the coffee trade during the period when world prices were high. At the moment, NWCA faces severe problems in meeting its obligations. The impact of NWCA has decreased considerably. Local NGOs are limited in their sphere of activities as a consequence of their weak organisational profiles. In contrast, international NGOs are very active in the area as a result of their high organisational profiles. Membership organisations except BVC cover the entire region. The BVC is based mainly in Mezam. The spatial influence of international NGOs is a result of their policy of support to local NGOs through financial assistance and the adoption of local NGOs and CBOs as co-workers.

The Tubah Watershed Project: A Model of Collaboration Between NGOs and Local Communities

For a period of thirty years, the international NGO, Helvetas (Swiss Association for Development and Cooperation), together with the Community Development Department (CDD) in the Ministry of Agriculture and a few local NGOs have constructed about 350 rural water schemes and 150 water points in the North West, South West and West Provinces, serving about 1.2 million rural people. The CDD and NGOs, as partners of Helvetas at execution level, design, plan, implement and monitor the performance of village-based water maintenance committees, which operate and maintain the schemes. Helvetas and its partners started a comprehensive process of information and sensitisation on improved water resource management for water maintenance committees, traditional councils and regional authorities. The villages are the project stakeholders and through their water committees (WMC) and caretakers mobilise local people to contribute in kind and cash for construction, maintenance and operation. Bigger villages require river intakes and water treatment for which sedimentation tanks and slow sand filters (SSF) are designed and constructed. Water intakes are classified as land of common interest and are controlled by local authorities like village and traditional councils. However, with increased agricultural activity in most intake areas and watersheds, water contamination in small streams becomes serious. The Tubah Project constitutes thirty years of experience in watershed protection by Helvetas. Some ten years after initiation, the benefits are already being harvested from this project.

The physical and economic benefits which will result from watershed improvement or improvement in land use practices include such matters as forest conservation, forest management, afforestation, grazing controls, agroforestry and soil conservation. The NGO strategies for watershed management derived from this study include:

• Development of local institutions: Formation of farmers' groups and federations in the programme areas as well as the formation of project and programme committees and training.

- Active participation by the target population: There is a clear definition of roles of various population groups, a participatory approach for planning decision-making, sharing responsibilities, promotion and communication. This also applies to equal access to benefits for all programme participants and active participation of all in the learning process. Women are empowered in land use management and production. This is accompanied by the development of self-help potential for the target population (formation of common initiative groups and creation of alternative income generation).

- Conflict management: Forums and mechanisms of negotiation have been developed. This requires the setting up of a comprehensive and permanent monitoring system to allow proper control of activities in target areas.

The role of NGOs, local communities and civil society is crucial in achieving sustainable watershed resource management. The strengths of NGOs in this direction are impressive but can be exaggerated. Local institution building has proved difficult and it is common for projects to fail when NGO staff have departed. A key issue is how to build on local successes in providing services nationally. The danger is that Northern NGOs will be used even more actively as channels for donor assistance, which would threaten to suffocate the flexibility, independence, and low bureaucratic costs that have made local NGOs effective. Helvetas is working alongside the government to develop the capacity of national NGOs. Training, technical assistance, networking to disseminate technical information among local NGOs and other activities are being pursued. However, it is difficult for local NGOs to know when financial support will be extended to them by northern NGOs like Helvetas. If it is too early, it may weaken the self-help motivation. If it is too late, it frustrates attempts to move ahead with schemes for water supply.

The issue of sustainability and independence of local NGOs therefore needs to be addressed. Partnership and participation are as important in the relationship between NGOs and the beneficiary communities as they are in those between the NGOs and the government. If projects are to be sustainable and yield long-term benefits, communities must be more explicitly involved in design and implementation and in defining their own contribution.

Most local NGOs operating in the region have sometimes unwittingly incorporated old-style management ideas such as strategic planning – now dismissed by development workers as having failed to live up to its promise when it was developed in the 1970s – rather than adopting the most up-to-date ideas. The most up-to-date mainstream management theory and practice is now concerned that NGOs themselves should incorporate flexible work teams, reduce hierarchies, and build on organisational values and cultures. This should improve their effectiveness and generate new ideas and approaches – ones rooted in different cultures and values, and in a genuinely developmental approach to overcoming obstacles to positive social change.

Discussion and Conclusion

The community of NGOs and civil society organisations is now far larger than it was a decade ago, as it is increasingly being felt that they have more advantages than disadvantages compared with government agencies which perform similar tasks. Donors and national governments therefore direct an increasing part of their funds to NGOs, which increases the likelihood of dependency on external funding. It also poses the risk of being more responsive to donors' agendas than to the need of their constituencies.

The issue of the long-term sustainability of NGOs is real. There is the fear that agencies funding NGOs in resource poor societies, where there is no evidence of medium-term capacity to absorb these costs, are simply reinforcing what some have termed the 'global soup kitchen', or the globalisation of social welfare. There is therefore a need to focus attention towards the goal of sustainability through local resource mobilisation. As of now there is no evidence in the country of such resource mobilisation through tax-based state funding, local philanthropic action or income-generating schemes. Under such circumstances sustainability is simply a myth. On the contrary, local NGOs are noted for their dependence on diplomatic services and perpetual support from international donor organisations.

With globalisation and international trade, NGOs have become increasingly influential in world affairs and are consulted by both governments and international organisations. These organisations exert a significant impact on the social, political and economic life of their target populations. However, there is the question of sustainability as local NGOs in Cameroon derive most of their inspiration and resources from foreign NGOs. In this way both foreign and local NGOs serve as agents of re-colonisation rather than as liberators, as they pose as new missionaries.

NGOs encounter a number of problems. Some local NGOs that gain access to official funds through related government projects geared at rural poverty alleviation report that they encounter bureaucratic bottle-necks in their functioning, which in turn may create room for masquerading to gain access to official funds. The majority of local organisations suffer from a weak organisational network. There is a need to appreciate the issues surrounding capacity building beyond technical and sectoral aims. Capacity building must contribute to the long-term organisational strengthening, or the institutional development, of civil society as a whole.

Local NGOs also suffer from management problems. NGO leaders and staff are sometimes reluctant to think about organisational questions because it might interfere with their primary task of using almost all funds for working with poor people rather than spending money on administrative questions. A second set of problems revolves around the view that many NGOs are established by people searching for alternatives to mainstream thinking and there is sometimes the feeling that management and administration, with its association with the business and the public sectors, is something NGOs could do without. Some NGOs have experienced rapid growth and change. Organisations which started out as small, informal structures in which management issues could be dealt with on an ad hoc, informal basis may grow in size and develop more complex, multi-dimensional programmes, and suddenly find that they need new ideas, systems and procedures to cope. Finally, as local NGOs have grown closer to official donors they have been required to develop new systems of accountability and their effectiveness has been questioned and challenged. This has led to the feeling that some of the impetus for the new interest in NGO management has come from the North, and has taken the form of an imposed marginalisation rather than being part of a local NGO's own agenda.

As a result of the above factors, there is the need for NGOs to confront the issue of their sustainability and to elaborate new management models.

References

Acho-Chi, C. and Ndenecho, E. N., 1994, 'Rural Development Survey of West Cameroon: North West Region Consultative Study for the Netherlands Development Association (SNV)', Yaoundé: SNV.

Ndenecho, E. N., 2003, 'A Landscape Ecological Study of the Bamenda Highlands', Unpublished Ph.D. Thesis, University of Buea.

Ndenecho, E. N., 2000, 'Appraisal of NGO Intervention in Natural Resource Management', Tubah Upland Watershed, Helvetas Sponsored NRM Formative Evaluation, 10-17 January 2000, Bamenda: Helvetas.

Tah, H. and Zimmermann, T., 1994, 'Report on the Evaluation Meeting of the Bambui Watershed Project', Bamenda: Helvetas.

Wiendels, M., 1993, 'Region North West/West: Institutional Infrastructure', Yaoundé: SNV.

Zimmermann, T., 1994, 'Project Proposal for the Conservation of the Bambui Watershed', Bamenda: Helvetas.

Zimmermann, T., 1994, 'Project Proposal for Rehabilitation of Bambili, RCA Bambili, IRZ Bambui Watershed Project', Bamenda: Helvetas.

Zimmermann, T., 1994, 'An Introduction to Watershed Management for Intake Areas of Rural Water Supplies in Cameroon', in Yebit, G. et al., Proceedings of agroforestry harmonization workshop, 4-7 May 1994, organised by RCA Bambili, USAID, GTZ, Helvetas.

Zimmermann, T., 1995, 'Project Proposal for Guzang Watershed', Bamenda: Helvetas.

Zimmermann, T., 1995, 'Project Proposal for Mbiame Watershed', Bamenda: Helvetas.

Zimmermann, T., 1996, 'Watershed Resource Management in the Western Highlands', Bamenda: Helvetas.

V

State–Civil Society Relations

10

Political Leadership, State–Civil Society Relations and the Search for Development Alternatives

John W. Forje

Introduction

At the dawn of a new millennium and descending from the hills of the lost decades for socio-economic transformation, all significant actors in the development process have converged on a new agenda – the role of civil society as a serious partner in the transformation of the society. Developing countries, Africa in general and Cameroon in particular, continue to struggle to identify developmental options, implement feasible growth strategies, and overcome persistent poverty and domestic social inequality. Industrialised countries, in turn, are beginning to realise that current consumption patterns are a liability in maintaining basic domestic standards of social equity, social security, and human development. Internationally, there is an increasing lack of control over future market directions, global trade, the capacity of countries and regions to sustain achieved levels of economic growth, and the rapid social impact of science and information technologies. That corruption, poor governance and underdevelopment combine to wreck Cameroon, is self-evident.

The general atmosphere that pervades today's Cameroon is that of uncertainty and misery. Pessimism, disappointment and total despair now take the place of the euphoria of the immediate post-independent and reunification era. The problem facing the continent is 'man-made' and requires concrete solutions from within and outside Africa. Many states have literally collapsed. More are daily being packaged for destruction, Cameroon included, because of its inertia and the attitude of recycling the political class. Cameroon now presents the gloomy picture of a corrupt nation that stands aloof from the problems of the continent. In short, it is an absentee country as far as African issues are concerned. This development raises the question: What is the way out? Very germane in today's Cameroon is the state of the devaluation of human beings. Let us start by recognising the present crisis in Cameroon for what it is: a crisis of leadership and development. Let me also grant that because it is a crisis of leadership and development, the problem is necessarily multi-dimensional. It is therefore political as well as economic. It is equally socio-cultural as well as moral. While it is also a product of Cameroon's chequered history, the contemporary Cameroonian environment largely shapes its present manifestations, globally and locally. To attribute the problems to external causes alone is to shy away from the problems. Rising frustration and despair have gripped the people and pushed them into a perpetual state of coma and inaction – a veritable state of 'inertia'.[1] Underneath that 'inertia' is a burning desire for 'greater achievements or ambition'[2] embedded in every Cameroonian. How to convert rising frustration into a realised ambition is the question. An authentic Cameroon 'glasnost and Perestroika' is needed to give the required dynamism and sense of direction for the emergence of a new society.

Cameroon stands the risk of disintegrating. The present ethnic patronage-dependent government-oriented relationship holds the country to ransom. Some ethnic groups have taken advantage of the existing state system to lord over other groups. This hostage taking or hijacking attitude bleeds the country dry. These developments not only undermine the pre-existing cultural models but also use them in a competitive divide and rule governance framework, which entrenches exclusion based on the conflict of ethnic identities. Of course, conflicts did exist in the pre-colonial setting, but the models used to resolve them were largely successful. The pre-colonial cultural institutions had a better record in managing cultural diversity and fostering nationhood when compared to existing governance models. Pre-colonial cultural institutions and patterns tended to favour inclusion as opposed to exclusion. Elements of exclusion were counterbalanced by elements of inclusion in which the individual always felt connected to a wider community. This is not the case today. Pre-existing indigenous processes and practices for creating unity and harmony among groups have been replaced by the centralised authoritarian and militaristic rule of the post-colonial state, whose public policy framework emphasises division and exclusion.

Independence was intended to provide an opportunity for a new governance form, to reverse whatever exclusionary public policy framework of the colonial state, and to make it more attuned to the cultural patterns of the new integrated nation; but that has proved elusive as ethnic hegemony has hijacked state institutions and confiscated state property as personal goods. So bad is the situation that ethnic hegemony has desecrated civic freedoms, rights and other instruments and today these fundamental tenets of democracy remain cosmetic. The result is that Cameroon has a constitution without constitutionalism and elections without democracy. The struggle among the various ethnic groups and sects over power, elections, government services and development opportunities, has further entrenched the politics of exclusion that greatly weakens the state internally and externally.

To compete in an increasingly knowledge-based interconnected world economy, Cameroon must improve its governance system, international competitiveness, adapt to rapid technological change and accommodate its production system to both external and domestic demands. It is a challenging process which the state cannot handle alone. Comprehensive and concerted partnership and participation are required from other key stake holders, civil society and the private sector. Instead, social safety nets are weakened, and social-sector reforms have been insufficient to strengthen these systems, due to the hegemonic attitude of the ruling class. The outcome is that available resources have been shifted away from social programmes and responsibility for the social well-being of the people is transferred from the state to the private accounts or to private sectors controlled and owned by the ruling elites, and profits are not ploughed back to address pertinent problems of the suffering majority. The effect of these changes is that greater responsibility for survival is placed on the shoulders of the poor and the communities in which they participate.

The holy (or is it unholy?) marriage between the state, ruling elite and some segments of the civil society in the early part of the post-independence era ironically took away the inalienable rights of the custodians of power in making choices on issues that best enhanced and harnessed their potential for mapping the proper road to the sustainable development. The alienation of radical segments of civil society saw the start of 'things falling apart'. There is now a new re-awakening and re-linking between state and civil society in addressing the needs of the people. The search for development alternatives assumes a central place in the emerging agenda of Cameroon in the twenty-first century.

In this framework, the challenges for social development and poverty reduction are seen as those of the availability rather than the redistribution of resources. Policy reforms are required and expected to maximize the use of resource - 'doing more with less'. The overarching issue of cultural orientation still needs to be addressed. The character of the new social ethos that should guide reforms must be geared towards a human-oriented development approach. This is an ethos that is increasingly determined by cultural values. Therefore, policy changes at the macro- and micro-levels ought to be promoted as good and desirable with one spirit directing the approach - 'human-oriented, human-faced' - and the people making the decisions in the process. Development so conceived is not to be taken as a synonym for economic growth although sometimes the line of symmetry here could be rather thin. Current development efforts could result in a qualitative increase or decrease in certain indicators, in inequality among the people, more or less marginalisation, or more democratic or authoritarian political regimes. Viewed this way, one point becomes paramount which is that development cannot 'be achieved by proxy' (Osia 1987:37). It is a process in which the people pursue objectives set by themselves and in their own interest and with their own resources (cf. Aragon's [1995] concept of autonomy). It is a tall order; and calls for astute leadership backed by positive responses from civil society and the private sector without, of course, excluding the role of the international community.

Making choices by the people implies a search for development alternatives for the common good. More than half a century of independence, of state intervention through a 'top-down' development approach have failed to meet the basic human needs of the people. Rising expectations only converged on destructive frustration, alienation, apathy, abject poverty and despair. In a way, inappropriate independence and failed policies ushered in affluence only for a few. Neo-colonialism replaced nationalism, while patronage, ethnicity, corruption, and clientelism overtook unity, nationalism, coherence, social justice, and inclusion. In the same vein, it also destroyed a national sense of belonging. Development cannot be sustainable when people feel they are strangers in their own country, and when the state adopts a discriminatory, victimising and punitive approach.

Civil society and the 'bottom-up' approach were removed from development, planning, formulation, implementation and execution of socio-economic related transformation as far back as the period of central state-driven planning of the three development decades (1960-1990). The majority of the people seem worse off today than before independence largely due to the politics of exclusion, social injustice, the absence of the rule of law, and divide and rule tactics that lead to the inappropriate utilisation of human and natural resource potentials. Of course, pockets of development have been achieved during the past four decades of independence although more could have been done if only state and radical civil society had not parted ways. The importance and role of civil society and the search for new development alternatives remain imperative for a country endowed with human and natural resources potential but with the vast majority of the population living in squalor and abject poverty. The country can only claim the twenty-first century when added value is given to its human and natural resources. In order to be part of the evolution under the canopy of information and communication technologies (ICTs) and the unstoppable forces of globalisation, the Cameroon state and people must rethink, reconstruct, and reconstitute the state and society as inalienable partners in development.

In short, a new development approach, one of inclusion – 'bottom-up' – involving all stakeholders can no longer be overlooked. The search and implementation of a new road map for sustainable development must not continue to be absent from the country. Many questions abound as to why development eludes Cameroon and its people. Apparently, it is evident that there is a failure of the conventional thinking and approaches so far adopted. Furthermore, those who pilot statecraft are totally detached from the predicament of the people, as government and other actors impose development, whether conceptualised as altruistic or exploitative. Knowledge of and links with recipients is often minimal. David Pitt (1976) indicates that the social distance between development planners and beneficiaries of development projects usually means that nothing is achieved.

What needs to be done to accelerate economic and technological growth and progress? To promote economic and social development and to reverse environmental degradation, crime, corruption, insecurity and other ills that have befallen the country, a new vision or road map needs to be articulated and aggregated. A new modus operandi for both the public and private sectors is needed to move the country forward. That road map must be constructed through the trinity of partnership, participation and responsibility sharing among the key players - state, civil society and the private sector.

Given the complexity of the cultural and strategic poles entangled with the issue in question, we should be realistic enough to admit that the problem requires a yet to be constructed political surgical theatre and a team of political surgeons yet to be trained to undertake the political operation in order to reconstruct the one and indivisible political landscape of Cameroon. Whether you adopt a Leviathan or Clausewitzian, a cultural or a strategic pole approach, the bottom line here is simply that of the 'politics of inclusion and exclusion'. Once people have been pushed to the margin, it is unlikely that any significant changes can result in terms of development. The moment now seems opportune. There is general consensus across a wide spectrum of opinion, institutions and scholars that development is essentially people-centred, 'the involvement and commitment to aspired living standards and not the amount of infrastructure that a society possesses' (Kiawi & Mfoulou 2002).

This article seeks to examine and address numerous questions related to the economic, political, technological and social transformation of society. The idea is to give renewed attention and focus to issues of 'inclusion, partnership, participation, responsibility and benefit sharing' in the development process. Thus, the focus of the study is also on policy formulation, implementation and evaluation. The aim is to shed some light on the failures and imbalances in government policy strategies, in its human capital resource development, and its social and development policies. State-civil society interaction is treated as vital to the creation of the necessary enabling environment for sustainable development and quality livelihood for the majority of the people.

Common Challenges for the State and Civil Society in Cameroon

With the transition from the colonial to post-colonial administration, social policy took on completely different functions and objectives. It became a means of legitimising the new regimes constructed by the African nationalist rulers of weak and fragmented post-colonial states. Two distinctive overlapping phases can be distinguished. The first is the early post-colonial period or the constructionist phase. The second is the crisis phase, which began in the mid-1970s and became evident and protracted in the decade of the 1980s. The 'constructionist' phase was one of consolidation and expansion of the neo-colonial accumulation model that characterised the development paths of many African political economies (Mbaya 1995). Coupled with this model was the legitimation strategy of the populist programmes of the nationalist movements that came to power after independence (Mkandawire 1995). Central to the legitimation strategy was a strong social policy tied to an essentially constructionist ideal of economic development, that is, building physical, social, and human infrastructures. This was also a period of 'constructing' major social programmes in education, housing, health, urban planning, and elaborate social subsidies, matched with the construction of new physical signs of nationhood – airports, five star hotels, expensive cars, elite residential estates, parliament buildings and government offices (Morales-Gomez 1999).

The policies and politics of 'indirect rule' (British Cameroons) and 'assimilation' (French Cameroons) respectively practised in the colonial entities piloted civil society in different directions. While civil society in Anglophone Cameroon has tended to play the role of participation in the manner of responsible partnership in the tradition of indirect rule (Temngah on trade unionism in this volume, Yenshu Vubo 1998, Chole 1991, Jinadu 1990, Mohammed 1991, Osei-Hwedie 1990), civil society in Francophone Cameroon has rather either acquiesced with the state or adopted a radical and often violent protest approach in the tradition of the Union Populations du Cameroun (UPC). Of recent, a most vocal civil society movement has arisen in the Anglophone territory and has been instrumental in advocating changes in the country. In all cases, it is the response to the state - whether colonial or post-colonial - that largely determines the emergence of these movements. In the one case the colonial regime's attitude led to improvement unions as in the British-administered territories, and in the other repressive French colonial policies led to a radical civil society. Judging from the first stage as earlier outlined, social policy and development were thus selective, discriminatory, and exclusionary, geared to protecting and advancing colonial interests (Patel 1992). The neglected majorities were forced to fend for themselves as there was a largely indifferent attitude towards grassroots initiatives. This brief journey through the evolution and development of civil society gives a bird's eye perspective of the 'actually existing' role of civil society in the context of Cameroon. It points in the direction and reality that Cameroon civil society, although sharing common characteristics with other countries, fails to operate in the same way as in the developed polities of Western Europe and North America.

One can advance the point that the existing leadership style in Africa encourages conflicts rather than bringing peace, development and national unity. The dividends of democracy do not exist. If there are pockets of democracy, they do not trickle down to the people who matter. The challenge of development facing the government comes from donor bodies and civil society organisations stressing the need to 'put people first' and to give development a 'human face' as a concrete and comprehensive road map for social development (Preston 1993, World Bank 1991, 1993 and 1996). There is a call to re-democratise and create a new and just society. However, that genuine call is not making the expected breakthrough to institutionalising democratic governance, due to a combination of factors.

Presently, social and human development inequalities remain untouched by the reform process, if any exists at all. The Cameroon government's 2005 budget with tax increases was not one geared towards development with a human face; rather, it was a policy approach that deepens poverty, social inequalities and intensifies class divisions. The poor are thrown further down the alleys of despair. It is difficult in this context to see how the government's aim to achieve social development objectives with more equity, effectiveness and efficiency can be achieved when the poor are further marginalised and excluded in the development process. It can be argued that with the transition from the colonial to post-colonial administration, development policy took on completely different functions and objectives. The same can be said of the coming into being of the monolithic party structure which legitimatised the regime constructed by Cameroon's leadership after independance.

From a broad and sustainable development perspective, policy reform must reflect a deeper shift that encompasses key actors especially civil society and the private productive sector, to help promote Cameroon's integration into the global economy (see Bonvin 1997:40). The collapse of civil society came with the formation or co-option of all political parties under the umbrella of the Cameroon National Union (CNU) in 1966, and intensified under the Cameroon People's Democratic Movement (CPDM) in 1984. This co-option shares some common trends. Firstly, the immediate objective was the forging of a nation-building project. Unfortunately, and seen from a long-term perspective, it had serious destructive effects on the economy, the social fabric and the nation's institutions. Secondly, the assessment of the available options to reform social policy systems under various forms of development strategy is, at best, constrained by financial factors, and is in most cases non-existent due to mismanagement. Thirdly, national wealth is still unequally distributed, and international development assistance, on which the country relies to implement human development programmes, is unlikely to increase. Government investment in social development is therefore unlikely to increase, particularly as the country is unable to meet its own share of the contract with the Bretton Woods financial conglomerates and other donor bodies. The return to political pluralism in the early 1990s has not ushered in the expected change.

Given the inter-related persistence of these trends, the need to examine the challenges posed by current policy is even more urgent. In light of the history of state-civil society intercourse since the return to political pluralism, Cameroon is not better placed to face the challenges of public policy reforms in the interest of the poor and forgotten majority. The 2005 budget with its more than a hundred per cent tax increase in many sectors, coupled with the fact that there has been no salary increase in the past twenty-three years as against a 70 per cent reduction in wages, constitutes a serious test case for state-civil society relations in Cameroon. The slogan 'great ambitions' constitutes therefore an anvil for serious confrontation (or is it acquiescence?) between state and civil society. By and large, these new tax increases further perpetuate, pervert and deepen the state of poverty and exclusion, and do not constitute poverty alleviation (as is claimed by the World Bank-inspired jargon). In short, the 'forgotten majority' was further forgotten and marginalised through poverty elevation strategies put in place following the budgetary plan of 2005. Government became too big, moving from forty-five to sixty-five ministries in that same year; axes are too high,[3] with dwindling social amenities and poor quality service delivery. It is glaringly contradictory that these increases are coming after the 11 October 2004 Presidential elections with the ensuing 3 November 2004 'Great Ambition' policy statement.

How is civil society going to act? No action by civil society consolidates the 'peace and stability' and the 'captiveness of civil society' thesis. On the other hand, reaction by civil society will entail exerting its independence and the 'role fulfilment' thesis as the custodian of power by popular will, which could lead to confrontation with the state - thereby dispelling the peace, stability and tranquillity thesis. Seen in either perspective, the nature, structure and functioning of the state in Cameroon is seriously put to the test. Can poverty be alleviated when policy measures are designed to hurt the poor most? What form of society is the state out to create? Changes in society that place people in a precarious mental and psychological balance plunging them into a situation of self-dissatisfaction, deprivation and disappointment, have put classical concepts of development into serious doubt. Hence the calls for an alternative development strategy that can best resolve the plethora of problems confronting the development path of Cameroon.

It is therefore imperative for Cameroon to strengthen its institutions and democracy in addition to promoting good governance. The performance of Cameroon in the process of democratisation has been mixed, at times dismal and marked by progress in some areas and failures in others. On the one hand, there has been some degree of shared norms of political trust, tolerance, willingness to compromise, and belief in democratic legitimacy. On the other, just the opposite makes it difficult for the country to bring itself together, thus failing in the process of transforming itself into a modern state. The democratisation process is derailed due to the impasse characterising the civil society and state relationship. Within the context of an 'autocratic regime', 'movement-government' and 'weak-state' regime forms, it is difficult to accelerate the democratisation process and to create an alternative development path. The absence of checks and balances breeds corruption which discourages investors' interest. This gives birth to an ailing economy and governance practices deeply threatened by the cancer of corruption. Government cannot win the fight against maldevelopment, corruption and poor quality service delivery without incorporating the services (participation, partnership and responsibility) of civil society and other key players.

A transformation that can only be realised through the interplay of the key actors in a spirit of partnership, participation, and responsibility must include equitable sharing of the wealth of the nation. It calls for democratic governance, accountability, transparency and a genuine reform of institutions and attitudes of the people. Not surprisingly, this provides plenty of scope for mounting criticism of statism, and such criticism has been readily forthcoming, assuming an almost ritualised character. The general point is worth restating in a slightly different way: most African states conform to the essentially coercive notion of power implied by the definition of a strong state vis-à-vis its people, but ironically, in the subtle meaning, they remain weak and collapsed states precisely for failing to address the real plight of the people. The state of complementary relations, participation and partnership between state and civil society does not exist to give the legitimacy and effectiveness much needed by the state for proper governance and the exercise of power.

Failure here could be traced to the multi-faceted role the state has taken, beginning from that of the 'monolithic state' that came into being immediately after independence, acquiring excessive 'strength', but a strength which was not able to be generalised across issue areas. The Cameroon state is not a unified organisation; some parts are stronger, others weaker. According to Skocpol (1985:17), 'one of the most important facts about the power of a state may be its unevenness across policy areas'. Government's effectiveness in letting people off the hook who embezzle state funds has not been matched in the area of sustainable development or even the domain of individual collective freedom. There is no equivalent in the state's capacity in unbalanced or selective discriminative development practices between the provinces. One can also point to sectoral evidence of exceptions to state strength and state weakness. The role of the ruling elite within the state and private sector takes centre stage.

The phenomenon of the foreign-funded civil society with its own political agenda different from that of the people places the country on a particular plane, where the kind of social contract between civil society and state does not genuinely exist to forge ahead. Operating under an autocratic state regime system, civil society is unable to play the input role it should in shaping public policy through critical, open and serious discourses between the state and the other key players of civil society.

Democratisation in Cameroon has brought with it debates over the very nature of that democracy. The nature of the state system dictates the pace and structure of the governance process. In this regard, civil society plays a key role in Cameroon's progress towards democratisation, unity and development. The active role and full participation of civil society is absolutely essential to the success of every progressive venture undertaken in the country. Reforming Cameroon's institutions is essential for balanced development that meets the basic needs of the people. What is fundamental is that government no longer sees itself as the sole supplier of social services. Given the new political dispensation that emerged in the 1990s, the option of incorporation and the search for partnership with the private sector and civil society remain vital in propelling the country into a modern state. It is only by breaking existing barriers that new hopes can be created.

The Need for Institutional Reforms

In a multitude of policy assessments African governments are classified as illegitimate, unable to implement policies, and unresponsive to the needs of their peoples. Reform is the best way out of the ongoing malaise. Reform should not only be directed to the government but should touch all components of society. Good governance is the key to institutional reforms and this should also impose demands on policy-makers in their exercise of power in the following respects:

- Creating an effective state possessing and exhibiting an enabling political, economic, legal and cultural environment that spurs economic growth and ensures equitable distribution.
- Ensuring the incorporation and representation of civil society and communities in policy articulation and aggregation processes, with the state accelerating and facilitating political and social interaction as well as fostering societal cohesion, stability, unity and a sense of belonging.
- Enabling a private sector to play an independent and productive role in the economic transformation of the country.
- Negotiating with an international community not hostile to the aspirations of the people but positively responding to the priority goals for economic transformation set by the government and people.
- Creating an enabling environment is vital for the economic take-off and political transformation of the country. The process requires a number of inter-related policy actions that should push forward the following developments:
- Creating accountable and transparent administrative structures;
- Ensuring the separation of powers between the branches of government, including the establishment and maintenance of law, order, and equal justice for all;
- Extending social amenities and infrastructure to the rural areas, protecting the poor and forgotten groups as well as including these vulnerable groups in the decision-making process;

- Drastic reforms within the structures and functions of political parties, civil society organisations and social movements;
- Paying greater attention to the development and utilisation of science, research and technology in the development process, bearing in mind the impact of knowledge-based development in today's world.

Cameroon is also in dire need of institutional reforms that should lead to inclusive democracy which secures people's rights and liberties. Reconstructing the state through reforming its institutions calls for inclusive democracy. Democracy presents the only form of political regime compatible with respecting all five categories of rights – political, social, economic, cultural and civil. Democratic governance presupposes the existence of effective domestic institutions. Currently, achieving good governance in Cameroon is an uphill task because of the complex hierarchical nature of the political power structures of government institutions, which is further hijacked by ethnic hegemonic forces, patronage and nepotism. There is a gross lack of political will in ensuring that representative democracy, with the people having the ultimate authority, takes hold in the country. The return to multiparty political pluralism has not reformed the legislative arm of government with the erstwhile monolithic party structure still enjoying hegemonic sway under the guise of political pluralism. Although 'good governance' remains an attractive concept, it equally implies value judgments that shift between communities and political parties. Achieving most of the precepts of good governance, such as increased public sector efficiency or reduced poverty implies a loss to some groups. For instance, increased efficiency in public service delivery implies curtailing the activities of rent seekers. On the other hand, poverty reduction calls for equitable income redistributive measures that obviously would hurt the interests of the affluent class.

Therefore, good governance and reformed state institutions cannot be attained in a vacuum. They have to be the product of a bargaining process between the various stakeholders in society – the state, civil society and the private sector – entrenched under the auspices of the 'will of the majority' as clearly, fairly and freely expressed via an electoral process based on pluralist political systems (see de Mello & Barenstein 2001).

At least two roles can be identified for civil society organisations in the democratic process of Cameroon, namely: (i) propagating democratic values, creating awareness and socialising their members in these values, as well as defending democratic principles and social justice in the society as a whole, as was demonstrated in the early 1990s with the return to multiparty politics; (ii) promoting democratic governance that entails serving as a buffer between the state and society through advocacy, monitoring and seeking to consolidate and strengthen good governance and transparency. For civil society to play this role requires access to information and the ability to disseminate it to its members and to overcome the handicap of total dependence on foreign sources of financial, organizational and other forms of support. To begin with, CSOs in Cameroon should endeavour to put their own houses in order by practising internal democracy, accountability and transparency (that is, developing a certain governance culture) as well as ensuring that their membership is as inclusive as possible so as to act as genuine instruments of national integration. They should take off from the basis of creating and strengthening mechanisms for peer group review. In short, they should monitor and police themselves. It is equally important for the state to learn to dialogue with civil society so that the different key actors can transform themselves into powerful agents of change that lead to and sustain democratic governance, accountability, transparency, inclusion and love for the country. The challenge to civil society, the state and other key actors in building and consolidating effective democratic governance is therefore enormous. Making the effort by taking the first steps in the right direction means a lot on the road towards effective democratic governance and building a better and bright and sustainable future for present and subsequent generations. Are Cameroonians prepared to begin on that long march?

Conclusion

Many factors need to be intertwined to create the necessary enabling environment for a country like Cameroon to be party to the globalised democratic world of the twenty-first century. As earlier indicated, government cannot alone create the playing field to ensure that inclusive democracy reigns supreme. Though government holds the key to opening up the gate to a level playing field, other actors must be ready to be participants and responsible players in the chess game of politics. As a way forward, it is imperative that a number of interrelated approaches be articulated and aggregated between the stakeholders.

Interrelated Approaches to Securing the Rights and Liberties of the People

Government credibility: The credibility and legitimacy of the government is primordial. Illegitimacy and low credibility of government exert high costs of implementation. The New Government of Achievement created on 8 December 2004 illustrates those high costs and relates to the inertia of incredibility that has gripped the governance form in Cameroon for the past decades. Failure is what characterises this regime form and this becomes self-fulfilling as resistance to new policies which force the government to constantly change cabinets yet with no concrete results being produced. Government needs to break away entirely from past practices to improve its reputation, to gain credibility and the confidence of the people.

Accountable Administrative Systems: Progress in the democratisation process, accountability, transparency and quality service delivery have been used by external donors as key elements of aid conditionality for financial support. The perception is that accountability and transparency increase public sector credibility. The government has been forced to enhance institutional accountability by increasing administrative transparency. The Cameroon Good Governance Report is a typical example. What are lacking are the implementation aspects of the report. The ongoing criss-crossing of newly appointed Prime Minister E. Inoni (8 December 2004) from one ministerial department to another to restore sanity, efficiency and productivity in the public service sector is part of the attempt to build confidence and credibility by the state. But accountability and transparency call for institutional, legal and efficient structures to ensure a functional and administrative input and output function. Public service output functions require credibility, sustainable procedures and verifiable standards.

Political and Economic Environment Minimising Risks: The political and economic environment should be such that it greatly minimises risk, acting as a bait for foreign investment as well as encouraging domestic mobilisation of scarce resources for long-term investment crucial for developmental purposes. There is a dire need for an effective regulatory framework to curtail the excess of monopolies or cartels. The behaviour of the political elite should be called to order in order to make the public sector more effective, efficient and appreciated by society. Therefore, quality services ad the judicious use of state property and institutions must be given priority. Low productivity and poor accountability within the public service sector is a deterrent to good governance. Government is required to adopt a more holistic measure of inclusion to restore confidence, credibility, accountability, transparency and quality service delivery.

Domestic Politics Encompassing Interest Groups: Bearing in mind that domestic politics encompasses most interest groups and that a functional political system is one that is open to contestation, the need for creating an enabling playing field is important. It is this enabling playing field that can show the path towards democracy, transparency and increased accountability. Although there have been strong external inputs for the country to walk on the path of pluralistic governance system, it is evident that sustainable political systems can be achieved only over a long period of learning on the job. But since government stands as a stumbling block in the process of creating a pluralistic system, it goes without saying that the learning process does not exist for the people to eventually cultivate a culture of pluralistic system of government. It is also a process that calls for the total engagement of civil society organisations, with their activities carried out unhindered, unrestricted, unfettered or unrestrained. Political participation by the multitude is required and must be encouraged by the key player - the state - and in partnership with others.

Governance as Part of the Political Process: Judging from recent debates, governance is part and parcel of the political process in which civil society is a major contributor. Generally, good governance cannot be sustained in a hostile environment characterised by the politics of exclusion. Much remains to be done in opening up the political space in Cameroon for the genuine introduction, articulation and aggregation of multiparty politics and for civil society and the press to operate unhindered. Only through an open door policy can the level of political accountability and transparency be elevated, so that political competition can prevail to give credibility and legitimacy to the system.

Notes

1. The idea of inertia was openly acknowledged by President Biya as being at the basis of poor governmental performance and stalled development.
2. The idea was launched by President Biya as a campaign slogan during the 2004 Presidential elections and to inaugurate his second seven-year term.
3. Fiscal stamp moved from 500 to 1000 CFA, tollgates from 500 to 1000 CFA; windscreen licenses from 15,000 to 25,000 and from 25,000 to 1000,000 CFA, and passports from 30,000 to 50,000 CFA.

References

Aragon, L. E., 1995, 'Building Regional Capacity for Sustainable Development in the Amazon', UFRJ Social Development, Challenges and Strategies, Rio de Janeiro: UFRJ/EICOS.

Bonvin, J., 1997, 'Globalisation and Linkages: Challenges for Development Policy', *Development*, 49, 2.

Chole, E., 1991, 'Introduction: What is Social Development?', in Mohammed, D., ed., *Social Development in Africa: Strategies, Policies and Programmes after the Lagos Plan*, London: Hans Zell, Publisher, ACARTSOD Monograph Series.

De Mello, L. and M. Barenstein, 2001, 'Fiscal Decentralization and Governance: A Cross-Country Analysis', IMF Working Paper WP/01/71.

Jinadu, G., 1990, 'Social Development in Africa: A Proposed Change Model', *Journal of Business and Social Studies*, Vol. 4, No. 1.

Kiawi, E. C. & Jean Mfoulou, 2002, 'Rethinking African Development: Social Science Perspectives', *CODESRIA Bulletin*, Nos. 1 & 2.

Mbaya, K., 1995, 'The Economic Crisis, Adjustment and Democracy in Africa', in Chole, E., and Ibrahim, J., eds., *Democratisation Processes in Africa*, Dakar: CODESRIA.

Mkandawire, T., 1995, 'Adjustment, Political Conditionality and Democratisation in Africa', in Chole, E. & Ibrahim, J., eds., *Democratisation Processes in Africa*, Dakar: CODESRIA.

Morales-Gomez, Daniel, ed., 1999, *Transnational Social Policies: The New Development Challenges of Globalisation*, London: Earthscan Publications.

Osia, Kunirum, 1987, 'Black Africa and the Dilemma of Development', *Journal of African Studies*, Vol. 14, No. 7, Summer.

Osei-Hwedie, K., 1990, 'Social Work and the Question of Social Development in Africa', *Journal of Social Development in Africa*, Vol. 5, No. 2.

Patel, L., 1992, *Restructuring Social Welfare: Options for South Africa*, Johannesburg: Ravan Press.

Pitt, David C., ed., 1976, *Development From Below. Anthropologists and Development Situations*, The Hague: Mouton Publishers.

Preston, L. T., 1993, 'Putting People First. Poverty Reduction and Social Reform in Latin America and the Caribbean', Paper presented at the Inter-American Development Bank. Conference on Social Reform and Poverty, February, Washington, DC: World Bank.

Skocpol, Theda, 1985, 'Bringing the State Back In', in Evans, Peter B., D. Reuschemeyer, and T. Skocpol, eds., *Bringing the State Back In*, New York: Cambridge University Press.

World Bank, 2000, *Can Africa Claim the 21st Century?* Washington, DC: World Bank.

World Bank, 1996, *World Development Report*, Oxford: Oxford University Press.

World Bank, 1993, *The Social Dimension of Adjustment Programme. A General Assessment*, Social Dimensions of Adjustment Steering Committee, Washington DC: World Bank.

World Bank, 1991, *World Development Report*, Oxford: Oxford University Press.

Yenshu Vubo, E., 1998, 'The Evolution of Official Attitudes towards Grassroots Initiatives in Cameroon', *Community Development Journal*, Vol. 33, No 1.

11

The Youth, the Challenge of the New Educational Order and Development Alternatives

A. V. Kini-Yen Fongot-Kini

SAP's Negative Impact on Education

Since the implementation of the Structural Adjustment Programme (SAP), which started in some African countries as early as the beginning of the 1980s, youths have for the past two decades been hard hit by the cuts in salaries of their parents and the ban on state employment imposed by the so-called adjustment strategies. Within this same period Africa has registered a net population growth of 20 to 30 per cent, that is, from 700,000,000 to about 1,000,000,000 inhabitants between 1980 and 2005. This rapid growth accounts for the very young population of Africa as compared to most countries of Europe and North America (especially the USA and Canada), that have very high and rapidly ageing populations.

The Bretton Woods Institutions and the United Nations Development Programme (UNDP) were quite aware of this youthful population growth in Africa, and indeed in all Third World countries, but did not put in place parallel alternative measures to make use of this dynamic human resource and render it more productive and self sustainable. Instead they concentrated only on financing the reproduction of the neo-colonial state system to maintain the tributary economic system imposed during colonial times. It was still the interest of the metropolitan capital of the neo-colonial structures that had to be taken into consideration and attended to. Therefore, the youth of Africa were still subjected to the type of colonial educational curriculum developed to satisfy colonial needs. Those youths whose parents could no longer afford this colonial form of education were forced to drop out of school, to join the growing jobless young population, who are popularly known as 'sauveteurs',[1] a 'survival of the fittest' category. In short, not even the colonially educated youth were saved from the unemployment problem. They swell the 'survival of the fittest' category of unemployed youths of Africa.

The high rate of unemployment of the youths and the very low rate of wage earning capacity of their 'extended family' mentors and providers of their basic survival needs create more dependence on meagre extended family budgets. Many local small businesses are forced to close down, especially the small and medium sized businesses, because the autocratic neo-colonial states are the sole providers of liquid cash that circulates in the community through salaries, wages, and payment of local contracting firms. There are thus no other alternatives for employment for the youths since the collapse of the entrepreneurial state.

This reinforces the grip of the autocratic neo-colonial state on civil society, since everybody, just like every business, depends on the omnipotent State for survival and performance. The SAP and the Bretton Woods Institutions' managers were quite aware that the colonial system set in place gave full rein to the state to be the sole employer. Even after so-called independence, no measures were taken to create alternative income generation and employment facilities. One would think, and rightly so, that the Bretton Woods' SAP was intended to prepare for the brain and muscle drain of African youths into the industrialised world.

With very minimal circulation of liquid cash and non-payment of services by the state, poverty becomes as biting as it is unbearable. Most state workers go for months without salaries; just like state contractors wait for months for payment of bonds. The situation is one of state delinquency, where the state is unable to honour its part of the contract both with the civil service for state-employed workers and the civil society of the free-lancers and self-employed. The result is a crime rate that soars, just as the state delinquency rate rises in corruption and lack of transparency. The state, in order to solve its financial and management delinquency problem, is forced by SAP to raise taxes even on basic commodities and services. This high tax raise is destined to garner revenue to pay the immoral debt of the Bretton Woods Institutions. There are no substitutes for the social welfare system where everybody is condemned to the 'survival of the fittest' make-shift strategy and behaviour. This situation strangles and gradually kills all private economic initiatives, especially the small and medium sized businesses and the self-employed who are endeavouring to make ends meet. It also affects the transparency and good governance of state business, thereby raising corruption to its summit. Finally, it contributes to poor productivity and poor performance of the economy at all levels of social participation in state management by civil society.

The salary cuts imposed by SAP to curb government spending so as to amass money to pay for the imposed debts, have earned it the name of "State Approved Poverty", which has created devastating results in the domain of reproductive health and in the general health care of citizens. It has also not only contributed to, but also hastened, the creation of the new brand of African youths popularly known as 'Bush-Fallers' (Natang Jua 2005:22-25) who are forced to expatriate themselves under all forms of hardships to look for survival havens in foreign lands. The brain and muscle haemorrhage of youths from Africa is very beneficial to the Western capitalist countries – Europe and the USA especially. These highly industrialised countries with rapidly ageing populations need not just the cheap labour and well educated youths to boost the population. They also need the colonially well educated and trained youths of Africa to contribute to the social security of the ageing populations of these countries.

With the present wealth and development of South Africa, it would be difficult to convince South African youth to migrate for good and settle in Europe, the USA or Canada as youths of other countries of Africa are doing today. Instead other African youths are trying to migrate to South Africa. Then just think of what would happen if other countries like South Africa developed in the African continent, or if all Africa became like South Africa. Would any African youth want to smell Europe or America, apart from those who might want to go there just for personal reasons and transactions? But Africa has been condemned to become the poor bowl-in-hand beggar of the world, willing to take whatever rubbish without questioning – the dumping ground for toxic, nuclear and all sorts of industrial wastes – thus becoming the most highly infected continent by the HIV/AIDS pandemic virus and all other health hazards.

With the breakdown of the pre-colonial cultural and traditional social security systems, the African socio-economic and political systems have not provided for an adequate and efficient social security system for all as the cost of health care and security have risen. Yet there is a clamour for the achievement of Millennium Goals for Africa by the year 2015.

The Need for an Alternative Structural Adjustment of Educational Policy for African Development

If we accept Amartya Sen's (1999:53) definition of development as freedom, then the fundamental question is: how does education fit into this scene? If education can be defined as the process of inculcating cultural and traditional values, skills and strategies into an individual to enhance his or her talents in capability towards livelihood-building, then one could agree with Sen that it deals with building the various dimensions of an individual's right to freedom. Anthropometrics implies that freedom is the foundation of being human. According to Amartya Sen:

> The objective of development relates to the valuation of the actual freedoms enjoyed by the people involved and the enhancement of human freedom is both the main object and the primary means of development. Individual capabilities crucially depend on, among other things, economic, social, and political arrangements. In making appropriate institutional arrangements, the instrumental roles of distinct types of freedom have to be considered, going well beyond the foundational importance of the overall freedom of individuals.

It is from this standpoint of Amartya Sen's that I would like to consider education as the liberating motor for capacity-building towards livelihood-building for the development of individuals and communities as a con-synergic whole. Since Africans through colonisation have been subjected both to mental and physical slavery, Africa's youth of the Third Millennium have the task of deconstructing its educational philosophy and curricula to recreate and reconstruct that liberating space conducive to productive business development. This means that Africa must review its imposed policy of 'education for all' by the year 2015 in the Millennium Goals and NEPAD's aims for Africa, for the youth especially.

The United Nations' development programmes in Africa and the Third World insist on literacy as if literacy alone is the solution to all development ills. This raises some critical questions and assessments, namely:

- Does it mean that all Africans must go through the same pre-fabricated literacy moulds imposed by the colonial and industrialised powers in the name of education before they can be developed? This falls in line with Paulo Freire's pedagogy (Freire 1985).
- If development is freedom, people-based and people-orientated, does it not mean that people be given the freedom to decide and choose the kind of education that will suit their development needs?
- Since the foundation of development is the participatory and transparent management of the natural and human resources of peoples and communities, is it not a top priority to develop strategic business management curricula for African educational systems?
- Should business management, business philosophy and ethics curricula not become the foundation of education in enhancing development in Third Millennium Africa?

The Need for 'Liberation Education' for African Development: The Question of Language

The problem of Africa's underdevelopment is the pre-fabricated literacy and educational programmes imposed on Africa from colonisation to the third millennium era. The literacy-imposed programmes as well as the education curricula in Africa have always been, and still remain, very alienating because the freedoms of Africans and their development focus on self-determination have never been given their rightful consideration.

Africans have been taught to communicate and think only in European languages; but never in African languages, except only when used to transmit dominant Euro-Americano-centric thought, cultural values and religious patterns of belief (witness the transmission of the sacred texts of the grand religions into local languages), behaviour and consumption. This is because they realise that language is the foundation of culture and cultural transmission of values and belief systems. As I indicated elsewhere (Fongot-Kinni 2004), the promoters of the dominant colonial languages are so aware of their superiority complex and want to maintain these languages at all cost, and at all times, as the foundations of all business management and communication management strategy.

From the intellectual and ideological standpoint, Africans were groomed and sometimes forced to adopt foreign ethnocentric, superior-rating ideologies, and accept bastardising their rich heritage as expressed through their spiritual and material cultures and languages. Intellectualised Africans were obliged to make room with any available space in their brains and souls only for the dominant thought patterns. The irony is that these foreign cultures and languages are very sensitive and protective of their heritage – to a point where they do not hesitate to manifest their hostility to other cultures that infringe on their integrity and survival (witness the work of the Academie Française and English purists in this regard).

Africans are made to believe that it is not proper to question the fact that English is the World Language and the Language for Business Management par excellence. But they forget to realise that languages rise and fall just as Empires and Civilisations have risen and fallen into decay. Once upon a time, it was the language of the Pharaonic Egyptians, then the Phoenicians, the Greeks, the Romans, the French, the British, and today the Chinese have come to stay. Tomorrow, it may be the turn of Africans if they want to liberate themselves from this cyclic domination of colonial and neo-colonial languages by adopting African languages with an international vocation.

But Africans are not trying to critically evaluate the impact the Chinese language will have on world business civilisation in the Third Millennium. As I have mentioned previously, language plays a foundational role in all communication and business management strategies of any people. The African youth of today refuse to question whether African business development would be possible without the enhancement of African literacy in African languages. However, Nigeria, the Congo, the Southern African countries, Tanzania and Kenya are well aware of the role of local languages in business development, and human development as a whole. This is because these countries believe that language is at the centre of every development and business management in progressive liberation terms and that the language that provides this forum or liberation space is the African language, wherever one might want to do business.

The mastery of many languages by businessmen and women is the key to success in business management, communication management and business development. All African long-distance and trans-border businessmen and women are polyglots and masters of many African languages, and are experts in communication management in business capability-building. These are the future liberating business designers and managers, as well as the liberating business educators in Africa for the Third Millennium.

Freedom to Decide and Choose the Kind of Education that Suits Africa's Development Needs

In talking about the new brand of youths in Africa whom Lapiro de Mbanga (1987)[2] identifies as 'Sauveteurs', 'Make-shift Survivor Businessmen/women', I inferred that they, like the new unemployed 'creolised geo-urban' social strata, are the capability-deprived category in African human resources, just as they are the greatest asset for enhancing creativity in business production, business management and communication management of Africa in the Third Millennium.

This dynamic youthful human resource is only waiting to be tapped and empowered through capability-building and livelihood-building strategies. The plight of this group is that they are still considered and treated like children or minors without the right to vote, or to decide on the kind of education or business strategy development that would be to their benefit and human development. The unfortunate creative category of this lot is recruited into the classical neo-colonial mainstream category, where they are transformed into inheritors and reproducers of the status quo type of education, for business managers of the status quo neo-colonial states in Africa. In most African countries the youth have been reduced to second-class citizens of executors, and just like the women, they do not have access to the decision and policy making machineries of the paternal state. They are only recruited in the youth wings of political parties which do not give them the liberty to decide on their fate and destiny as the 'so-much-acclaimed' 'leaders -of-tomorrow', by the very leaders who do not give the liberty for deciding on their destiny and future. The tendency of the neo-colonial mercenary states in Africa is to brainwash the youth and transform them into the mass handclapping machine road-side-lining flag wavers for the autocratic and folkloric democratic leaders and Heads of States of Africa. To brainwash the youths the more, these political leaders and Heads of State are perpetually re-elected into power through the established mechanism of the folkloric democracy monsters, while at the same time re-assuring the youth that they are the leaders of tomorrow. At best they are treated as a subaltern socio-political category (vigilantes and vanguards of parties) or relegated to a dependent civil society that only serves to perpetuate personality cult worship – witness the case of President Biya's Youth (PRESBY) and Jeunesse de Chantal Biya (JACHABI).

In short there is no participatory discourse and constructive space between the youth and their bought-off natural 'mentors/teachers' and politicians. Such a discourse implies that the education of youth should follow the andragogic Socratic and Platonian continual, critical and discursive approach or Freire's model of humanising pedagogy (op cit.:55) and not the pedagogic approach. It also obliges educators to give the orientation and freedom to youths to develop their teaching materials and to engage in peer teaching to enhance their freedom of creativity, critical thinking and choice of areas of education that they believe are relevant to their future needs for developing their capability-building, livelihood-building and well-being. In this regard I would again take the advantage and liberty to call on Amartya Sen (1999:51) to instruct all African educators and development scientists in this regard when he insists on development as freedom:

> The ends and means of development call for placing the perspective of freedom at the centre of the stage. The people have to be seen, in this perspective, as being actively involved – given the opportunity – in shaping their own destiny, and not as passive recipients of the fruits of cunning development programs. The state and the society have extensive roles in strengthening and safeguarding human capabilities. This is a supporting role rather than one of ready-made delivery. The freedom-centred perspective on the ends and the means of development has some claim to our attention.

This means that education curricula for the youths of Africa today and the future should respond to the demands of the youths of today and their destiny; with regard to their future needs and their critical approach in evaluating and reconstructing the classical forms of education dispensed in African schools and universities. For instance, most subjects that are studied in schools and universities are very environmental and human-based: whether when dealing with medicine management, technology management and application, natural and human resources management, or business management, one has to deal with the anthropometrics and environ-metrics of capability-building, and capability-provision for individuals and communities in their natural habitat and their socio-economic world.

The pertinent questions of advocacy for change in policy and approach to African education of youths for development in the Third Millennium are:

- How can African youths be expected to be the leaders of tomorrow, and address the needs of their livelihood-building and capacity-provision for the development of Africa if they are not given the freedom for critical discourse on the educational systems that condition their destiny and development process?
- Have African youths ever been given the chance to critically appreciate the anthropometrics and environ-metrics of managing business in Africa?
- If African youths are not given the critical freedom space to deconstruct and reconstruct their colonial and neo-colonial educational curricula, how can they reclaim their own destinies and autonomously determine the development goals of their generation?
- If African youths are not given the critical freedom to experiment on and apply new theories for appropriately creative and productive development, how can they respond adequately to the challenges of the Third Millennium?

Developing Strategic Curricula for African Educational Systems: The Case of Business Management

The Third Millennium Goals for Africa require among other priorities new strategies for developing education curricula that will lay emphasis on developing multiple talents of young Africans right from the cradle. This will reorient the content of curricula in the domain of pedagogy itself, the basic and applied sciences, social sciences, philosophy, the arts and management. There is a need to give an African dimension to these disciplines and integrate local knowledge systems and technologies within their core content. The case of business management needs some special attention.

The rationale of this proposal is motivated from the anthropometrics of African societies. It has been observed that geo-ethnic communities and socio-economic groups that initiate the mastery of business management right from the cradle, thereby making the acquisition of the techniques of business manage-ment as a necessary component in life, are generally richer and develop faster than those that do not. This is the case of communities like the Igbos, the Hausas, the Malenke, the Fulanis/Fulbe, the Ewes, the Ijaws, the Yoruba, the Fon, the Bamileke, the Kongo-Ba-Kassai, and the Wolof, whose business acumen is universally acknowledged. The secret of their success can be said to lie in the fact that they start early in childhood integrating and honing skills and strategies in marketing, money management through savings, banking, lending and investing in other forms of income generating business. These categories of Africans tend to be multi-faceted and multi-dimensional in whatever production they engage in and are also very gifted in com-munication management and business management. They are essentially multi-lingual in African languages and are experts in cross-cultural management.

Anthropometric observations confirm that these categories of African peoples adapt easily to other African cultures and to Western cultures without necessarily losing their cultural identities. They are more African-inward-looking in development skills and strategies but also more cosmopolitan than most of the other geo-ethnic categories of Africa.[3] They tend to behave like the Jews, the Arabs, the Chinese, the Indians and Pakistanis of Europe and Africa who insist on inculcating their children with their cultural philosophies and values alongside the European and African cultures. These geo-ethnic cultural foundations, alongside with the cross-cultural enhancements, have rendered these particular peoples ex-perts in domestic and world business wherever they are found. In Africa, only the geo-ethnic communities th at integrate business management from the cradle as a part of life can rival and even challenge the Jews, the Arabs, the Indians, and Chinese who tend to control even to the extent of monopolising business mana-gement in Africa.

Anthropometrics points to the fact that life is the continuous process of acquiring skills and strategies on livelihood management which solely depends on the management of the natural and human resources for profits from the surplus value of production and for the sustainable development of resources. Pre-colonial Africa provided the space for acquiring the foundation skills on the management of the natural environment and the natural and cultural resources of every people. This enabled the individual to acquire the minimum skills in self-sustainable management, production, distribution and business within the corporate community. For education to be productive and sustainable to development in Africa, the youth must be educated to re-incorporate the African cultural skills in management and create new appropriate curricula for African ongoing development in the Third Millennium.

When Tony Blair takes it upon himself to advocate equipping African youth with skills for developing Africa in the Third Millennium, I seem to believe that he has recognised that the colonial and the neo-colonial syllabi for Africa have not been orientated to respond to and address Africa's development needs. In 'The Blair Report on Africa' (Babendreier 2005) the prime minister of Great Britain insisted on the need to educate African youth and advocated '... Providing funding for all African boys and girls in Sub-Saharan Africa to receive free basic education that equips them with skills for contemporary Africa'.[4] But before Africans should hope and wait for Blair's education funding for Africa that might come too late, or just with other strings attached, it is high time Africans themselves start laying the groundwork for recreating the new curricula for educating the youths of Africa. As the leaders and managers of African resources tomorrow, the youths must be schooled, among other educational requirements, in the basics of business management and resource management in general, as essential tools for sustainable development in Africa in the Third Millennium

Ethics in the Curricula: The Foundation of Education for Africa's Third Millennium Development

There is a need to infuse ethical values into the curricula at all levels. This ethics could be developed from a variety of sources: primordial African cultures, core universal values derived from the so-called grand religions, social and political philosophy based on rationality, and existential praxis. Bernard Fonlon (1967) highlighted the aim of education as recreating and moulding the spiritual soul in the educated memory in a healthy body.

There is also a need to develop an African philosophy of education, which insists on incorporating spiritual-building and cultural-building values. It is the recognition of this African social and philosophical value of ethical education and its incorporation in all aspects of human and resource management that leads to business management and development of the individual and the community in a sustainable manner. Such an African philosophy of education should consider education as a holistic enterprise of moulding the individual to imbibe the values that will render him or her an ethical being first before anything else. Therefore, any education that does not lead human beings to fulfil life missions

(Fongot-Kinni 2002), which should be the enhancement of human and social life on earth, is of no value.

It is within the social matrix of corrupting colonial and neo-colonisation ethics that it could be confirmed that Africa needs a new mental-liberating and soul-liberating ethical educational order before anything else. This new African Business Ethical Order – (ABEO) – must be founded on the indigenous African social and cultural values of communalism and solidarity. These values must be integrated in the educational curricula with emphasis on human and cultural resource management, for effective international business management, to attain sustainable humane development of Africa in the Third Millennium.

This calls for the designing of curricula for the training of trainers in the new African Business Ethical Order in general and management, whether in public office or private business, bearing in mind the cross-cultural diversities and complementarities of the normative orders and behavioural patterns that build up African civilisations in marketing and exchange in commodities: in real and artificial capital.

Conclusion

If it can be accepted that the youth of Africa of the 1980s to the Third Millennium are the 'lost generation' (Nantang Jua 2005), the factors contributing to this impasse are basically structural. The Structural Adjustment Programme imposed by the Bretton Woods Institutions in Africa was more preoccupied with one aspect: the recuperation of the debts owed to the World Bank and the International Monetary Fund. It did not care about the fate of the youths who were an important stakeholders in the SAP business. It did not carry out a situational, structural as well as a systemic and anthropometrical analysis to measure the impact its policy would have on the youth sector of the population. It did not care at all to carry out an impact assessment of its policies on the entire systemic interconnected structures of the stakeholders as government decision-makers and executors and the stakeholders as civil society and victims. It did not create alternative structures within the system to address the problem of unemployment of the youths, nor did it create alternative structures within the civil society that would generate employment for the youth. Instead it wasted energy and money on what appeared to be mere mouthwash propaganda on transparency, democracy, the fight against corruption and good governance of the same inadequate structures that were reproducing them. The SAP created a system that was in essence corrupting and enhanced the very endemic corruption that has been promoted by the colonial and the neo-colonial system and the Bretton Woods Institutions in Africa since 1884 through 1945 to the present day.

SAP promoters were and are aware that the education curriculum imposed on the youths from the time of the colonial exploitation of Africa was intended to respond to the needs of colonial exploitation and never for the self reliant and sustainable development of Africa. This curriculum contributed to transform

African youths into Eurocentric clowns, copy-cats, Fey-men and Fey-women,[5] who constitute the growing categories of 'Bush-Faller' outcasts of all sorts, even to the point of becoming mercenaries against their own countries and peoples, in the name of 'going hunting in greener pastures' in Europe, the USA and Canada. The mentality is corrupting and unethical as youths invent compensatory alternatives when they fail to fall within the classical systemic chain of school to work as Nantang Jua has demonstrated. This corrupting and unethical attitude is boosted by the neo-colonial curriculum which has obliterated all fear and respect for ethical values.

This is the reason why the African education of youths for development must be inward-looking for the interest of Africa and Africans; and for the building of the complete human being, spiritually and materially. Africa must develop a new liberating education curriculum for its youths, which must take cognisance of the African values of appropriate proactive development for Africa; and integrate African values of communitarian solidarity. For all is not just economics and unethical capitalism, if at all we must first seek the economic kingdom; nor is all just selfish politics, for the political kingdom of self aggrandisement; it is also for the religious kingdom, a 'City of God' on earth (St. Augustine), with an African religious tolerance that builds on solidarity and communitarian development for the good of all Africans, all Humanity.

Notes

1. Local term for hawker.
2. Local popular musician.
3. Warnier attributes entrepreneurial spirit of the peoples of the Cameroon Grassfields (West and North West Provinces) to a combination of values of hard work, an inward-looking spirit and cosmopolitanism derived from a long historical past (Warnier 1985, 1994).
4. When Blair limits his attention to 'basic education' it carries with it an evident colonial tinge. One is left to wonder whether basic education can lead to development.
5. Local term for con-men.

References

Amin, Samir, 1972, *Développement Inégal*, Paris :Editions Maspero.

Bernstein, Henry, 2000, 'Colonialism, Capitalism and Development', in Tim Allen and Alan Thomas, eds., *Poverty and Development into the 21st Century*, Oxford: Oxford University Press/The Open University.

Blair, Tony, 2005, 'The Blair Effort To Fund The Education Of African Children, The Report On Africa', *The Nation*, Nairobi.

Fongot-Kinni, A. V. Kini-Yen, 1988, L'Idéologie, Pouvoir et Droit: Le Cameroun, la Construction de l'Etat et la Danse des Masques, Thèse de Doctorat d'Etat en Sciences Politiques, Université de Paris I, Panthéon-Sorbonne.

Fongot-Kinni, A. V. Kini-Yen, 2002, 'Mbum Ideology, Philosophy and Democracy: An Ethico-Historical Anthropologics of the Pharaonic Dynasty of Nganha' (Unpublished).

Fongot-Kinni, A. V. Kini-Yen, 2004, 'The Anthropologics of Doing Business in Africa', Mikkeli Business Campus Lectures: University of Helsinki.

Freire, Paulo, 1985, *Pedagogy of the Oppressed*, New York: The Continuum Publishing Corporation.

Hewett, Tom, 2000, 'Half a Century of Development', in Tim Allen and Alan Thomas, eds., *Poverty and Development into the 21st Century*, Oxford: Oxford University Press/The Open University.

Jua, Nantang, 2005, 'Differential Responses to Disappearing Transitional Pathways: Redefining Possibility among Cameroonian Youths', *African Studies Review*, pp. 13-35.

Sen, Amartya, 1999, *Development as Freedom*, Oxford: Oxford University Press.

Warnier, J.P., 1985, *Echanges, développement et hiérarchies dans le Bamenda précolonial (Cameroun)*. Stuttgart: Franz Sterner Verlag 76.

Warnier, J. P., 1994, *L'Esprit d'Enterprise au Cameroon*, Paris: Karthala.

12

Towards a Synthesis

Emmanuel Yenshu Vubo

In an attempt to write a synthesis of contributions to a book of this nature there is always a risk of repeating the conclusions already made in the individual presentations. In order to avoid such a temptation the best approach would be to present a summary of the debates that took place during the workshops to discuss contributions and evaluate the level of the work covered. We will start with a presentation of the conclusion of the workshop debates and then proceed to an evaluation of the work. We will conclude finally with the question of whether the civil society is searching for development, is it posing alternative development actions or is it merely a pointer in the intellectual (theory, policy, programmes) and practical reformulation of development?

I

(i) There is widespread disenchantment with Non-Governmental Organisations (NGOs) and other modern sector organisations (common initiative groups, economic interest groups, cooperatives and associations) after a period of initial euphoria and exaggerated optimism. Some NGOs tend to lapse into 'briefcase' organisations while others simply function as branches of external NGOs. This is principally the result of initial attempts to restrict civil society to the legalised domain and modern structures that were the source of official support and lavish external funding. For a long time the enthusiasm for creating these structures was both funding-driven and prompted by opportunism rather than by a genuine attempt to contribute to shaping an alternative sector. In this regard the complicity and complacency of transnational NGOs and funding consortiums of the North only exacerbated the ensuing crisis of legitimacy and performance. In fact, the modern civil society sector was a veritable underground economy providing untaxed earnings and enriching promoters (Yenshu Vubo 1998a), constituting as it were a new white-collar sector. Its failure can thus be said to have been predictable as can be said of 'euphoric' (Tostensen, Tvedten & Vaa

2001) and 'angelic' (Houtart 1998) visions of civil society. The outcome of the performance of NGOs leads us to contrast this largely 'invented civil society' with civil society that emerges from local forces. The future outcome of this sector will therefore depend on its capacity to anchor itself in the social fabric and stand the test of time. In the process, connections with the other sectors of civil society, especially the endogenous, will be vital as has been suggested elsewhere for the women's movement (Yenshu Vubo 1998b). In the same way the reform of the NGO sector should revisit the model of existing partnerships and division of labour marked by the subordination of local NGOs to agendas set by external agencies and dependency vis-à-vis external funding (Yenshu Vubo 1998a:47, Mohan 2002). For it to stand on its own feet, this sector must both be indigenous and exercise a large measure of autonomy. The whole process will imply synchronising the activities of the multi-layered civil society world, structured in local, ethno-regional, national and transnational strata in the image of Touraine's (1996) multi-layered world of locals, nationals and cosmopolitans, in order to achieve equilibrium and a balance of forces.

(ii) The state exhibits differential attitudes towards civil society organizations (CSOs) depending on whether they are hostile, docile or collaborative towards a state characterised by repression, indifference or attempts at cooptation. There is also a discriminatory application of laws. For instance, while previous legislation was inspired by an environment characterised by overarching state security issues inspiring the laws against subversion and state security, recent worries are about terrorism, especially after the famous 9/11 events. As such, groups can be prohibited and tagged when their objectives and actions are not favourable to the regime. This situation is compounded by the wide-ranging discretionary powers wielded by administrators in offering accreditation - all this dictated by a fear that civil society organisations will get involved in politics, especially of the anti-regime type. The group was of the opinion that these fears were unfounded since all civil society activity was potentially political if politics was to be defined as the competition over the management of public life. A tightening regulation over civil society in the name of security is a violation of citizens' rights in their claim to manage their affairs.

(iii) There is dispersed and uncoordinated legislation and judicial processes governing civil society organisations (CSOs). This leads to legal confusion in the domain of civil society as well as confusion in administrative coordination. The accreditation process was tight in some cases and extremely loose in others. As NGOs needed to survive for three years before obtaining accreditation, this drove many of them underground. Moreover, one legal obstacle to the blossoming of some CSOs is the abnormally long period it takes for the application guidelines ('textes d'application') to be enacted, even when a law governing a form of CSOs has been passed by the legislature and enacted by the President of the Republic. In contrast, there is a vast domain of unregulated or loosely regulated associational life in the so-called 'informal' sector, community development associations, improvement unions, cultural associations, local solidarity societies etc., where it suffices for a people to constitute themselves into a group to gain de facto recognition from administrative authorities. Most of these structures function on the basis of by-laws or internal rules and regulations alone. The space of unregulated organisations is vast and provides a potential for liberating action. Such self-sustaining associations should not be the subject of administrative control.

The group recommended that it was instructive to learn from international legislation in the matter and institute a single legal instrument, a Charter, which would spell out the general guidelines according to which all CSOs should operate. These principles can then be adapted to specific types of organisations. In this context the bi-jural nature of the state was not likely to be of assistance while lifting parts of foreign legislation and transposing them to the local context was going to be prejudicial to any reform process. Besides, the civil society itself should be instrumental in advocacy for improvement in types of legislation relating to itself in particular and the legislation process in general.

Traditional associations, movements and organisations are the source of vitality within civil society because of their strong social bonds, their capacity to act as social solidarity funds and their capacity to mobilise, although they may be misinterpreted by the state. They derive their legitimacy from their historical depth and need to be given administrative recognition. They stand in an ambiguous position between tradition and modernity and are instrumental in building old and new social ties in the society. Concerning the question of the traditional aspects of civil society and the issues of identity. Vilas (1998:69) has remarked that the most salient aspect of the recent concern with civil society has been the increasing importance of the socio-cultural framework of collective action. Meanwhile Touraine (1996) argues that one of the important stakes of contemporary social movements even in the West has become the question of culture. Our concern with this domain also answers the question of the historical dimension of civil society as posed by Mamdani (1995:613-614) and Mohan's (2002:135) call that civil society be interpreted 'through culturally relevant norms and practices'. They become part of Osaghae's positive ethnicity (1998) or progressive action by the claims they make on the state and the argument for the right to self-organisation within the polity in line with Touraine's conception of historicity (1974:94) presented as 'cette action de transformation de la société par elle-même' (that process of the society transforming itself) as opposed to nefarious forms of ethnicity, which are the source of inter-community strife, animosity and conflict. This is where an essential dividing line has to be drawn between the two phenomena, which are the source of intense ideological confusion. Craig (1998:12) argues rightly as many others that 'identity politics is not itself necessarily the basis for progressive forms of action', but we also agree with Breytenbach (1998:40) that ethnic forms of action 'should not be excluded simply because they are ethnic'. Touraine's model considers identity as one of the three constitutive principles of social movements alongside opposition and totality (Ferréol et al. 1995:157-158). Touraine argues that identity is not a simple reflex action, the discovery of social coordinates, the assumption of roles and statuses, but the birth of a social movement in itself (ibid.:185), and that a cultural fall-back position always challenges the political system that takes responsibility for social organisation (ibid.:206). Néveu (2000:81), for his part, argues that the identity dimension is an integral part of social movements and that social movements are also the special moments for the construction and maintenance of identities. He goes on to indicate that protest is a fertile ground for identity formation. It is in this light that one has to interpret the local women's movement covered in this volume. In the African context local institutions became civil society (and not simply Breytenbach's proto-civil society) from the time the modern state excluded them from the modern sphere of governance.

(iv) Informal financial institutions tend to replace the formal banking system because the latter are procedural and cumbersome while the former are flexible, accountable and quick at problem-solving. They are credible forces that transcend ethnic boundaries. They are collectors of small savings, offer loans at very considerate interest rates and operate on a self-help basis. They offer services that banks in the main are unable to offer mainly because of the restructuring undertaken within the reforms of the financial sector. The banks have become more prohibitive to the common man in terms of preconditions for opening accounts, saving and obtaining loans. The so-called informal sector has become the common man's financial market in the increasingly precarious situation of the economic crisis of the 1980s and the early 1990s and the SAP imposed by the Washington Consensus.

The study confirms the fact that these structures are more anchored in the social context than the formal or, more still, formalised sector. The social networks, social solidarity, the safety networks and the self-help spirit are the cardinal points at the basis of their operation but they are also the basis of small-scale investment necessitating relatively little capital as well as investments in social consumption, well-being and cultural capital. In this way, they are contributing to individual personal development, firstly by serving as palliatives and safety nets in a context of increasing poverty, and secondly by contributing towards the improvement of people in low income categories. They stand in clear contrast to big financial institutions, which contribute only to accumulation for the rich and discriminate against (by eliminating and disqualifying) the poor. That is the law of the system. Moreover, the inability of the banks to thrive in the local context scares away even those local people who can afford to operate savings with them.

The question arises as to whether we can classify the informal financial institutions within civil society. To the extent that they are associations situated outside the family/kin group and the state, they are civil society. In the same vein they are civil society because they are situated outside the global market (especially the global financial market), although constituting an alternative and budding financial market of their own. Their ability to compete with the mainstream modern financial sector (although not in a brutal or confrontational manner) puts them along other civil society organisations that are in search of alternative visions for society. They may form the basis of the future markets of local capital that can be classified with the other sectors of the economy as the market (in the sense of an overarching sector of the modern economy), but for now it is out of that sector and can be classified as an indigenous civil society sector. When compared with the other sectors that are not strictly formal (cooperatives, NGOs, credit unions) they are definitely the pointer to a new direction that has to be harnessed. This most neglected sector has only been the subject of much negative appraisal by the state whose only craving has been to regulate it. Ways must be explored to integrate this sector in the official local financial market and very much in the direction of solving its problems.

(v) State interference tends to disempower civil society (either by capturing vital segments and subordinating them to partisan interests, by the demonisation of critical elements or administrative harassment) while certain forms of civil society are overtly rebellious (either due to the ignorance of their roles or a reaction to administrative hostility).[1] These two trends constitute obstacles to a rapprochement between the two. The ideal in state-civil society relations is that they should be complementary and not mutually repulsive or distrustful of each other. Moreover the tendency for civil society to be split along regime-opposition lines does not serve the interest of development or the future of society as such. The state has to allow the civil society its domain for it to play a meaningful role.

(vi) There is a need to be more focused on what form of development one is concerned with. There have been too many fluctuations in the mood of development thinking and practice over the past decade. The search for development alternatives should be inward-looking with the watch word being self-reliance and autonomy first as a challenge to dependency. External inputs should be a catalyst rather than the main thrust of development. The main goal should also be general human welfare.

(vii) Religious organisations and other forms of associations provide a much-desired ethical dimension to society that is generally absent in public life. They are first and foremost schools of management and accountability. The current configuration of the religious organisations situate them clearly within civil society by dint of all definitions whether systemic, radical, or reformist. While some are involved in the social mission of alleviating poverty among the poor or instituting social welfare programmes among the faithful, others are involved in gospels of prosperity (and hence accumulation) as a solution to current problems of poverty. One is critical of the state and market policies in a critique that one would characterise as internal to the system while others are facilitators of the market via the adoption of accumulation as a creed. One can fault some of these policies for being inscribed in welfarist notions of development marked by traditions of gender imbalance and couched in traditions of insulation from global issues. In this regard they are sectarian and evidently partisan as they target only the 'faithful' in their specific zones of influence despite their universalising message. In their own light they are complementary coping strategies that have not been integrated into overall development strategies. There is a need therefore to integrate these strategies into overall development policies and programmes as is the case in the domain of health and education. However, one needs to commend these organisations for their early tendency to tackle the gender question by designing gender-sensitive programmes, however limited in scope they may be. The same has to be said about the quality of social services (education, health) that are universally considered to be the best, even ranking above public and private services.

(viii) In terms of performance one can contrast external NGOs and home-grown or local NGOs and home-based associations or solidarity unions, the labour unions and the professional unions, religious organisations and private or state social services, etc. There is a need to compare all of these trends. There is therefore differential performance with each structure having a comparative advantage over the other, needing to learn from each other and therefore complementing each other.

(ix) There is a gap between the content of pedagogy in the modern school system and the milieu in which the youth are situated. This gap tends to relegate rural peoples to the fringes of modern life and widens the village-city gap, generates unemployment, alienates the youth, reproduces redundancy through educated unemployment and orchestrates a new wave of massive expatriation of vigorous youngsters to the North. There is also a tendency towards capability and livelihood deprivation that not only puts the youth in crisis but jeopardises the very future of African societies. These developments necessitate a reorientation of the educational system and a re-situation of the school system within the community. This will be much in the direction of 'functional training... a continuity of moral values derived from the indigenous cultures and the transmission of economically useful skills' (Yenshu Vubo 1998c:21). The arguments of the workshops and presentations argue for 'the younger generation [to] be given autonomy and individual initiative in the process' (ibid.). The radical reform process will also recover talents that risk being rejected by the modern school system. This will be based on and serve as the basis of an inward-looking philosophy of education and development that integrates ethics and local knowledge systems and skills in the content of curricular, the model of development and the management of affairs (both public and private business). Such a vision challenges the prevailing monolithic thinking that serves as the building blocks of the current one-dimensional world order in the name of globalisation.

One often repeated objection to operating in African languages as pedagogic and management tools is extreme diversity and a multilingualism considered as perverted (evidently a modernist bias). This very obstacle is not alluded to when fundamentalist religious messages are translated into every language that has at least 25,000 speakers. This simply means that mono-lingualism only serves to transmit dominant visions of development. On the contrary, functional literacy and authentic education is best in no other language than that of the speaker. Moreover the experiences of trans-ethnic and trans-frontier polyglot businessmen in Africa point to the fact that 'polyglotism' and not mono-lingualism is a viable solution. In other words, cultural diversity will not cease to be problematic when it is inscribed within stifling mono-lingual spaces. Diversity management as cultural development will only benefit from experiences in multilingualism.

This vision of development seeks to restore autonomy chiefly from the ideological and hence pedagogic standpoint. It is perfectly in line with Paulo Freire's (1985:55) humanising pedagogy taking the youth as a creative starting point. The cardinal point is autonomy in which people assert their right to historicity or the capacity to produce their orientations and give meaning to their actions (Touraine 1974). Amin considers this to be the radical break operated by the development of modernity when

> ... humanity was called to the knowledge that human beings make their own history, that they can and even must do so, and that to do so they must choose ... To say that human beings make their history is to propose an organized social frame which facilitates the creation of an emancipatory project (Amin 2000:590-591).

It is in such a context that any current African renaissance project should be inscribed.

II

What can be deduced from the present work is that we have only covered a fragment of the civil society domain and only a tiny aspect of development, although an important one. The papers have each in their own way attempted to cover as wide an area of the national territory as possible. Even then we have only scratched the vast terrain of civil society as it is blossoming in Cameroon. What this points to is that the task is essentially an unfinished one and that this is only one in many of the works that have been and are yet still to be undertaken in the domain. A lot has actually been left out: the cooperative movement, the peasant movement, the syndicates of businessmen, the motor car drivers' unions, the sectarian autonomist or secessionist movements, traders' unions, etc. This shows that civil society is a vast field that would take more than one volume to cover.

This is also true of development. We have only concentrated on those aspects of development that the civil society of the nature we identified could handle. We have explored the labour question, social development, environmental and watershed protection, civil or civic rights, small-scale financing, gender issues, land rights, coping with economic crises, relations to the state and citizenship. We have not been able to explore the question of industrialisation, public works, peasant concerns with commodity prices (see the concern with cotton prices within which Cameroon's voice is virtually eclipsed), consumer concerns with quality and prices (indeed quite a few consumer associations have been formed of recent), decentralisation, traders' concerns with the tax burden and duties, and many other social development issues. However, we have been able to examine certain hitherto unexplored dimensions such as the traditional aspects of civil society, the issue of identity within civil society, legal reforms around civil society, an evaluation of civil society, a comparative analysis of religious organisations as civil society bodies, and the question of alternatives to the current revisions that have characterised development over the past four decades. This has given us the possibility of determining to some extent the contribution of civil society to development. We can say that the most visible contributions of this dimension of civil society are in the domains of the social (provision of social amenities, development of a corporate spirit, self-help insurance schemes) and the political (citizenship, civil rights, contribution to public debate and advocacy). It is also showing signs of contributing to a budding alternative financial sector that is at the basis of much-needed funds for development. This may not be much but the very awareness of the need for mobilising funds is a step in the right direction.

Imperfections and insufficiencies abound, especially in the very problematic state-civil society relations and the legal framework. The one remark that can be made is that this is due to the state scepticism about civil society and its assimilation of all forms of protest to anti-regime activity with its consequences in terms of change of regime. This brings us to the question of the role of civil society. Can civil society become an autonomous domain? If so, what will be its role? This takes us to the issue of whether civil society is an alternative vehicle of development, either in posing acts or proposing new visions. Evidently, civil society promises new approaches to public performance but is limited by the very dimensions of its capacity. It can and is active in social and political development but cannot substitute for the state in its sovereign and collective function, or even propose new regimes. The functions of the state are far-reaching and too vast for civil society, while regime issues are questions of the development of political classes.

However, the style and vision of civil society can be a catalyst in determining the directions a society and its state apparatus take by shaping legislation, political awareness and style of political practices. As Vilas (op cit.:73) has posited, civil society is distinct from political society but is not a stranger to politics because the term civil society has clear political undertones. Among the potential functions of civil society (to be contrasted with the political manipulations of certain sections of the civil society) one can identify three: creation and expansion of democratic space through civic education and mobilisation; involvement of civil society in radical political reform; and development of political forces that will emerge and detach themselves from the civil society stream. In the last case mention needs to be made of intellectuals and trade union leaders who have moved from the protest dimension of civil society to occupy the centre stage of politics as reformist leaders, for example, Lech Walesa (Poland), Vaclav Havel (Czech Republic), Fernando Cardoso and Ignacio Lula (Brazil), Frederick Chiluba (Zambia), Tom Mboya (Kenya). In that regard, the civil society is a complementary arm of the public sphere that has to be recognised by the state and given free vent by all regimes. In fact, Vilas (ibid.) concludes that it would be unwise for the state to seek to politically neutralise civil society. It is also incumbent on this civil society to be respectful of its limits and its catalytic (rather than replacement) role. The civil society has its advantages that it must jealously protect and which it must not lose by trying to engage in two competing public spheres, namely the modern economy as separated from the domestic sphere (in the Weberian sense of capitalist development) and politics as the public sphere for the exercise of power. These advantages are neutrality, non-profit and low cost. Where civil society engages in partisan politics or engages in the market economy by way of an underground economy, it loses in credibility. The partisan messages of partisan politics corrupt the transcendental message and posture of civil society movements, which only succeed by providing moral censure to public life.[3] Market competition will lead to a loss of low cost, non-profit and philanthropy that are other transcendental aspects of civil society. The rise of civil society adds a third sector or dimension to society besides the state and the market.[4] These three domains act as checks to each other: the state provides the orientation and framework (policy, legislation, judicial) for the deployment of economic activity and the emergence of the civil society; the economic sector organises the production and distribution functions fashioning consumption patterns and determining well being; civil society provides the domain of free association and the moral and social framework for the state and the market. Distortions arise when there is interference across domains; hence the need for mutual respect of domains. Such mutual respect is necessary for the advancement of society as an integrated structure and not an entity fragmented along opposing lines.

Notes

1. In fact the dream of the regime has been to put civil society to its own uses and place it at the service of a neo-liberal political frame in the style of what Samir Amin calls 'low intensity democracy' (2001), that is, 'exclusively a political democracy' (2000:592).

2. For more on the transcendental nature of civil society see Gramsci in Tejada (1998:31-32).

3. This view is in opposition to the much publicised and depoliticised domain which goes under the name of third sector.

4. We are following the footsteps of Houtart (op cit.:19) who argues that civil society is situated at the crossroads between the state and the market (another name for the dominant capitalist economy) and existing in a dialectical relation to the two: '... la société civile se situe bien au carrefour du marché et de l'Etat, distincte mais en relation dialectique avec les deux, c'est-à-dire en étroite dependance de la manière dont ils sont définis, mais aussi capable d'agir sur l'un comme sur l'autre, en fonction des forces existantes'.

References

Amin, S., 2000, 'Economic Globalisation and Political Universalism: Conflicting Issues', *Journal of World-Systems Research*, Vol.1, No 3, Fall/Winter.

Amin, S., 2001, 'Une radicalité démocratique', http://humanité.fr/journal/2001-01-29/2001-01-29-238694.

Breytenbach, Willie, 1998, 'The Erosion of Civil Society and the Corporatisation of Democracy in Africa', *QUEST*, Vol.XII, No. 1, Special Issue: Proceedings of the Interdisciplinary Colloquium on State and Civil Society in Africa. Abidjan, 13-18 July.

Craig, G., 1998, 'Community Development in a Global Context', *Community Development Journal*, Vol. 33, No. 1.

Ferréol, G., P., Cauche, J-M., Dupez, N., Gadrey and M. Simon, 1995, *Dictionnaire de Sociologie*, Paris: Armand Colin/Masson.

Freire, Paulo, 1985, *Pedagogy of the Oppressed*, New York: The Continuum Publishing Corporation.

Houtart, F., 1998, 'Editorial', *Les Cahiers Alternatives Sud*, Vol. V, No. 1.

Mamdani, Mahmood, 1995, 'A Critique of the State and Civil Society in Africanist Studies', in Mahmood Mamdani and Ernest Wamba-dia-Wamba, eds., *African Studies in Social Movements and Democracy*. Dakar: CODESRIA.

Mohan, Giles, 2002, 'The Disappointments of Civil Society: the Politics of NGO Intervention in Northern Ghana', *Political Geography*, 21.

Néveu, Erik, 2000, *Sociologie des mouvements sociaux*, Paris: La Découverte.

Osaghae, Eghosa E., 1998, 'Structural Adjustment, Civil Society and National Cohesion in Africa', AAPS Occasional Paper Series, Vol. 2, No. 2.

Tejada, Aurelio Alonso, 1998, 'Le Concept de société civile dans le débat contemporain: les contextes', *Les Cahiers Alternative Sud*, Vol. V, No. 1.

Tostensen, A., Inge Tvedten and Mariken Vaa, 2001, 'The Urban Crisis, Governance and Associational Life', in Tostensen, A., Inge Tvedten and Mariken Vaa, eds., *Associational Life in African Cities: Popular Responses to the Urban Crisis*, Uppsala: Nordic Africa Institute.

Touraine, A., 1974, *Pour la Sociologie*, Paris: Seuil.

Touraine, A., 1991, 'Entretien', *Revue Sciences Humaines*, http://www.cybertribes.com/touraine.htlm

Touraine, A., 1996, 'Entretien avec Alain Touraine sur "Smart Geneva" et la société de l'information', http://diwww.epfi.ch~galland/articles/Touraines.htlm

Vilas, Carlos V., 1998, 'L'heure de la société civile', *Les Cahiers Alternatives Sud*, Vol. V, No. 1.

Yenshu Vubo, Emmanuel, 1998a, 'The Evolution of Official Attitudes towards Grassroots Initiatives in Cameroon', *Community Development Journal*, Vol. 33, No. 1.

Yenshu Vubo, Emmanuel, 1998b, 'The African Woman and the Development Crisis: An appraisal of Changes, Constraints on Empowerment and Prospects for the Future', in Simo, David, ed., *La politique de development à la croisée des chemins: le facteur culturel*, Yaoundé: Goethe Institut/Editions Clé.

Yenshu Vubo, Emmanuel, 1997, 'Democratizing Development in Sub-Saharan Africa: Imperatives and Possibilities', *Scandinavian Journal of Development Alternatives and Area Studies*, Vol. 16, No. 2, June.

www.ingramcontent.com/pod-product-compliance
Lightning Source LLC
Chambersburg PA
CBHW021901020426
42334CB00013B/425